Our Special Child

Bette M. Ross, M.Ed.

OLIVER
NELSON

THOMAS NELSON PUBLISHERS
NASHVILLE

*for the parents of
today's children with special needs*

Published in Nashville, Tennessee, by Oliver-Nelson Books, a division of Thomas Nelson, Inc., Publishers, and distributed in Canada by Word Communications, Ltd., Richmond, British Columbia.

The Bible version used in this publication is THE NEW KING JAMES VERSION. Copyright © 1979, 1980, 1982, Thomas Nelson Inc., Publishers.

The names of some persons used in anecdotes in this book are fictional. Any resemblances with persons living or dead who have had similar experiences are coincidental.

Printed in the United States of America.

Library of Congress Cataloging-in-Publication Data

Ross, Bette M.
    Our special child / by Bette M. Ross. — [2nd rev. ed.]
      p.   cm.
    Includes bibliographical references and index.
    ISBN 0-8407-9201-8 (pbk.)
    1. Mentally handicapped children. 2. Child rearing. 3. Down's syndrome. 4. Child development. I. Title.
HQ773.7.R67 1993   93-7357
649'.1528—dc20   CIP

1 2 3 4 5 6 — 98 97 96 95 94 93

Koch, Richard, M.D. "Feelings and Their Medical Significance." *Ross Timesaver,* Vol. 16, No. 5 (September–October, 1974). Copyright 1974 by *Ross Timesaver.*

"Overprotectiveness" and "Independent Living." *Patient Care,* November 15, 1978. Copyright 1978, Patient Care Publications, Inc., Darien, CT. All rights reserved.

Ludlow, J. R. and Allen, L. M. "The Effect of Early Intervention and Pre-School Stimulus on the Development of the Down's Syndrome Child." Copyright 1979 by J. R. Ludlow.

Spock, Benjamin, M.D. *Baby and Child Care.* New York: Pocket Books, 1976. Copyright 1945, 1946, 1957, 1968, 1976 by Benjamin Spock, M.D. Reprinted by permission of Pocket Books, a Simon & Schuster Division of Gulf & Western Corporation.

Turnbull, Ann P. and H. Rutherford, III, see The Helsels.

Van Wogner, Dr. Benjamin. "Guidelines for Working with Students with Disabilities." *AIMS Newsletter,* May/June 1991, Volume V, No. 10.

The author also would like to express her appreciation for the short excerpts from the following:

Brecker, Don, Ph.D. Address to the Fourth Western Regional Conference on Services for the Profoundly and Severely Disabled. Los Angeles, CA, 1979.

Carhart, Bev. "High Country Classroom." Special Education Program, 1977–1978.

Interviews with Judy Cook and Mary Boyd Merrill of Project COPE, Tami Yamaga of Huntington Beach Union High School District, Gay Parrish and Marcy Page of North Valley Regional Center, and Donna Ewing, Director of Curriculum Technology, Newport Mesa Unified School District.

Contents

Foreword

I t was a glorious morning, the day after my second son's birth. I was feeling vital, a little smug, if you want the truth, and peaceful. What could be better than to be the mother of two healthy children? Yet that peace was about to be shattered for many months.

When the doctor came into my hospital room, his pleasantries did not prepare me for these words, "Mrs. Ross, your baby has Down's syndrome."

Down's syndrome! The room started to vibrate. The shock of his words blurred the sunlight and color of the day. The rest of his words drowned in the roaring in my ears. Down's syndrome!

I knew about Down's syndrome. In school I had gone on a field trip with my psychology class to a state hospital, and the doctor had shown us the kids who were mentally retarded. I remembered thinking if ever I had a baby with a handicapping condition, it would be okay as long as his mind was all right.

And now in this bright, cheery, bustling hospital, a doctor was talking about my son, who was only forty-eight hours old. In my grief I could only think that it just couldn't be true. But even then, the doctor's unsmiling gaze and the cold core of fear inside me said it was true.

I had the impression that the doctor stayed a long time, droning endlessly at me when all I wanted was to be left alone. How could I call my husband and tell him this news? After receiving his kisses and nuzzling good-night, his "Sleep well and sleep warm, little mother," how could I tell him about our son over the telephone?

The doctor left. I got out of bed and put on my new lavender robe. I have hated the color lavender ever since. My roommate came back. We looked at each other without speaking. Finally, she said,

"Would you like to be alone a little longer?" I said, "No, I'm leaving."

I started down the hall. A nurse hurried after me. "Can I get something for you, Mrs. Ross?"

"I'm going to see my baby."

"You come back to your room," she said, turning me around. "I'll bring your baby."

Tears were pouring down my face. "But it isn't visiting hours."

"Don't you worry."

My roommate was gone again. I sat in a big wicker rocker with faded chintz covers of splashy flowers. A very mothery chair. I felt so small, all folded in. I held my breath. Maybe I could just disappear. Maybe I could make myself grow smaller and smaller and just go away.

The nurse came back with her small bundle. "Do you want to hold him in the chair a while?" I remember how gentle her voice was.

I nodded. She lay the baby on the bed and brought me a pillow. She put the baby in my arms and waited a moment, watching me.

I tried to blot my tears on my sleeve. They refused to stop. She brought me a handful of tissues.

"Are you all right?" she said in that same soft, gentle voice.

I nodded. She left. I looked down at that little yellow-red face in the white flannelette wrapper. Someone had combed his dark hair and parted it. There was enough for that. His eyes were open. The whites were yellow with the jaundice. But the doctor had said that would clear up in a few days. I uncovered his little fists. I held the baby close and rocked, with each rock driving my sadness deeper and deeper. I felt him squirm. His tiny mouth was moving, seeking. The fist curled around my finger. Gently, I pried the little fingers away and opened my robe. Through a blur of tears, I guided the little mouth to my breast.

Years later, talking with other parents of babies who were mentally retarded, I would discuss whether it is easier to learn of the baby's disability all at once or little by little. Whether the hard, quick blow bleeds less and heals faster than the slow, gnawing fear that something is wrong but no one will come out and say exactly what. After thirty years, I still don't know the answer, except that there is no easy way.

When Mike was born, he was called mentally retarded. A few years later he was called a mental defective, then mentally handicapped, and then developmentally disabled. Now children like Mike are called developmentally disadvantaged or children with special needs. Ways of looking at the problems and ways of coping change, but problems remain the same.

Thirty years ago, books available to parents of children with disabilities showed an appalling lack of imagination. They displayed lurid photographs of institutionalized children, helpless, never engaged in productive activity. Any studies done comparing the progress and potential of those children to nondisabled children of the same age invariably left parents feeling without hope for the disabled child's future. Parents then had literally no idea what to expect if they undertook the challenge of raising a child with a disability at home.

Today, that isn't true. Somewhere along the way, individual parents and parent groups began to say, "Hey, wait a minute! The problems we are facing are the same parenting problems we have with our other children, only intensified. Why are so few support services available? Why are persons with handicapping conditions, even ones who are severely disabled, shunted off to institutions and segregated schools? Why are their needs and especially their potentials being minimized?"

Gradually, state legislatures responded. The series of bills sponsored by former Assemblyman Frank Lanterman of California made that state a pioneer in the fight for the rights of developmentally disabled persons with the creation of a statewide network of centers that offered a complete range of services to clients. This network now includes twenty-two Regional Centers administered by the Department of Developmental Services.

Other states have similar programs under varying titles. A letter to the National Association for Retarded Citizens can bring you the information you need about your own state. (See the Appendix for the address.)

Referred to Regional Centers or their equivalent in other states, newborns and older children can receive evaluations, diagnosis, health counseling and, where necessary, advice about placement. Frequently, parents can be put in touch with parents of children with similar disabilities. Parents can also receive information about family planning, genetic counseling, and supportive family counseling. More about each of these specifics will be discussed throughout the book.

As more parents today refuse to hide their disabled child's light under a bushel, parent groups are becoming more numerous and more active. In most states now there are parent groups concerned with Down's syndrome, autism, cerebral palsy, epilepsy, spina bifida, and many other disabilities.

Even today, however, some doctors and other professionals aren't aware these groups exist. Knowledge of resources for bewildered parents to draw upon varies drastically from doctor to doctor, hospital to hospital. A few years ago it was not uncommon for doctors to gently tell parents that the best thing for them was to institutionalize their disabled child before they became too attached to make the break.

So much information, so many supportive services are available now that no parent need ever feel helpless or abandoned in facing the future with a child with a disability.

When professionals make negative predictions about your child's potential, sometimes they know less than you do. When experts tell you something will not work, they may mean only that they have never tried it.

When you have learned all you can about your child's disability, have evaluated the testing done by professionals involved in the child's life, and have integrated it all with your own parent-sense, no one may know better than you what may be possible through a strong, positive faith, honest acceptance of your child, optimistic attitudes toward his life and yours, and willingness to work for his right to live the most fulfilling life he is capable of living.

Millions of kids, like our son Mike, would never have made the grade if one needed to be "perfectly normal" to inhabit this less-than-perfect world. As psychoanalyst Dr. Karen Horney observed, "A perfectly normal person is rare in our civilization."

Ninety percent of parents never have to face the knowledge that their baby has a disability. For them, such a fear is no more than a nameless, needless goblin that creeps in at three o'clock in the morning. To the rest of us, the fear became a manageable reality.

The first International Year of Disabled Persons, as proclaimed by the United Nations, was 1981. The purpose was "to improve the lives of the world's 400,000,000 disabled persons." Isn't that great? Perhaps it would also be appropriate to have a Year of the Parent with special blessings for natural, adoptive, and foster parents of children who are disabled in any way. These parents have had to learn deeper meanings of the words *love, adventure, faith, compassion,* and *courage.*

And God, who studies each commonplace soul,
Out of commonplace things makes his beautiful whole.
—Sarah Chauncey Woolsey

Preface

to the Second Edition

*T*his edition of *Our Special Child* grew into reality because of the continuing impact of our son Mike's book over the past ten years and because of Mike himself.

Letters have come to us from readers from all parts of the United States and from other countries. Many parents shared stories about their children with special needs. And many letter writers asked questions: Is Mike living at home again? Is he out there and independent? Does he have a job? A girlfriend? Does he drive? Would we follow the same path again, or do my husband and I regret choices we made to prepare Mike to leave home at his maturity? What, if any, has been the downside of this journey that began thirty years ago when Mike was born?

This edition adds two new paths. The first path tries to answer some of these questions as the story follows Mike into independent adulthood—his successes, his adventures (some harrowing), and his struggle to understand who he is as a man.

The second path details strides being made today in accommodating children with special needs as they venture further into mainstream living. In education, particularly, computer technology plays a significant role, thanks in part to changing attitudes and the evolution of computer technology that makes it better able to serve our children.

BETTE M. ROSS
Newport Beach, California, 1992

Acknowledgments

With great gratitude I wish to acknowledge my debt to the following people who made time in their busy lives to share with me help, advice, and materials: from Covina Valley Schools, Dave Golden, Harry W. Krall, and Doris Wheeler; from San Gabriel Valley Regional Center, Ron Woods, Michele Ritchie, and Howard Chudler; from Children's Hospital of Los Angeles, Richard Koch, M.D.; from California State University at Los Angeles, Dr. Alice V. Watkins; from Ontario-Pomona Association for Retarded Citizens, Joanne Travers and Judy Cook; from Cameron Christian Pre-School, Betty Harris; from Valley Light Industries, Adrienne Brooks; parent Faith McLaughlin; and all others who shared their stories.

BETTE M. ROSS
West Covina, California, 1981

Introduction

This book is written for parents of a child with a handicapping condition, but it is of great value to all professionals as well. The author has beautifully presented her reactions to the birth of a baby with Down's syndrome and how she and her husband wrestled with early decisions regarding their son Mike's care at home. It is difficult for those whose children do not have disabilities to appreciate the pain, frustration, and special joys and challenges experienced by parents who raise such a child. Bette Ross's book helps us to see all this.

She takes us through her son Mike's early preschool years, emphasizing the importance of infant stimulation programs to help any child reach full potential. The story continues through her struggles with the educational establishment to achieve a broader program for Mike. Mrs. Ross eloquently presents the problems of raising a disabled child through the adolescent years, including ways to deal with sexual awakening and to encourage development toward independent living as a young adult.

Our Special Child should be on the "must read" list for teachers in special education. It provides a rich understanding of how to better utilize the energy and talents of the parents of the children they teach. The message for all professionals is that they should be alert to new ways to help parents work realistically with their disabled children instead of discouraging them and denying opportunities to their children.

The book will be an inspiration to parents. It illustrates how much can be accomplished by faith, knowledge, determination, and hard work in raising the potential of a person who is mentally retarded. At the same time, the author shows the innumerable ways that parents can work with schools, community, and informal mutual support groups of parents such as she works with in California.

With humor, rich insight, and sound practical advice, Mrs. Ross helps parents help their disabled child take a fitting place in the community. In this process, she tells us that parents can also help the community better understand and accept that people with special needs can make valid and valuable contributions to society.

RICHARD KOCH, M.D.
Division of Medical Genetics
Children's Hospital, Los Angeles, California

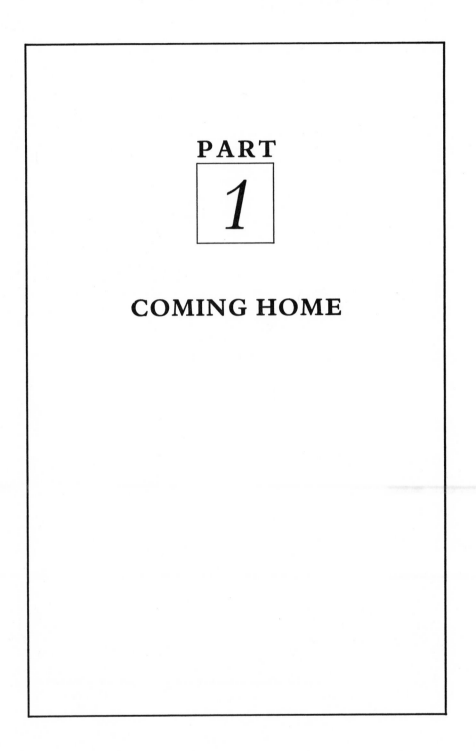

PART

1

COMING HOME

CHAPTER 1

Making a Decision

T here is no way I will take that baby home," declared Joe Curtis to the doctor as they stood in a corridor of the maternity ward. The distraught young father faced the older man, whose hands were jammed into the pockets of his lab coat. "This is the worst day of my life."

Joe Curtis was an intense man. He ran a small business fixing farm machinery. In his town in Kansas, people had babies every day. But not babies like his.

Joe's voice broke as his heart was breaking. His first son. He had just taken flowers to his wife in the maternity ward. He was still haunted by her eyes, which had been dark with sorrow, full of the stunned surprise of someone who doesn't know why she's hurting so badly. Bring that baby, who caused all this grief, home? Never!

Joe brought Evelyn home two days later without their son. "Wait till we decide what to do before we bring him home," Joe had told her. It was the same thing he had said when she had tried to get him to agree on a name for him.

Joe was confident he could find a better place for the baby than in their home. Over the next week he drove miles to visit places that offered care for babies like his. Evelyn went along when he visited the state hospital for mentally retarded persons fifty miles away.

"That was all I could take," she said later. "I just knew we could give our son better care than that. After all, those people had whole wards of babies to care for. How could our son get care as good as we could give him?"

At the time Evelyn was also going daily to visit her son in the hospital. Although she had made the decision not to breast-feed, in her sorrow her arms ached to hold her baby. She would sit in the nursery feeling a fierce protectiveness. This little one! So much against him!

For days, she said nothing to Joe of her visits. Finally, one evening she could put it off no longer. Joe had just come in from visiting the last of the placement homes on their list. The best that he had found with an immediate opening was a resident school where 160 children lived. It was high on the state's list of approved institutions. The cost of keeping a child there was nearly $1,000 a month.

"But even at that," the words came out of Joe as though he were unwilling to say them, "it was nothing like a *home* home."

"I couldn't *put* him there," said Evelyn.

"There are foster care homes," said Joe. "But he'd have to go on a waiting list to get in. He'd have to go to an institution first." He looked anxiously at his wife.

"But if he's going to be cared for in somebody's home—when he gets in—wouldn't it be best if it were our home?" Their eyes met.

"Is that what you want?" said Joe.

"Yes. Oh, yes! Is it what you want?"

"I don't want you to be sad."

"I am sad. If we gave our baby to someone else to take care of, I would still be sad, but I'd feel guilty, too. It's not like he's going to need constant medical care . . . it's just that I truly believe we are the best parents for him. Oh, Joe, I love him no matter what's wrong! I can't help it!"

"Then I want him home, too," said Joe.

And they decided to name the baby Robert, the name they had chosen before he was born.

Joe and Evelyn Curtis are among thousands of parents who have gone through this painful experience. Though much of the information in this book comes from our own family's experiences, our mentally retarded son, Mike, is now an adult. Our learning experiences with him do not always offer helpful direction to today's parent. Therefore, I've also investigated much that is new in research and programs for individuals who are mentally retarded, and I've asked many parents like the Curtises to share their stories, too.

At a time when they are reeling emotionally, all parents of children with disabilities face the same decision: Should they take the baby home? If they do, how will the situation affect their other children? Children yet to come? Will one parent gradually give up other activities to devote a lifetime of care to this one child? Will the expense and the extra care and the emotional load on the family impose stresses that could endanger the fabric of the marriage itself?

WHERE IS HOME FROM HERE?

"Don't take him home," the obstetrician says. "You'll all be better off if you place him in a residential facility immediately."

Then the pediatrician says, "You had him. It's up to you to take care of him." Other professionals may propose a host of intermediate solutions.

But this child has a disability! It isn't that he wasn't planned for. You just hadn't planned that he was going to be imperfect. Now what? Toss him back and try to land another, more perfect?

The crush of problems that come when a child with a disability is born is so heavy and so emotion-laden that it is unwise to rush into a decision regarding your child's future. The Curtises preferred to leave Robert in the hospital while seeking a decision, but many parents take their babies home while not actually committing themselves to keeping them there. This approach removes the time pressure of having to reach informed decisions before they have investigated all the alternatives.

The best source of informed help and support during this period and later is often parents who have children with similar conditions. They can tell you what to expect if you rear your child at home. Your doctor may not be aware of existing parent groups, but making telephone calls to local service agencies, such as the public social services department, may help. If your town has no such listing, call city hall and ask for the name of a group, public or private, that serves children who are mentally retarded. After you get in touch with one appropriate agency, the personnel will be able to refer you to others. Be patient. Other people are busy, too, and they may sometimes seem to be unfeeling. What is a devastating problem to you may be only a routine referral to them. Try not to let it get you down. Once you locate the right group, chances are you will find the solid comfort, inspiration, and reliable information you need as you struggle to reach a decision both parents can live with.

One of the most valued leaders in this field when Mike was a baby was Richard Koch, M.D., of the Division of Medical Genetics at Children's Hospital of Los Angeles. Regarding placement, Dr.

Koch felt that "if out-of-home care is required, foster home or family care is recommended, rather than institutional care. At the Regional Center for Developmentally Disabled, Los Angeles, it has been several years since a young child with Down's syndrome was placed in an institution."[1]

The key is having help and support for the parents, particularly the parent who will be most involved with the child, usually the mother. If you take your child home to rear, be prepared for more traumas, more sorrow sometimes. However, the lows may be lower, but the highs are so much higher!

IN HOME—OUT OF HOME—WHICH IS BEST?

As you consider what is best for your child, ask yourselves, Given the nature and degree of severity of the disability, where will our child have the greatest chance to become a well-adjusted person?

Perhaps it will be your home and perhaps not. Dr. Koch has pointed out, "A loving home or foster home, combined with early education techniques, can result in an intelligence quotient (IQ) 20 to 30 points higher than that of the child reared in an institution."[2] New research on measuring intelligences will be discussed in chapter 10.

Professionals working with youngsters with disabilities in out-of-home placements say that they can always tell the children who spend their first years in family homes: They are emotionally more stable and can usually do more for themselves. (Children brought up in institutions from birth haven't learned to do for themselves because staff members sometimes don't have time—or always patience or interest—needed to train children to feed and dress themselves and to become toilet trained.)

If you decide to place your child in a state facility, acquaint yourself with the laws regarding care of wards of the state. Different agencies may tell you conflicting things. The best way for you to discover which of the child's rights you are relinquishing is to call the local office of the state legislator representing your area. Ask someone in that office to find out for you which laws apply to children being made wards of the state and to send you copies or summaries of what they cover.

Make certain before you sign anything that your decision can be revoked if you later change your mind. Ask the social worker, or whoever is handling your case, to show you the section of the document that specifically states it. If the document does not state that the decision is revocable, or if there are confusing portions, it would be well worth your peace of mind to consult an attorney and ask for an explanation of the document. Then if you do place your baby out of home, whether in a private or state facility, and come later to believe that you can do a better job raising the child at home, you can still do so.

People like you and me, making all kinds of interesting mistakes, can work wonders. No professional will have the interests of your child more at heart, no matter how impeccable the professional credentials. To professionals, your child is of necessity one of many in their care. Experts in any field come and go, transfer, get promoted.

Parenting is a deeper experience. You don't switch children as you become more proficient in parenting. You get to keep the ones you made the first loving mistakes on and experience the joy of realizing that those mistakes were not crucial—merely part of the parent growing, too.

> Do not worry about tomorrow, for tomorrow will worry about its own things. Sufficient for the day is its own trouble.
> —Matthew 6:34

CHAPTER 2

Getting Organized at Home with Your Baby

I saw a delicate flower had grown up two feet high between the horses' feet and the wheel track. An inch more to right or left had sealed its fate, or an inch higher. Yet it lived to flourish and never knew the danger it incurred.

—Henry David Thoreau

*W*hen we brought Mike home from the hospital, an unavoidable task was telling those we loved that our new baby had a disability. Some already knew it. They had visited us in the hospital, had been met by my tears, and had left in sorrow and, often, in guilt. (I guess guilt plays a part because our first reaction to this sort of news is to be grateful it happened to someone else.)

We already had a two-year-old son, Jimmy, a sturdy, bright, and active child. Jimmy was too little to understand much about his baby brother, but he didn't really care. To him, babies that small were only good for looking at anyway, and for holding gingerly, like they were company.

Grandparents are a different matter. Tied into grandparents' love for grandchildren is their love for us. During our growing years, our parents could usually make things right. Now, they see not only the baby's problems but ours as well, and they are helpless to do anything about it. No wonder they often have a hard time accepting the situation.

We did it all wrong. In the heat of our distress, we dumped the news on the grandparents without warning. Their shock led to denials, recriminations, and unhappy feelings that lasted for months.

With a little more thought we could have chosen other ways to inform the grandparents. How would I suggest doing it today? If they lived out of visiting range, I would put off telling them of the birth for a few days until I could learn more about my child's disability and possible potential in order not to paint a totally bleak picture. Even if they lived nearby, I would write to them rather than call to give them time to grieve alone before sharing our grief.

The opening words of Dr. Benjamin Spock's third revision of his world-famous book *Baby and Child Care* are, "You know more than you think you do." A few pages later he says,

> Love and enjoy your children for what they are, for what they look like, for what they do, and forget about the qualities that they don't have. . . . The children who are appreciated for what they are, even if they are homely, or clumsy, or slow, will grow up with confidence in themselves—happy. They will have a spirit that will make the best of all the capacities that they have. . . . They will make light of any handicaps. But the children who have never been quite accepted by their parents, who have always felt that they were not quite right, will grow up lacking confidence. . . . If they start life with a handicap, physical or mental, it will be multiplied tenfold by the time they are grown up.[1]

These comments apply to all persons, not just those with special needs.

SETTLING INTO A ROUTINE

A bit of a song from the musical *West Side Story* talks about time to love and time to care spent just being together, without pressure. You want to capture this feeling now. Although your emotional state may be anything but calm and happy for a while after you come home from the hospital, allowing yourselves to settle into a comfortable routine has several benefits. If your baby has no life-threatening problem that requires extraordinary care, your doctor will probably tell you to treat him as you would any new baby. If you have other children, this will be easier than if you are establishing a "new baby routine" for the first time.

Mom, there always seems to be something that needs doing when a new baby enters a family. Even so, when the baby naps, you rest. Get a good book if you like to read. Do something personally pleasurable for yourself. Establish the baby's nap time as your free time. Don't cram in a few more of those endless household tasks; care for yourself; make it a recreation period for your intellectual, physical, or spiritual well-being.

While helping your baby to work around to regular eating and sleeping hours, try to keep other variables of day-to-day living at a constant. I wouldn't tear into a remodeling project, for example, repaint the walls, or do anything else that introduces temporary physical clutter. It's always more difficult to carry on routines when the house is torn up. The assurance of outward order right now is just one more thing that may help you relax and feel more able to deal with your chaotic feelings.

Was there some favorite activity you shared with your other children before the arrival of the baby? A favorite TV show you and your spouse rarely missed? Did you go out shopping and have dinner at McDonald's on Friday nights? Did you regularly attend worship services?

Yes, you are feeling so tired, so fatigued. And you know why. It's not merely the physical exertion of having a baby; it's the fact he has a handicapping condition. If he did not have the condition, what would you be doing now? Let me guess: planning to get your figure back in a hurry, promising yourself a clothes-shopping spree in a few weeks. Good idea! Plan it. Put it in your mind. Look forward to it.

Dad, did you regularly play tennis or bowl with your friends on your day off? But you haven't played in a few weeks, not since the baby? If the baby's mother has difficulty getting out of the house, you may feel you should stay home on your day off and give her a breather. Good for you! But you need R & R (rest and recreation), too. The comfort and support of your friends are as nourishing as the exercise. Perhaps both parents can manage time so that you help each other with the baby and chores at home and each get some time away.

Having fun, relaxing with each other away from the children, is good, too. Yes, you've probably spent more time together since the baby came, spelling each other, caring for the infant and the other children. But now try to arrange to spend time with and for each other, as you did before the baby. Social workers point out that divorce rates for parents of babies with disabilities are much greater than for the general populace.

RESPITE CARE

A social worker told me of a mother who had not been apart from her two children with disabilities and their brother for ten years, defeating her husband's every effort to lure her away. Finally, he gave her an ultimatum: "Either you go with me [to an expense-paid company vacation and convention across the country], or we're through."

The wife was outraged. The poor woman felt torn in two. She said, "As if I haven't enough to cope with! How could he be so callous? So selfish! It isn't enough I'm giving my life to the children—"

The social worker cut in gently. "Yes, it is," she said. "It's too much. Your husband loves you. He sees what you are doing to yourself and to the marriage by doing everything for these two kids. What about your other child? What about him?"

Convinced her husband meant what he said, and persuaded by the social worker that other people were capable of caring for her children in her absence, she was at last able to let go.

When the couple returned two weeks later, the wife was able to view her children with a fresh perspective. For the first time she was able to see their disabling conditions as a problem, shared by her husband, but not the central fact of her existence. Their marriage improved from that point.

Parents who rear youngsters with disabilities will always have more stress, more problems to cope with. Generally, when you meet well-adjusted children, you assume their emotional stability comes from being blessed with well-adjusted parents. But becoming well-adjusted parents doesn't just happen. You must work at it. You learn to include consideration for your physical and mental health and that of your spouse along with the rest of the family's. This element includes having vacations and also regular hours during the week free from care of your child or children with special needs.

Such care is called respite care. *The Random House Dictionary of the English Language* defines *respite* as a "delay . . . for a time, esp. of anything distressing or trying." Respite care is coming to be a vital adjunct to the health and well-being of families of children with handicapping conditions. An outsider provides care for a few hours a week or a few days a month. In every state, parents and parent groups are demanding that state funds spent for care of persons who are mentally retarded include money set aside to pay for regular periods of respite care. In many states, private charitable organizations or church groups offer brief respite stays, a weekend or a few days, for children year-round.

THE POWER OF LOVE

Reading Dr. Spock gives you a great feeling of reassurance. You come to realize that your baby is disabled in only specific areas; in other ways, she is not disabled. If it is difficult at first to separate the child from the disability, try to think consciously of each positive attribute. Does the baby sleep well? Does she have good skin tone or pretty hair? As she grows older, does she respond to your voice or your smile? Is she eager to be fed?

"The natural loving care that kindly parents give their children," says Dr. Spock, "is a hundred times more valuable than their knowing how to . . . diaper just right or how to make a formula expertly."[2]

If a few weeks or months passed before you learned of your baby's disability, you had an advantage over the parent who learned from birth. Uninhibited by feelings of helplessness, you were able to freely enjoy the infant.

Doctors have noted that sometimes the birth of a baby with a disability causes the parents such despondency that they stop talking to her, even ceasing to react to her as a person. Care becomes mechanical. I suppose part of this reaction is a parent's effort at self-preservation, an effort not to care so much, not to love, to protect the self from even more hurt.

But as you become more involved with your baby, your love grows, whether you realize it or not, and so does your sense of pride at her progress. Loving your baby, feeling the need to comfort and protect her, you will naturally stroke her limbs, hug her gently, touch your lips to her, and talk and perhaps sing to her. All of these natural actions are the best possible ways to stimulate the baby to reach full potential within her limitations.

As with any baby, stimulating the senses helps the infant progress better than those who are left alone. This interaction accounts in part for the startling differences found in physical and mental growth between babies with similar disabilities reared in institutions and home environments.

"IS HE GOING TO BE ABLE TO . . . ?"

It is hard to adopt a wait-and-see attitude about your baby's potential development. There are so many unasked questions you would not have considered had the baby been born without the disability. You would not look down the years and think, *What if one of us gets sick or dies and there is no one to care for him? What if the money runs out? What if his sisters and brothers resent him?*

When I used to find myself slipping into the what-ifs, I grew into the habit of asking, *Would I be wondering about these things if they concerned my other children?* I was the world's busiest worrier. Before we even brought Mike home from the hospital, I was worrying about what would become of him when he was grown.

It took a fortuitous remark by Dr. Richard Koch to start me on a different path of thinking. Mike was in for his six-month checkup when Dr. Koch commented, "What beautiful eyes he has."

Well, I'd been so busy worrying about Mike when he would be eighteen that I'd never really noticed his eyes. They were beautiful— brown flecked with gold and black. How could I have missed it? That was the beginning of learning to separate the child from the disability.

I felt a strange, inordinate pride driving home from the doctor that day. Mike was doing better than had been expected. Looking back, not knowing then, I see the beginnings of a realization. I was beginning to think of Mike in terms of the possible, comparing him to his own potential.

DISABILITY AS A PERMANENT GUEST

When we first brought Mike home from the hospital, I can't recall doing anything right. I remember I was tired all the time. I craved the plunge into sleep. True, with Jimmy still under two, it was a busy time. Having two in diapers always is for a mother with no help. But it was more than that. Mike's Down's syndrome weighted my walk, my thinking, my actions.

More than tired, I could not involve myself in anything else. I was not even sure I loved Mike. Years later, reflecting on Mike's early days, my husband confessed that he, too, had had difficulty loving Mike. Each had kept those feelings from the other. I saw myself then as trapped, hopelessly, forever. No doctor we went to felt Mike would be better off in an institution; he was too "high," almost borderline Down's. We could not afford private residential care. We brought him home, decided gradually to rear him at home, almost by default, and only because searching deep within ourselves, Guy and I could not honestly believe that at that point in Mike's life anyone else was better equipped to care for him than we were.

This statement sounds terribly blunt, but it is also true. I resented Mike terribly. We would never be the image of the two-car, one-dog, 2½-kids, and big-backyard family that I had always envisioned. I was not prepared to be part of one of those families where disability is a permanent guest. I had always felt that such families were "different" first, and that's why such things happened to them. It didn't happen to nice people like us, who went to church on Sundays and had the grandparents over for dinner regularly.

I don't like to recall those first six months, having blocked them out for many years. The city we moved to, a poorer city, was near a waste treatment plant and an oil refinery. When the wind swept in off the ocean, the stench was terrible. In summer it was a breeding place for mosquitoes. Our house was situated near the crossroads of two major highways in a heavily industrial sector. Ambulances screamed by two or three times a night. Guy's new job was in a city nearly an hour's drive away. He was usually gone from seven in the morning until past eight at night. I knew no one in the neighborhood.

Yet, despite the nightmare quality of my recollection, I must have done something right. The person I shortchanged was not the baby but me. And that only out of a collection of circumstances such as having no relatives or trusted friends nearby to lean on for support, a hostile neighborhood, and a money shortage that made it unthinkable as far as I was concerned to spend money on myself or for baby-sitting, especially since I had nowhere to go anyway.

Dutifully, I nursed Mike, spooned strained food into him, gave him vitamins, kept him dry and clean, and attended to his numerous wants. His bad temper was the result of a bowel problem that necessitated suppositories and occasional enemas to help him eliminate. (That would give anybody a foul temper.) Although Jimmy and I took him for walks in the stroller, it was not a safe neighborhood, so we usually stayed in the yard.

Nevertheless, when I took Mike in for the first checkup, the doctor seemed amazed by his progress. He was responding well to his environment, he was a happy baby, he had gained weight, and his muscle tone was improving—all encouraging signs for good potential development.

"I'm glad to see you are talking to him," the doctor observed as I dressed Mike.

"Why wouldn't I?"

"Some mothers give up. They become so convinced that nothing can be done, they stop talking to the child."

It had never occurred to me not to talk to Mike. Just as it had never occurred to me not to nurse him. I had nursed his brother. And being a lazy person, I found it so much easier to give him milk already warm and sterile than to fuss with bottles. I was being a good mother in spite of myself. What a shock!

"CAN'T WE HAVE AN OPERATION TO FIX IT?"

Remember the joke about the little kid who asks where he comes from? Conscientious Mom drops everything, sits down, and gives an explicit explanation of where babies come from. "Oh," says the kid. "My friend Kevin's from New Jersey."

Most parents with children give considerable thought to telling them about the coming baby in such a manner that they feel part of the experience. They learn that the new addition will be "our baby" and that they will get to help Mommy and Daddy with the baby's care.

One thing that worries parents of babies with disabilities is how to tell their other children that their new baby has a handicapping condition that won't ever go away.

Well, don't forget Kevin from New Jersey.

Frank and Dora Thompson worried about telling their girls, ages six and seven, about their newborn daughter's Down's syndrome. For weeks, they put off telling the girls, debating the right approach to avoid trauma. When they finally explained it, the girls said merely, "Oh, you mean like the kids at school in the special room!" Then they wanted to know if their new sister could have an operation for it or if it would go away when she got bigger.

Depending on the ages of your other children, keep your explanation to just the facts you feel they need to understand how the disability affects the baby and them.

"He's paralyzed on one side. That means his left arm and leg don't work too well."

"Can he have an operation to make them work right, like mine?"

"Not yet, but maybe someday there will be a way. We just have to help Tommy learn to use his other arm and leg as well as he can."

When Jimmy was about four, we told him about Mike's disability. Until that age he could not really discern any difference between Mike and other two-year-olds. "Mike has a disease called Down's syndrome. It doesn't mean he's sick exactly. Just that he won't grow as fast as you did."

"Not ever?"

"Probably not. It's not anybody's fault. It's just something that happened."

Give your children time to think things over. They will probably look more closely at the baby for a while, trying to decide how this new information makes a difference. They may ask more questions later, and they may not. I suspect that when a baby is born with a disability, other children in the family may feel they are to blame. Maybe they didn't want a little stranger to come into Mommy's and Daddy's lives, and somewhere deep inside they fear that their bad thoughts caused something to happen. I never knew if Jimmy ever felt that way, but I went out of my way to assure him that it was no one's fault.

Children can accept almost anything if their parents treat it in a matter-of-fact manner. They will accept the new baby and love her as they would any new sister if these are the vibrations they feel from their parents.

Whether or not the parent really believes the disability is a matter of fact, or a fact that overwhelms the rest of family life, is important to the future well-being of the family.

One thing parents can do to emphasize their healthy attitudes toward their youngster with special needs is to try to provide special, separate times to share with each of the other children.

If you tell them that Tiffany's cerebral palsy doesn't make a difference in how much you love the rest of the children and then spend all your time with Tiffany or all your conversations with others discussing Tiffany's condition, your other children may become confused. They may feel that you do not really believe that Tiffany is no more special than the rest of them. They may feel bad about it and yet feel guilty about their feelings because they do realize that she has a disability and they do not.

Gradually, you will come to appreciate the help and support your other children can give you. Tell them frequently how much it means to you and what a joy they are to you. (How many times have you confessed to friends, "I don't know what I'd do without my children's help!" and yet neglected to tell them?)

In addition to telling your immediate family about the baby's disability, you must speak to your friends. They will be eager to see your new addition to the family. Help them to see what you see. If they are truly interested and sympathetic, tell them in detail what you know, what he has, and how it manifests itself. It's easier for them to understand and be supportive when they are in your confidence.

"HE'S STILL A GREAT LITTLE KID"

Children are so full of curiosity that any unusual situation arouses their interest. When Guy and I went to visit some old friends who had not yet seen Mike, their ten-year-old, Walter, was intensely curious. I sensed disappointment when he looked at the baby. He whispered something to his mother. She laughed. "Walter's disappointed because Mike looks the same as all babies."

"How did the doctor know there was anything wrong with him?" Walter blurted.

I hesitated. How much should I tell him? He was a bright child, and he was my friend. And I was beginning to be aware that I wanted people, children in particular, to understand about Mike so that they would not be afraid of his differences as they grew older. Walter and I sat on the couch with Mike on my lap. I explained about the epicanthic fold of the upper eyelid that accounted for the slightly oriental look, and I showed him the somewhat stubby fingers and toes. Then I demonstrated the Babinski reflex on Mike's foot. Walter took it all in.

When I had finished, he said, "He's still a great little kid, Mrs. Ross."

"That was nice of you," his mother said after Walter had gone off to play. "I was ready to wring his neck."

Sometimes the telling backfires.

When the Sandstones, a middle-aged couple from Phoenix, saw their granddaughter for the first time at three months, the grandmother gazed at her in tight-lipped silence, then exploded in anger, "There's nothing wrong with that baby! Why are you persecuting her?"

The baby's mother was shocked and hurt by the outburst. The irony of it! Being forced to defend a condition that had all but towed the family under! She gave up, the mother told a parent group years later, ever trying to explain it rationally to her parents. For years after, every time she'd call her mother to report some new accomplishment by her mentally retarded child (always amid news of the other children), she'd say, "See, I told you there was nothing wrong with her."

Another parent at the same meeting, full of anger, related how her father reacted on one occasion when he dropped in while she was playing the guitar. Her two-year-old son had cerebral palsy. He loved music and was rocking and waving his unimpaired arm to the

17

music. The grandfather had been a concert pianist. The mother assumed he would be delighted at the child's evident enjoyment of the music. His response was a shock: "Why not? He's going to be a pianist. He's going to gain full use of that hand."

The mother would have laughed had the grandfather's delusion been less tragic—not in terms of the baby's paralysis but of the man's inability to accept the baby and love him as he was.

"I SEE WHAT IS BEHIND MY EYES"

With great insight the daughter of the concert pianist helped us realize why relatives sometimes are unable to accept our children's disabilities. "Your mother needed more information," she told the first parent, "just like my father. When you say 'retarded' or 'disabled' to grandparents, they think of a crazy person or they remember the town where they grew up and the 'kid not right in the head' who wandered around town with nothing to do and nowhere to go. Not living with your child and knowing him like you do, the image they build is their own stereotype. The Chinese have a proverb for it: 'I see what is behind my eyes.' Not what is, but what I believe.

"And you have to remember," she said, "your parents are in pain not only for their grandchild but for you, their child. They know your pain, and no matter how old you are, you are still their child. They can't help you or do anything to change the fact that you have a disabled child, and they know it."

Relatives seem to come in different varieties, like salt for a water softener. Best of all, of course, are the salt of the earth, who learn to treat your child like all the other nieces and nephews or grandchildren without special favoritism or the opposite. Cherish these relatives and friends like them.

Lean on them for emotional support when you need it. Encourage your spouse to do likewise. A sympathetic listener can help you keep the problems attendant to your disabled child in perspective. But don't expect sympathetic treatment as a way of life. That gets stale quickly.

A second category of friends and relatives includes those whose sympathy unfortunately gets in the way of good sense. No one consistently spoils a child and expects the child to exhibit good manners and reasonable behavior. Yet sometimes friends are so overcome with sympathy that they cannot resist favoring the child with special needs. This treatment can be demoralizing to the brothers and sisters.

There are a few relatives or acquaintances you can do without. This person is so entangled in her own hangups that the thought of coping with a genuinely disabled person is actually upsetting. Or he is depressingly fascinated with the deviations of behavior or mannerisms that loving parents overlook, such as rocking, or differences in appearance. Or she acts worried—perhaps the condition will rub off on her! If only such people could by some miracle briefly stand in the shoes of a person with a disability and know how hard the person tries to do everyday things.

Do you convey to others a sense of being a whole person rather than being merely the parent of a disabled child? "Merely?" you say. "It's a rather big job!" Yes, but not the whole of your life. An acquaintance is also the parent of a child with a handicapping condition. Our children have grown up in the same schools. In all the years we have bumped into each other, she never mentioned having any other family while bubbling over with news of Lucy. She was involved constantly in school, workshop, and recreation activities for her Down's syndrome daughter. Imagine my surprise upon learning just recently that she has two other children and a husband. The word from the husband (via my husband) was: "Far as me and the other kids go, she's never home. I try to make it up to them."

Getting organized at home with your baby means getting your life organized, too. If you have no family member or friend who will sit occasionally with your children, begin now to locate a sitter. If you cannot afford to hire one, consider going to work for pay a few hours a week. If your salary does no more than pay for your travel, the sitter, and a few hours away from home, it will be worth it in terms of your health, your self-confidence, and your outlook on life. Spending time away from your baby will help you work with her more confidently and more lovingly.

"The more people have studied different methods of bringing up children, the more they have come to the conclusion that what good mothers and fathers instinctively feel like doing for their babies is usually best, after all."[3]

CHAPTER 3

Coping with Grief and Stress

R ampaging tropical storms drenched southern California last winter. Homes perched on hillsides slipped from their foundations, breaking apart. Other homes were viciously undercut by the fast-moving currents of swollen washes. Hundreds of homes and mobile home parks built in the flatlands were flooded out.

Who says tragedy builds stronger foundations?

A stone house built on granite may resist catastrophe better than other types of housing but not better than the same house unhit by tragedy.

What is the point?

For years, psychologists have been fond of saying that tragedy welds a family together. Not without a terrific struggle, it doesn't! If a family is strong to begin with, it may eventually become stronger. But in the meantime you feel that your soul is being ripped apart, that you were never so alone; and here comes some person who's never been through it suggesting that everyone but you is coping beautifully!

Grieving over a child's disabilities compounds the natural stresses that occur when a new baby comes home. Sol Gordon, in his book *Living Fully*, notes, "Occasionally [the birth of a baby with special needs] has added strength and new spiritual dimensions. In these situations, husbands and wives accept the challenge involved, support each other, and think themselves blessed for what they've got. But more often, stress occurs."[1]

As you settle in at home with your baby, you find you need great tightrope-walking skills. Minor irritations become magnified; simple accidents become catastrophes; disagreements explode into dreadful arguments. Families are asked to cope with a situation not of their making whose resolution is rarely in sight, something dumped more or less permanently on them. No wonder its waves wash over every corner of their lives.

It's hard to overestimate the power of forces hidden behind that simple word *stress*. Webster defines *stress* as "strain; pressure; especially a force exerted upon a body, that tends to strain or deform its shape." That's quite a weapon.

My world went out of order when Mike was born. I saw no way to make it right. So for a time I became obsessed with order. I folded and refolded diapers endlessly, stacked and restacked them, squaring the corners, seeing how high I could make the stacks without them tipping.

I became totally autocratic with my not-yet-two-year-old son, Jimmy. I had decided that if you train little ones strictly, their good habits will lead them in the right direction when they are growing up, and the parent will not have to do further work.

I began insisting Jimmy always replace the soap in the soapdish in the bathtub, never in one corner or the other where he was prone to leave it. The washcloth always had to be folded and the ring scrubbed away before he climbed out. At the same time, any little tumble he took from his tricycle or off furniture (he was a climber) filled me with remorse all out of proportion to his bumps and bruises. I was a bad mother...I couldn't do anything right...I let my son fall and get hurt...how could I expect him to bathe properly when I was a bad mother?

One day Mike cried with colic—nonstop. By late afternoon my nerves were so frazzled they were ready to rip like silk at the slightest snag. Jimmy came in from playing, happily dirty from head to bare foot. One look at him and I began screaming, "Don't you care about making Mommy more work? What a bad little boy you are...," and on and on and on. Jimmy just stood in the middle of the kitchen floor trying to stuff all ten fingers into his mouth.

Suddenly, I looked at him, really looked at him, and there was a frightened, adorable child, wide-eyed, having not the least idea why his mother was screaming. I burst out crying and went down on my knees to hug him and tell him Mommy was sorry, it was all her fault. After that I began conscientiously thanking God for Jimmy. And I began trying to thank God for Mike, for God's believing we were parents enough to make our circumstances a growing experience for our family and, ultimately, a triumph of love.

Stress doesn't always come out in screams. It surfaces in unpredictable ways. My misdirected anger and irritability toward Jimmy came, I believe, out of my frustration at being thrust into a situation I could not control, the presence of an immutable imperfection in Mike. Stress makes that inward turn and punishes the body with ulcers and other disorders (more frequently in men than in women) while the outward person presents a capable facade to the community. Stress commonly produces symptoms of headaches, nausea, and muscle tension.

It's not hard to pinpoint the causes of stress. Most obvious is the inescapable distress over the baby's condition. Guilt, no matter how short-lived, produces stress. Feelings of inadequacy: that you as parents will fall short of what you need to be in the challenge ahead. Fear of the unknown: incomplete knowledge of what the baby's disability means to your family in terms of your other children, your relationships with each other, your finances. Anger: the injustice of it all. The ambivalent feelings you may be having toward your child or your spouse or your other children are all capable of producing stress.

If you cannot bare these feelings to your spouse or someone in a parent group or your friends, find somebody you can relate to. Don't wait until your feelings are compounded by the inevitable problems that will arise naturally, as with any child, as your disabled child grows older. Release them now so that you, too, can begin to heal emotionally.

An emotionally healthy parent is more able to rear emotionally healthy children. You must fight for your emotional balance so that you can be an effective parent.

Your family doctor may be able to help you, depending on how much experience she has had with what you are going through and the degree to which she has earned your confidence. Your minister or rabbi, a trusted friend, or a family guidance counselor may also help you find enough that is positive about your situation to give you a foundation of support, peace, and stability so that you can go forward again.

YOU ARE GRIEVING THE LOSS OF A PERFECT CHILD

Grieving over an irremediable imperfection is normal. For nine months, parents anticipate the arrival of a perfect infant, and in one short hour the shape of their hopes, dreams, and plans for the future is changed. Shock, disbelief, denial, anger, and guilt arise in a welter of confused feelings.

Many professionals working with families of persons with permanent disabilities are fond of explaining that sorrow or grief, once "worked through," is then somehow laid to rest and everything returns to normal. But many parents of children with disabilities deny that they ever worked through their grief.

Simon Olshansky, M.S.W., agrees with them. A well-respected social worker, Olshansky is one of the few doing research in the field of chronic sorrow in families of mentally retarded children. In a study carried out while Olshansky was study director of Children's Developmental Clinic, Cambridge, Massachusetts, he found that chronic sorrow is a fact of life for the parent of a mentally retarded child. Olshansky explains,

> This sorrow is a natural response to a tragic fact. If the professional worker accepts chronic sorrow as a natural, rather than a neurotic, response, he can be more effective in helping the parent achieve the goal of increased comfort in living with and managing a mentally defective child.... Most parents who have [such a] child suffer chronic sorrow throughout their lives regardless of whether the child is kept at home.... The intensity of this sorrow varies from time to time for the same person, from situation to situation, and from one family to another.[2]

Until Olshansky put a name to it, chronic sorrow was called unresolved guilt by too many psychologists. One parent crystallized the disparity of parental and medical opinion in this manner: Doctors and psychologists see the onset and relief of grief, stress, and guilt as occurring in a straight time continuum, like a bone that is broken, set, heals, and becomes perfect again.

Parents, on the other hand, see grief and stress as a circle, a vicious circle sometimes, in which the grief and stress are coped with successfully for a time but crop up in different circumstances.

What is more normal than to feel a limited return of grief when one son is romping on a football field and the other is forever sidelined? You don't "grow out of it" because the situation is never grown out of. The relapses come, most parents agree, in reaction to definite time-limited situations.

Evelyn, mother of an adult son who is autistic and aphasic, says, "After coping with an episode of chronic sorrow, I feel I am stronger than when I went into it." She is an older parent who has done a fine job with her son, in the opinion of an experienced parent counselor, and she developed a good theory along the way. You can accept chronic sorrow, Evelyn found, in the spirit of grieving for someone gone. There remains a real bonding with your child, and there is nothing negative in that.

Professionals and psychologists tend to think some strange thing takes place. Well, it doesn't at all. Sorrows come to everybody. So although mourning what might have been, you still love and enjoy and appreciate your child for what he is—and that is true bonding.

"HE SAYS HE DOESN'T NEED TO TALK ABOUT IT"

Sylvia's reaction upon learning after four months that her infant son had cerebral palsy was to head immediately for a library. Only the information about CP was outdated. It just frightened her more. Sylvia needed a year to cope with her initial grief.

"But my husband never mentioned the baby's problem, not from day one," Sylvia told her parent-group friends one evening. "He's never cried. He says he doesn't need to talk about it. I don't know; it seems to me everybody has to talk about their grief, y'know? Get it out from inside. It's been two years now since we found out. . . . I mean he treats the baby okay and everything, so he's gotta be feeling something, right?"

The next month when the group came together, everyone noticed a special quality about Sylvia, a kind of all-over shininess. We asked her about it.

"It was the darndest thing," she smiled. "We were watching the cerebral palsy telethon the other night, my husband and me. I figured we could learn something; and I mean, it was really something, all those pledges pouring in. It made me feel good. And then at the end, they started bringing kids onstage who had cerebral palsy, and all of a sudden I looked at my husband and he was crying. He was just sobbing! And for once, for the first time in our marriage, he let me comfort him. It had always been the other way around. So many times when he'd been feeling bad, I wanted him to let me help, and he never would."

They had talked for hours after the telethon. Sylvia learned something about her husband that astounded her. He was afraid that if he broke down in front of his wife and cried, there would be no one to pick up the pieces.

"What a terrible burden for anyone to carry," one of the other parents said softly. "Whoever said that to be masculine you shouldn't cry? Or that you never break down in front of your woman, you never can be weak or ask for help or say, 'What are we going to do?' "

The group was silent a moment, feeling the enormity of carrying a weight like that. "Life is bad enough," said one. "But when you have a disabled baby. . . . And it's not a situation that goes away."

The women in the group seemed especially subdued for the remainder of the evening and the men rather abashed that one had broken ranks and shared with his wife, his closest and most beloved friend, his terrible need for comfort and reassurance. Maybe it would take a long while for any of them to feel secure enough to break tradition again. But someone had made a beginning.

Some parents delay coping with their grief over a disabled child because the baby also has serious medical problems, sometimes of a life-threatening nature. One father expressed it this way: "Somehow, when the little guy is fighting for his life and you are fighting right in there with him, you find yourself hoping so badly he'll pull through that you don't care if he's going to be mentally retarded. You just want him to make it."

Typically, parents respond to the immediate need, putting aside for a time worry about the long-term problem. Many say this has helped them to cope with their grief. A partnership develops with the infant struggling so hard to survive so that when the immediate battle is won, the permanent bonding of parent and child has already begun.

Fathers especially have expressed the view that their fear of losing their child played a strong part in being able to accept the fact later that the child had developmental disabilities.

"WOMEN ARE STRONGER THAN MEN IN EVERYTHING BUT THE BENCH PRESS"

Some men still feel that part of their responsibility as head of the house is to be a rock that a grieving wife can cling to. But this image binds them to other "rock" properties: hard, unmoving, nearly impossible to break down without shattering.

But men do feel love, grief, exhilaration. Though some may still conceal them, today's men—fathers—feel more comfortable acknowledging their emotional needs. Both sexes need to be strong, loving, caring human beings; they need to vent the emotional elements of their natures.

At no time does a man caught in the rock-bound image suffer more than when he has a child with a disability. Not only may his ego suffer from the mistaken notion of having fathered imperfectly, but if he perceives himself as not being allowed to show grief, his troubles are compounded. Just how disastrous this culturally induced restriction can be is revealed in statistics that show a far greater incidence of heart disease, ulcers, and other stress-related diseases among men than among women.

Women, not having to protect a stereotypical image that inhibits display of emotion, are generally more able to share grief and other emotions with one another. They know how difficult it is for their men to share grief. The day is closer when sharing all emotions is a two-way street, with the wife in partnership, strong and available and able to comfort her husband as her husband comforts her. The result of women's unrestricted emotional development is, as a psychologist visiting our parent group wryly observed, that "women are stronger than men in everything but the bench press."

Talking it out is the only way to get through the phases of grief, many psychologists believe, even if you have to grab someone off the street to listen.

Comedians love to play skits off the comical relationship between a man all tied in knots with a problem and the friend he corrals to listen, who never gets a word in. When the lopsided exchange is over, a vastly relieved man walks away from the encounter saying breezily, "Thanks, Jerry! You've really taken a load off my mind!" And there's Jerry, palms out, mouth open, wondering, "What did I say?"

Last spring I spent several afternoons in the company of a young woman I barely knew. She drove the delivery truck for a dry cleaner and was returning my draperies. She and I hung them together; then I invited her to sit with me at the kitchen table for a cup of coffee before she went on her way. She'd been in California only two years, she told me. She and her husband moved when she was three months pregnant. They didn't decide to marry until just before the baby's birth.

When the baby was born, she had a cleft palate and other physical problems. Suddenly, the words were spilling from Lana. She had not been able to get out of her mind the feeling that the baby's condition was punishment for her getting pregnant when single. She felt unable to express her feelings to her husband.

Lana had to leave before she finished her story, having other stops on her route to make. She promised to come back the next day.

Over the next couple of days I listened to all the details. My heart went out to her. So much of her grief about her child was reminiscent of my own, and I carried her needs in my prayers those two nights. By the third day, she was no longer sobbing, and the words were flowing more like a calm tide than a rain-swollen creek. Lana decided all by herself that she wasn't to blame for her daughter's cleft palate. She had wanted with all her heart to bear a perfect baby, had eaten well, and had taken vitamins, even though she did not see a doctor. And she decided that God was not punishing her by giving her a baby with disabilities.

When she left for the last time, Lana was a different person. Her voice had a ring to it as she swung up behind the wheel of her delivery van. It was the voice of a confident young woman better able to move forward in practical fashion with the problems she faced. Her thanks were effusive to the point of embarrassing me. What had I done? Offered a kitchen table, a full pot of coffee, a few hours of time, and my undivided—quiet—attention.

I've not seen Lana since, but I know that if we should bump into each other, the warmth we shared would still be there.

PHYSICIANS DON'T ALWAYS TELL YOU THE TRUTH ABOUT WHAT TO EXPECT

Doctors may be surprised to find themselves singled out as a cause of stress among parents of babies with disabilities. The discussion in our parent group one day centered on how much doctors should reveal to parents when a baby with a handicapping condition is born.

"If we had known the whole story, maybe we wouldn't have been able to handle it. It's better to learn a little at a time," was one parent's feeling.

But another parent disagreed: "We kept asking our doctor questions, and he kept saying, 'Wait and see.' Doctors don't realize that parents are scared. When we are given such sparse information, we head immediately for the library and read from cover to cover information that is badly out of date. And that frightens us all the more."

"All we ever got from our doctor was a closed door. He'd come in for five minutes, look at the baby, and leave." Those parents felt the doctor's actions expressed tacit disapproval over the way they were caring for the baby.

In some cases the doctor had recommended out-of-home placement and showed his displeasure that they had not taken his advice by withdrawing his moral support.

"My pediatrician took care of the baby's needs. My gynecologist and obstetrician took care of my physical health. What was needed was some kind of overall attention to us as a family. Our nights were sleepless, our emotions unstable, our stomachs upset. Our sense of routine was interrupted. Our relations with each other, even with our other children, were terribly difficult. If our doctor had told us we could expect all these other things to happen—call them psychosomatic if you will—maybe we wouldn't have thought we were the only ones in the world going crazy," stated one mother.

Most doctors seem surprised at the widespread feelings of anger and frustration by parents who see them as uncaring or too busy to answer questions. They respond,

- "It's the first time most parents come up against something the doctor is helpless to cure. They have to get angry at someone."
- "We may not know a maternity patient as well as we should, in terms of the whole person. When we deliver a baby with a congenital disability such as Down's syndrome, we don't know how the mother will respond to the news. Many times it's better to say too little than too much."
- "Sometimes I really don't know the answers the parents are seeking. How can anyone say what a child's condition will be in one year or five years after birth?"

Dr. Richard Koch, having dealt with hundreds of parents of developmentally disabled babies, commented, "As soon as the physician is certain of the diagnosis, both parents should be told. The sooner parents become aware of the problem, the better their chance of accepting it and working toward constructive solutions. Initial counseling requires delicate understanding of what it means to parents to be told almost immediately after delivery that their child is abnormal."[3]

Doctors, too, are human and can be touched by human frailty. Their unwillingness to burden parents who are in shock with details of the child's disability may be founded on compassion, especially if they consider the parents unable to cope well with the whole situation. Sometimes, doctors' lack of communication is based on the frustrating awareness of the dearth of medical knowledge about that particular disability. Frequently, there is a real gap in research information upon which to base predictions of the child's potential.

Perhaps some doctors hide behind their professional demeanor because they cannot afford to let themselves care for their patients as individuals. If they feel like that, they are like the husbands who cannot afford to let their wives see their grief. What have they to lose but the wall that shuts them off from other people?

If the amount and kind of information your doctor gives you about your child cause you stress, seek other opinions. Call your local public health department or a local hospital and ask for the names of societies that deal with your child's handicapping condition. Parents in your parent group can often give valuable insights about doctors in the area with whom they have contact. With persistence you can usually find a doctor who is willing to take you into her confidence and will give you the time and consideration you need and deserve.

Also, if there is no parent group in your area, write to the nearest one, attend some of their meetings if possible, and think about organizing one in your area (see chapter 4). Big problems become bigger when hoarded. Shared, they diminish.

THE MYTH OF PARENTAL GUILT FEELINGS

Why do some psychologists assume that the basis for our grief and stress is always our guilt at producing a less-than–perfect child? Parental views of grief, stress, and especially guilt are often at variance with views held by a majority of psychologists.

Listening to a panel in which parent after parent told of negative experiences with psychologists and pediatricians, one doctor who teaches pediatric medicine at a large university teaching hospital exclaimed that she had failed to teach interns one crucial aspect of pediatric medicine: respect for parents.

The professionals who had counseled the parents on the panel had consistently adopted the attitude that they knew what was best for the parents in their grief or stress, often without ever listening to the parents. They consistently denied that parents felt what they said they were feeling and tried to force the square peg into the round hole by insisting that all the parents' feelings of stress or bewilderment were based on guilt. Once they rid themselves of guilt, so the professional line went, all parental stress would magically go away, too.

Parents are sometimes made to feel, in the words of Tillie Olsen in her book *Silences,* "guilt where it is not guilt at all but the workings of an intolerable situation." Which is more normal—to react to grief and stress over an intolerable situation, or to be convinced in therapy that you are harboring hidden guilt over causing the intolerable situation? Why do some psychologists so insist upon it? Especially with mothers. They may try to convince us we are feeling guilty and won't feel better until we admit it! Such an attitude undermines parents' confidence and ability to deal with situations realistically.

How has this sometimes superior attitude of professional toward parent come about? Ann P. Turnbull, writing as a professional *and* parent in the excellent book *Parents Speak Out,* believes it is because interns spend weeks studying the "psychological insight approach to parental guilt" while very little attention is directed toward helping parents solve day-to-day problems. Many such courses are a fraud, she claims, and tend to ensure further conflict and unsatisfactory relationships between parents and professionals. Extended work with actual families of children with disabilities should be a standard requirement for courses that purport to prepare students for working with parents.[4]

All professionals should accept parents as full-fledged members of the management team for their child. Parents have much to contribute, spend more time with their child, have more opportunity to observe, and are more sensitive to the nuances of the child's condition. They are the ones, after all, who have the longest time of responsibility for the child with special needs.

While strong positive relationships between parent and professional are vital to a stable family, stressful relationships of a more personal nature can impede a family's growth toward stability.

Unthinking friends and relatives with nothing but goodwill in their hearts can unwittingly create stress. Few who have not parented a child with a disability can truly appreciate the degree and kind of stress the birth puts on the parents.

For the first few months, perhaps a year or two, we fight private battles for self-control so that we can present a capable, unflappable front to the world. "How do you do it?" says an admiring friend. What does that do to the parent? It reinforces the feeling that such self-control is admirable. It's also very comforting to the friend, who is probably somewhat uncomfortable dealing with such stressful situations anyway. A simple, silent show of support could be better for the parents.

In the early months after Mike's birth, this kind of unthinking praise made Guy and me feel we were martyrs. Suffer and keep a stiff upper lip and the world thinks you're wonderful. Someone should have put us on to George Bernard Shaw's witty aphorism: "Martyrdom is the only way in which a man can become famous without ability."

I think then we would have sooner understood the need to talk about our grief with others. All that our own parents and close friends remember of that period is a vague, "We thought you were wonderful young parents. Were you really in as bad shape as you say you were?"

But then, twenty-odd years ago, there were few parent groups around to offer the knowledgeable and appropriate support available to parents today.

Dr. Koch always insisted that supportive services should not be limited to the disabled child but must include the parents as well: "The presence of a retarded child in a family does not necessarily have a detrimental effect on happiness and welfare of siblings or the family as a whole, when appropriate guidance and support are provided the parents."[5]

THE POSITIVE SIDE OF STRESS

Once you begin to develop confidence in your ability to cope with your child's problems and your family's emotional stresses and can feel the positive support of professionals, friends, and relatives, you will discover that your energy is returning.

Stress is not all bad. Stress can infuse you with tremendous amounts of energy. Directed now into positive channels, it can help you achieve wonderfully gratifying goals.

You can go for the biggies. Organize a campaign to fund research to learn more about your child's disability. Write to all available sources, such as health foundations, corporations involved in genetic research, drug companies, and medical journals, for updated information. Begin to gather a file relating to your child's disability. Include community resources, educational and recreational opportunities, and profiles of outstanding people in the field. Make it available to other parents and professionals in the area. Join a parent group or help to organize one through which counseling and information can be made available to other new parents.

Your energies should not all be directed to areas affecting your disabled child. Volunteer to be a Little League parent or serve on PTA for one of your other children. Teach lessons if you have a skill others need or want to acquire.

One woman, though she worked all day, still wanted to be useful to the community in the evenings. She no longer went out in the evenings, so she opened her home to committee meetings from her church; they always needed new meeting places. "Just give me a few days' notice," she'd say. Her calendar looked like a convention of chicken scratches. Every available space was filled. And she was as happy as a meadowlark to be sharing her beautiful home.

Even short-term bursts of activity are good stress relievers. Clean out the garage; strip off old wallpaper; wash the dog. Learn a new hobby or sport. Do anything that provides physical and mental exertion with what you consider a worthwhile goal. The fruit of your labor will give you positive feelings of accomplishment as you begin to regain your self-confidence and a more balanced view of your world.

Some relaxation techniques taught in aerobics or stretch classes can also be helpful in relieving stress. And don't forget sports, from organized to just a simple walk. The parent who works away from home may recover more quickly from the effects of grief and stress than the parent who spends every waking hour in company with the disabled baby. It is vital to the mental health of the homebound parent to plan a definite period each week free of cares.

"But I feel guilty hiring a sitter just so I can go browsing through the stores!" one young woman said. She was not paying a sitter just so she could browse the stores. She was paying a sitter to relieve her for a specified time that she could look forward to every week, free of any worry or care or responsibility for her family. It was time to turn her mind to herself.

Getting away from a trying situation periodically will bring one back refreshed, physically and spiritually, in a better mood and better able to cope. And in the words of Project COPE director Mary Boyd Merrill, "Coping is not a destination; it's a road."

CHAPTER 4

Parent-to-Parent Power

Oh, the comfort, the inexpressible comfort of feeling safe with a person, having neither to weigh thoughts nor measure words, but pouring them all right out, just as they are, chaff and grain together; certain that a faithful hand will take and sift them, keep what is worth keeping, and then with the breath of kindness blow the rest away.

—Dinah Maria Mulock Craig
"A Life for a Life"

*T*he first time I sat in on a parent group I didn't know what to expect. There we were, a circle of strangers. Some were in jeans and embroidered shirts, some in business suits. One young couple looked no more than eighteen. Yet we all had one thing in common: the birth of a developmentally disabled baby. One thing is certain: Disability strikes without prejudice for race or class or color. We were all in it together. And all of us by our presence were saying we needed one another. We wanted the comfort and strength and sharing of experiences to make us strong again. Within a few months, I knew I had found that "inexpressible comfort" Dinah Craig wrote about.

Perhaps the specialness of parent groups can be realized best in this retelling of an old folk tale. Once upon a time a traveler entered a small village. It struck him that there was no laughter. No children were playing. Men and women went about their work with grim faces. He approached a dour-looking woman hanging washing on the line. As the wet sheets snapped gaily in the tart breeze, he asked her, "Why are you so unhappy?"

"Oh, my cow got out last night and trampled the neighbor's vegetable patch; and now my neighbor refuses to give me back my cow until I pay for the vegetables, and I must have the cow to sell the milk before I can pay for the vegetables. No one has such troubles as I!"

"Would you like to be rid of your troubles?"

She peered at the stranger suspiciously. There was a kindly glint in his eyes. "How?"

"List your troubles on a bit of paper. In two days I will tell you how you may be rid of them."

The woman did as he said, and the stranger went on to a farmer bent over a broken plow. He heard the man grumbling as he approached.

"What is the trouble?" he asked.

"The rocks in the field have bent the blades of my plow. I have hammered them back into shape so often they are falling apart. No one in this village has it as bad as I! If only I had good ground to plow, all my troubles would be over!"

"Would you like to be rid of your troubles?" asked the stranger.

"Yes. I'd gladly trade my troubles for anyone's!"

"Very well." And the stranger told him to do exactly as he had told the washerwoman. During the rest of that day and the next, the stranger moved leisurely through the village, hearing everyone's complaints and promising everyone the same thing. Then the day arrived when everyone was to get rid of troubles. Early in the morning, the villagers began trooping over to the washerwoman's yard, their papers in hand telling all the details of their troubles.

One by one the stranger hung them on the line, until a blocklong line of troubles fluttered in the March breeze. The villagers watched uneasily. Was he a magician? Could he make their troubles just disappear?

"Soon," the stranger told them, "I will call a signal. Then you may all go to the line and pick out any trouble you would rather have than your own."

Smiles appeared here and there. It was so simple! Why had they not thought of it themselves! They began reading their neighbors' troubles to decide whose they would choose. The sun rose. The stranger did not call the signal. They waited. The sun began to descend and still the stranger did not call the signal. Finally, the washerwoman cast a sidelong glance at the farmer with the broken plow. *Poor fellow,* she thought. *All his field is so stony, and he has a bad back to boot. I wouldn't want his troubles, not if my cow and my pig got into the neighbor's vegetables.*

Next to her, a woman was covertly reading the washerwoman's list. *Poor soul,* she thought. *If she had fine strong sons like I, she wouldn't have to worry about a poorly made pen that doesn't keep her cow out of the neighbor's vegetables.* And the woman began to think about her own troubles. Yes, one of her sons was troublesome now and then, but at least she had children and didn't have to take in washings! And so down the line it went.

But a strange and wonderful thing began to happen. As the villagers toed the line, waiting for the signal, they began to look again at their own troubles. Amazingly, they had begun to shrink right before their eyes. Then the villagers began to shuffle in place, glancing nervously at one another. What if someone outraced them to the line and exchanged his or her big troubles for their own smaller ones?

Finally, as the sun was setting and time neared for farmers to feed flocks and washerwomen to take their clothes off the lines, the stranger gave the signal. Away dashed the villagers to recapture their own troubles. So happy they were and were ever after that they never noticed the stranger had vanished.

Strangers coming thereafter to their village, always made welcome, were heard to remark, "What a happy place this is! Not a trouble in the world! Ah, what a delight!"

I thought about this tale sometimes after Mike was born. But I never really appreciated it until I joined a parent group. Listening to those young parents gave me an entirely new perspective. I almost didn't go to that first parent meeting. A friend had told me about her only experience with a parent group: "Right after my baby was born, someone contacted me and asked if I wanted to join a parent group. I jumped at the chance. At the first meeting they gave me a list of jobs that were open and asked me what I'd like to sign up for. I just didn't go back."

Was she being selfish? Of course not! Parents of newborns are so busy, especially if they have other children, that asking them to serve on committees is thoughtless. They frequently haven't any energy left over. Coping with a baby with special needs, their own emotional stress, their families, has drained it all. What they need is something handed to them: a parent group where they can go and receive support with no strings.

We who are parents of older disabled children are in a unique position to understand and help new parents. Time enough in the years ahead to involve young parents in issues that concern them all. But now they need that concern, that support. No one can help a young parent as much as one who says, "I've been there. Can I help?"

HOW TO FIND A PARENT GROUP

There already may be an active group for parents of children with similar disabilities in your area, or an advocacy group for children with wide-ranging handicapping conditions where you would fit in. To find it, begin at the hospital. Sometimes volunteer services at the hospital maintain lists of parent organizations. Your church is another possible source. Or call your local school district office to find out if the district offers an infant training program for children with special needs. If so, it probably has a parent auxiliary. Or even though your child may be an infant, you might call local sheltered workshops (also listed as training workshops or vocational workshops). If they have been in existence long, they are doubtless aware of a number of parent groups serving various purposes. Finally, try social service departments or local branches of national associations for particular disabilities.

If there just isn't any group close enough in distance or purpose, consider starting a group yourself.

STARTING YOUR OWN PARENT GROUP

How do you reach other parents who may be interested in becoming part of your group? Agencies may not share names of families they serve, but they may be willing to distribute your message. And you may be able to insert a message in school and preschool newsletters or spread the word with your social worker if you have one.

A second way to locate interested parents is through an ad in your local paper: "Now forming: A parent group for families of children with special needs," or "Wanted: Contact with other parents of children with cerebral palsy." Be sure to include a telephone number. You may receive one call; you may get a half dozen. Take their names, addresses, and telephone numbers, and give them a date, time, and address of the meeting place. Think before the meeting about what you want most out of your group and ways in which belonging to the group will benefit everyone.

Try to enlist an agency to sponsor you, such as a Regional Center if you live in California, or some other group that is an umbrella agency for all disabilities. The name will give added stature to your group. Winning the group's support may include some monetary support or use of facilities for meetings or use of computers and copiers to put out your newsletters.

The first meeting Invite a member of your sponsoring agency to attend. Name tags are a good idea. Dig up some goodies. Remember, everyone is as nervous as you. But all attendees are probably grateful that someone thought up the idea of getting parents together. Pass around a sign-in sheet, including space for telephone numbers. A good opener is to introduce yourself and your spouse, tell a little about yourselves and all your children, and a little about your child with special needs. Then invite another parent to share. Not all parents will be comfortable sharing at this first meeting.

Here are some ideas to start the discussion: general community news, Little League, good bargains that week at the supermarket, things that establish your commonality as parents before you ease into specific problems. It is likely that someone else will begin talking about a child first. Some questions you can feed into the group might include these: How were you informed your baby had a disability? How satisfied were you with the information your family doctor or pediatrician gave you? What kind of program is your child in now (for older parents)? Are you pleased with it? How have things gotten better the past few years?

Then ask parents to think of their primary goal for their children with special needs. (Again, don't expect everyone to share. Be cool!) Encourage diversity of opinion. Smile! Show you mean it. Keeping an open mind at each step of forming and maintaining your parent group is essential. Each parent has had different experiences. Establish from the outset that this group will be the place where anyone can air feelings. Be supportive of other parents, even if you don't agree with everything they say.

At the conclusion of the meeting, ask parents to repeat their goals so you can write them down. This step gives everyone a chance to reshape thoughts and rephrase them more specifically. Your group's goals may include better community transportation (from the parent of a teenager), better preschools, more medical allowance for expensive drugs, parent education, and periodic meetings with other parents to exchange views and information.

Before everyone leaves, be sure the parent list includes everyone's address and telephone number, and ask for names of others who might be interested in future meetings.

Future meetings Decide before the parents leave where and when the next meeting will take place. Work for a more public meeting place, such as a church, bank, library, or community room.

Later you will want to devise a complete membership application that includes space for number of children, child's disability, special interests and abilities of parents, suggestions for future programs, and areas into which they'd like to see the parent group move.

ONE STEP AT A TIME

Don't be in a hurry to establish priorities among your goals. Take time to get to know one another, to discover who are your workers, your idea people, your planners, and those with strong community links. The most important thing in setting up any fledgling group is to proceed in small enough steps to ensure success, as you do with your children.

You may want to adopt several small goals to work on and achieve while you are also tackling a biggie. For example, you might engage in a bake sale to raise money for stationery and mailings, locate a permanent meeting place and a reliable baby-sitter, and at the same time work on bylaws.

It's better to work as a whole group the first few months rather than choose a board. When you start to grow—and you probably will if the atmosphere is friendly, informal, and nonthreatening—those who are interested in being on the board, working on obtaining interesting programs, or setting up bylaws will let it be known. As group members work without job titles for a while, the strengths and weaknesses of each will begin to emerge and become apparent to the majority. Taking it slowly this way allows "best friend" loyalties to evolve into support for people with outstanding qualities that had not been recognized before.

When you've established in your bylaws the officers you need, you're ready to consider who will run for each office. It's a good idea to present a complete slate to the general membership and ask for additional nominations.

By the time your first board has been selected and your bylaws approved—having met several times by now—you may find definite priorities emerging among your goals. These goals will determine the programs you select and how much money you need to raise.

Communication is your strongest tool for a vigorous and grow-ing membership. You will need almost immediately a telephone chairperson who is conscientious, who likes to talk to people, and who will call all members to remind them of each meeting and each special event. After several months, when your group is flourishing, you may evolve to a telephone tree. It is *always* a good idea to contact those who miss meetings, not to check up on them but to see if everything is all right (children with disabilities being more prone to medical emergencies than many children). Remember that a parent group is a caring group. Taking care of one another, being genuinely concerned about one another, and sharing the good and bad will strengthen the family feeling of your group.

Perhaps a member who likes to write can publish a monthly newsletter. Encourage input from other parents, but don't depend on it. Many parents do not feel comfortable broadcasting personal information. And (I found to my surprise) not all parents like to write things down. Get on the mailing list of other clubs or groups whose doings may profit your readers. Fill the newsletter with community happenings that affect the parents in your group, pend-ing legislation, information about leaders in the field, recreational outings or camps available for children with special needs, and especially doings of parent families in your club, such as parents attending symposiums about special disabilities or news concerning their children's well-being. Always mention your program for the coming month, presented in a way that makes it irresistible.

If communication weaves the links, money greases the wheels. Here again, start small with ventures almost sure to succeed. Truly, nothing does succeed like success. A small successful bake sale does as much for morale as it does for the treasury. From the beginning, be aware that some parents have a lot of time to give while others are heavily involved, especially those with several small children, and that money circumstances are equally diverse. Try to see that no one person volunteers to do everything. (Axiom: Don't burn out your best members.) Also, take care that no one is too overtly generous with a checkbook. Does that sound strange? Generosity is a marvel-ous thing but not at the expense of making members who must budget closely feel that their contributions of time and talent are of less value than a fat purse.

One successful fund-raising idea thought up by enterprising members of our own PATH (Parents Acting for the Handicapped) group was a monthly raffle. Members took turns donating a craft item such as a wastebasket, potholders, a pillow, a dried flower arrangement, or baked goods; members and guests attending the meeting could buy raffle tickets at twenty-five cents each. This money, each month, always covered the expense of our paid baby-sitter.

A baby-sitter? Yes, many young parents must limit their outside activities because of the expense of a sitter. We felt that it was in the club's best interest to have all our young parents attend without thinking that the expense of leaving the children constituted their night out for the month.

Having the raffle was also, inadvertently, a fun way of discovering one another's talents.

We had such a good time with the raffles that someone dreamed up the idea of making an old-fashioned patchwork quilt. An artistic member designed a log cabin pattern and figured out the number of squares needed. Everyone took home a pattern and background fabric for one or more squares. Then they were assembled by another person who was trained in quilting. A local business donated printed raffle tickets, and the quilt brought in several hundred dollars.

Raising money raises another issue: For your donations to be tax exempt for the donor, your organization must become incorporated as a nonprofit, tax-exempt organization under federal and state laws. That also exempts you from paying taxes on donations received.

Through patiently culling our resources, we found an attorney willing to donate his time to prepare our incorporation papers. He did need a copy of our bylaws. To become incorporated, you need to do the following:

Obtain state charter A state charter is a state document verifying the existence of your organization. It's a good idea for any parent group to get one. It's a necessity if you intend to do major fund raising or lobbying. To apply, write to: Secretary of State, State Capitol Building, (your state capital and state).

Register as a nonprofit organization If you are going to solicit funds, you should also register with your local U.S. Attorney General's Office. Write to: U.S. Attorney General's Office, State Capitol Building, (your state capital and state).

Obtain tax-exempt status from the Internal Revenue Service
1. Get several copies of Form 557, "Tax-Exempt Status for Your Organization," from your local IRS office for general information, and several copies of Form 1023, "Application for Recognition of Exemption."
2. Form 1023 needs to be filled out by an attorney. This is important, as proper terminology must be used. Call IRS Information

at 1-800-829-4477 and ask for Topics #109 and #110 for more information or additional publications.

3. Remember that the IRS is forbidden to give a tax exemption to lobbying organizations. Therefore, lobbying activities must appear minimal on your application. You should stress your group's educational activities.[1]

WHERE DO PROFESSIONALS FIT IN?

Some new groups are eager to attract professionals in their field to the group, counting on the prestige of a few well-known names to give them instant credibility. Think carefully about this step. It may be better for the organization if the hard workers who do the tedious work—the phoning, the patient working out of meetings or goal setting or the legwork on fund-raisers—are the ones who bask in the praise of their accomplishments rather than some professional figureheads.

Not only for your internal morale but for all practical purposes, the parents who do the work should be the people in charge. If a professional is eager to be identified with your group (for political reasons or whatever), accept the offer graciously, and assign him an advisory position rather than a role as a working officer. In this way he will be able to do projects on his own or draw in publicity that may benefit the group, but in the meantime, the press of his schedule will not impede your forward momentum if he is busy elsewhere when action is needed.

GETTING UNDER WAY

We are creatures of habit. The establishment and repetition of certain functions will help people become accustomed to the fact that your group is here to stay.

1. *The informative, upbeat newsletter.* It's surprising how many people have eventually come to our meetings because they had been added to our mailing list by a member and had seen something that caught their eye—usually an upcoming program of interest to them or that pertained to their own child's disability.

2. *A wide variety of programs.* The local public library, chapter of the National Association for Retarded Citizens, vocational rehabilitation, or social service offices may have videotapes or films that can be borrowed. Always preview them. Some sound terrific in description but are outdated, poorly conceived, or poorly made.

You cannot afford a poor program when you are just starting out.

Draw on community experts. The Chamber of Commerce and local professional organizations, such as the American Medical Association chapter, maintain a speakers' bureau, as might any local college. If possible, someone from your group should find an opportunity to interview or listen to an address by the person under consideration. A speaker who is entertaining as well as knowledgeable is ideal.

Take a field trip. A trip to a preschool or a local school with good interactive media programs for children with special needs is a wonderful way to plunge into the world of possibilities awaiting your child with special needs.

3. *Fund-raising.* Look for ways to tap the community rather than your own membership. Tie the size of the fund-raiser to the ambitiousness of the goal for which it is intended as well as to the capabilities of your members.

4. *Training.* Seek to train new parents to move confidently into positions of greater leadership and responsibility. One basic concept of developing a strong organization is to train as many people to do as many jobs as possible. The one-man or one-woman club will sometimes flourish and then go under when that person decides to quit. Or the person may refuse to relinquish control.

A parent group is about parents growing, too, parents gaining capability and being able to battle authorities when need be. When your membership grows large enough so that you need new positions filled—membership chairperson, for example, or ways-and-means and publicity chairpersons—seek out new people rather than draw from those already active. And when someone does a good job for the group, do as Ben Franklin said, "Be hearty in your approbation and lavish in your praise."

HOW TO MAINTAIN YOUR MOMENTUM

Some parent groups organize for one particular purpose, such as the establishment of an infant intervention program in their area, and when that has been accomplished, they disband.

It's a shame to let all that newfound expertise go to waste! When parents have learned how to work together and organize for a common goal and have tasted success, why not continue with a further goal? They might set as a new goal to secure a van to transport infants to the new development center or undertake a community survey of the education offered for their children when they graduate from the infant intervention program at three. Most parent groups plan to continue.

For those who view themselves as part of an ongoing organization, a periodic review of original goals is wise. They may discover that several of their goals are related. Two goals of our PATH group were parent education and the establishment of a parent network. They combined in the following way. To develop a pool of experienced parents who could go out and offer help and support to new parents, we felt we needed professional training. A combination of donations and fund-raising enabled us to hire a team to teach us the rudiments of listening skills, the psychology of grief and stress, a little about various disabilities, and ways to go about compiling a list of our community's resources for new parents.

Having trained parents led naturally to another goal, the establishment of our own speakers' bureau to address other community groups. Some parents just naturally enjoy telling others about their experiences with their children with handicapping conditions and will be eager to "go on the circuit" in behalf of their parent group or to address issues that need to be brought to the attention of the community. Groups such as PTAs, Rotarians, Elks, Lions, Moose, Kiwanis, Shriners, businessmen's and businesswomen's organizations, professional groups, and other parent groups are always looking for speakers. Spreading the word in the community will also help you become familiar with sources to draw upon for help in fund-raisers or speakers for your own group. At the very least, you will raise community consciousness about children with special needs.

Finally, a vital part of keeping your group alive and well is presenting consistently interesting programs. A good video followed by a question-and-answer period with a knowledgeable person on hand, an absorbing speaker, or a panel with a hot topic will bring out the membership. Occasionally introduce topics featuring the parents as speakers. For example, what do you do when other children in the neighborhood are hostile toward your child? It's important to feature parent members as experts, too. How often—still—do we hear, "The experts say...," and we are quiet? Encourage parents to express their feelings and discuss how they have handled problems. Speaking out helps them gain confidence in their views, actively think about what they really feel, and grow comfortable expressing these views.

As parents become more skilled at accepting themselves as authority and expressing their views, more of them will be willing to volunteer for more demanding roles.

PART

2

WE HAVE LIFT-OFF

CHAPTER 5

Infant Intervention— The Three R's Before Three

B ambi, ten months old and full of gaiety, hauls herself up the three short steps to the platform, wiggles across, and belly flops down the miniature slide to land in a soft pillow-size bean bag. Pushing up on her tanned arms, she smiles triumphantly at her mother (whose hands have hovered near throughout Bambi's adventure).

Bambi has Down's syndrome. Her quick smile, firm muscle tone, and strength are outstanding. Twenty years ago, what would this ten-month-old have been like? Probably a grateful mother would have characterized her as "a good baby—just lies in her crib and smiles at everybody." Twenty years ago, that might have been an acceptable blessing. No longer.

Today, infant intervention programs are designed to help babies with disabilities go through the developmental cycles on a more nearly standard timetable than they might otherwise. Through the use of exercises and skills training, undesirable sensorimotor patterns are interrupted.

THE THREE R'S: ROUTINE, REPETITION, AND RELAXATION

Judy Cook was formerly a public health nurse whose work as a home health nurse with Lanterman State Hospital in California brought her in close contact with parents of babies with special needs.

47

Visiting a mother with a beautiful child of six, Mrs. Cook found him still being bottle-fed. She said, "The mother explained that the doctor had told her the child would always be a baby, and it was better for her to accept it. So the mother never tried to teach her baby to chew solid food. As her son grew, the mother merely punched larger holes in the nipple and added cut-up bits of solid food to the milk, which the boy learned to swallow whole. By that age, of course, the boy was habituated, and it became very hard to retrain him to chew."

From that and similar experiences, plus an awareness of the work others were doing in habit intervention, grew Cook's belief that such behavior could be sidetracked by substituting habits that would contribute to normal development patterns—intervening with undesirable behaviors before they happen.

Cook organized an infant intervention program for babies with special needs: "We saw habits that needed to be interrupted—like two- and three-year-olds not willing to learn to chew food. And being able to anticipate habits that need to be cultivated—like chewing—we started babies on textured foods early, at six months. We encouraged mothers to grind their own food rather than using the prepared strained food, which loses texture and is all the same bland consistency. We even had them tasting lemons for the contrasting taste. Also at six months some babies are ready to drink from a straw. You can teach the skill easily while they have the initial sucking reflex. If you lose that opportunity, sometimes it takes several years before the child is ready again. All babies are different. Nothing works equally well with all babies."

The program Cook helped found is no longer in existence, a victim of state budget crises. Cook herself has moved on to San Gabriel Valley Regional Center where she recruits and trains retired persons to be surrogate grandparents to children with disabilities. However, many associations for retarded persons have referral services. Parents may call when their babies are only a day or two old. The Ontario-Pomona Association for Retarded Persons (OPARC) offers a referral service and parent training. Called Project COPE, this organization brings parents together in a series of meetings with nurses, doctors, psychologists, physical therapists, and attorneys, who donate time to share their knowledge with the parents. These parents, as they become more confident and comfortable with their situation, often go on to become part of a volunteer group, which matches more experienced families with parents whose newborns have similar needs. For further information, write Project COPE,

8930 Vernon Street, Suite H, Montclair, California 91763, or call 714-985-3116.

One outstanding source for parents who live in southern California is St. John's Child Study Center, 1339 Twentieth Street, Santa Monica, California 90404. (The phone number is 213-829-8921.) "Dedicated to the preservation and improvement of human life in all its forms and in all stages of development," the Child Study Center includes programs in infant enrichment (birth to three years), parent-child interaction, sensory motor play groups, parenting and support groups, adult programs for persons with developmental disabilities, and individual therapy.

A visit to the Child Study Center will help parents see what is now possible. Every year the Center has twenty thousand visits from families and children who have special educational, psychological, or physical needs. The Center has been offering a comprehensive range of diagnostic, tutoring, therapy, and parenting services to families for more than twenty-five years. With a staff of credentialed professionals from more than a dozen disciplines, the Center addresses the needs of children from infancy to adolescence.

At this writing, a bill based on the federal Public Law 99–457 is working its way through California's legislature. Its objective is to close the gap in services for all children with special needs from birth to age three. Proponents hope the bill will pass in 1993. One component of the bill will be to develop a statewide system of family resource centers.

At present, few school districts have infant programs, and children are not eligible for federally funded Head Start programs until the age of three. Parents have developed most of the community programs. Many private groups, meeting in schools and churches, have continued the work of infant intervention.

In a typical classroom, one might see two mothers working together on an angels-in-the-snow exercise on one baby while the other baby catches a quick nap on the rug. Elsewhere mothers exchange feeding hints while they sit with year-olds who are demolishing crackers at the table. Eight to twenty babies and their mothers may occupy the classroom any one morning, together with student volunteers from a nearby college, an interning occupational therapist, and sometimes a parent counselor. Most of the parent counseling is done by the parents. When one parent feels confident enough to bring up a particular problem, usually some other parent picks up on it because she has experienced something similar.

"Parents are the experts," says Cook. "They have all been there. The support and help they give one another is terrific."

In one infant program started by a retarded children's association parent group with the aid of federal grant monies, babies and toddlers attended from the age of three months to three years. In the classroom for two- to three-year-olds on one morning, seven toddlers sat in a row. A mini-obstacle course was laid out on the carpet with wide strips of masking tape. At one end of it was a balance board twelve inches wide, six inches high, and eight feet long. Along either side of its carpeted length were strewn a half dozen bean bags.

While the others waited their turns, one toddler was given a basket and told to "knee-walk" the length of the board, lean over (while maintaining his balance on his knees) to pick up each bean bag as he went along, and put it in his basket. After he finished, he was instructed to walk sideways on the tape (a step-slide) to a row of four nursery-size chairs. Carefully, he climbed up on the chairs, using the backs if he needed to maintain balance, switching his little basket from hand to hand as necessary, crossed the chair bridge, and climbed down. Still following the tape (each step encouraged by the teacher's praise and her firm insistence that every skill be performed correctly), he then stepped up on a rocking board made of rockers about the size of standard chair rockers supporting a platform, balanced a moment, and stepped down the other side and onto a second rocking board. Finally, the tape led him to a one-two-one pattern of step-blocks. Balancing from the last lower step, he then threw his collected bean bags, one by one, at a basketball hoop suspended shoulder height about a foot away. Mission completed (to much clapping from teacher and other children), the child turned back, still poised on the step, and retraced his path, repeating all the walking, climbing, sidestepping, knee-walking, and balancing skills. The entire procedure took about ten minutes. It was a performance worthy of any three-year-old, and it was performed by a moderately retarded toddler of thirty months.

In the classroom the children were also introduced to cutting and pasting skills, fitting of wooden shapes into boards, reaching readiness activities, and other skills designed to prepare them for preschool.

THE CASE FOR FAMILY INVOLVEMENT

Parents working together, supporting each other, provide the greatest gains for baby and mother, and the most positive reinforcement, believes Cook. She comments, "Leaving your baby with the professionals said to the parent, 'See, the pros can do a better job.' Parents are already feeling inadequate. They don't need a stranger coming in, taking over, and telling the parents she can do a better job."

Cook's view is supported by a number of studies that have found that when the parents are part of the team, the child makes the best possible progress. Involved parents are more nearly on target as they go home and continue the work with the baby. The work also increases bonding between parent and child.

But even the training and support parents receive working side by side with teachers in infant intervention programs may not be enough to enable them to function effectively as intervenors at home. If parents have other related problems, such as difficult financial or family situations, often the resolution of those problems must come first. Most parents, once their other pressing problems are relieved, can become effective trainers and teachers in changing and improving their child's motor and sensory behaviors.

DOES INFANT INTERVENTION REALLY MAKE A DIFFERENCE?

In 1979, two English medical officers, supported by a grant from the Department of Health and Social Security, Great Britain, published results of a massive study on the effects of early intervention. Joyce R. Ludlow, Assistant County Medical Officer, and L. M. Allen, Senior Assistant Medical Officer of Mental Health, for Kent County Council, involved all the children with Down's syndrome living in Kent County and born between 1960 and 1969 in a study that covered the next ten years.

They compared three groups of children with Down's syndrome to estimate the effects of early intervention and planned preschool stimulus on their mental development. Supportive counseling and training were offered to mothers, while children received an intervention program. They compared a group of seventy-five children with Down's syndrome receiving such stimulus with two other groups: one of eighty children who attended no preschool program or play groups; the other of forty-three children who were institutionalized shortly after birth. The actual program included children with all disabilities, but the study concentrated on children with Down's syndrome because they are a uniform and easily recognizable group.

Children and their mothers in the group of seventy-five attended the Development Clinic two hours twice weekly. The clinic was run on regular play-group lines but with a ratio of adults to children of one to one. The children received speech stimulus and training in self-help and locomotor skills. In addition there were group play, music and movement, story time, and nursery rhymes.

During part of the morning, mothers took a break together in another room, giving them an opportunity to share their various problems. That was probably one of the most valued aspects of the clinic. Repeatedly, mothers said how much they had been helped by other mothers. Mothers' attendance was considered essential so that the stimulus given two days a week could be continued at home. The goal was that attendance at the clinic would help the children reach such a degree of independence and social acceptability that at three years they could participate in a regular play group for two or three mornings a week while continuing to attend the clinic.

The main results of the study confirmed that early intensive preschool stimulation, coupled with parental counseling and full maternal involvement, reduced the decline in development of children with Down's syndrome and enabled them to more nearly reach their potential.

The possibility of integrating the children into regular play groups also increased. The policy was to treat them as much like nondisabled children as possible and to make them so socially acceptable in behavior and attainments that they could be integrated into play groups, nursery schools, Sunday schools, and similar groups. Mixing with their peers gave them additional stimulation. *In every case such integration resulted in marked improvement in language development.*

In the study, the much larger number of children, among the seventy-five in the clinic program, who could read and write and participate in community activities such as Brownies, Cubs, Guides, and dancing, confirmed the value of preschool stimulation and underscored how wrong it is to deny to any of the children the maximum opportunity of which they are capable.

One of Ludlow and Allen's prime conclusions was that "in the baby's first five years of life, the most important speech teacher and physical therapist he has is his mother."[1] To their comment might be added that fathers are playing an increasingly important role in their children's early years.

England is far from the only place where interested people have been studying the results of infant intervention programs. A study at the Model Preschool Center for Handicapped Children and the Child Development and Mental Retardation Center, University of Washington, Seattle, found that early enrollment in infant intervention programs was of definite value. Children with Down's syndrome who did not attend any preschool program leveled off at about 61 percent of standard development, researchers discovered, while children who attended the Model Preschool program appeared to level off at approximately 95 percent of standard development!

Parents are learning that intervening in health-threatening situations has a beneficial effect on their babies' future development. Disability is no longer believed to be a static condition. Studies from Great Britain, Argentina, Canada, and elsewhere overwhelmingly indicate that wherever infant intervention programs have been established, they result in greater growth for the child.

Dr. Maria Montessori was the Italian educator whose pioneering work with young children early in this century proved that children learned best when they were given a chance to use their physical senses along with mental ability in the learning process. She discovered that certain simple yet carefully selected educational materials provoked in children a deep interest and attention not previously believed possible. Children between ages three and four might work at tasks from fifteen minutes to an hour without tiring or losing concentration. In addition, behavior problems frequently disappeared.

Dr. Montessori's first work, from which her methods were developed, came from her teaching of developmentally disabled children she took in from the streets of Rome, children who were refused entry to the schools of that day.

A few years later, Jean Piaget, the eminent Swiss psychologist, went even further. He felt that there is a fundamental continuity between physical and mental functioning, that one helps the other at each stage of a child's growth.

Infant intervention programs use elements of both Montessori's and Piaget's work. Modern research shows that environment can profoundly alter the brain's growth processes. "Furthermore, it has been shown that brain processes present at birth will degenerate if the environmental stimulation necessary to activate them is withheld," writes neurobiologist Timothy J. Teyler.[2]

In other words, stimulation from the baby's physical surroundings can affect the baby for good or ill. From that point, it is not hard to understand why babies placed in institutions from birth do so poorly compared with babies raised in loving homes. And stepping up the stimulation of babies who are suspected of congenital disabilities can significantly increase their chances for normal growth.

Becoming aware of the exciting progress in the field of developmental disabilities during the last few years, parents are correct in wondering why the information has been so long in becoming more widely known.

Part of the problem still is getting medical people—especially pediatric residents—interested in the area of prevention of mental disabilities. In addition, psychologists traditionally have not been too interested in mental problems that are not 'mental.' They find studying psychoses more exciting than studying forms of retardation. And physicians tend not to be interested if they can't cut it out or prescribe a pill.

It is to be hoped now, with dramatic changes in the field of mental disability being proved possible in study after study, that more of the good minds of medicine will be eager to join those of education in alleviating the problems too long associated with mental disability, for child and family.

The success of infant intervention programs has brought a greater demand for them. Parents living in large cities may be fortunate in locating good existing programs, but families in rural areas may not be so fortunate. If your doctor is unaware of such a program in your community, the department of special education of the nearest university will likely have the most up-to-date information on the program closest to you or suggestions for parents wanting to start their own program. If you draw a blank, next try a hospital, your local association for retarded citizens, or the public school system's special education department.

INFANT STIMULATION ACTIVITIES IN THE HOME

You can develop a program with your baby. Simple exercises can be incorporated easily into the baby's routine once you understand what you are doing and why that particular intervention skill is important. Some literature is available for parents' use. Although not new, one basic book is *The Baby Exercise Book: For the First Fifteen Months* by Dr. Janine Levy. All the exercises she describes can be performed at home.

If your special needs baby has Down's syndrome or another disability that renders him poorly coordinated but otherwise unaffected physically, the exercises suggested in Dr. Levy's book will probably work well.

Before doing any exercises with a baby with cerebral palsy or any physically handicapping condition, check with a doctor or a physical therapist under a doctor's approval.

Exercises can be incorporated into daily routines like diaper changing. Aided by her mother or father, the baby can do from five to eight sit-ups at each changing unless she has a medical condition that makes this activity unwise. Sit-ups promote head control and stimulation of the muscles that will later be needed for balance and sitting alone. With a hand supporting her neck, the first step is to raise her by the shoulders to a sitting position and lower her again. As she becomes stronger, let her curl her fingers around your thumbs as you raise and lower her.

Another good one for diapering time is to grasp both legs gently at the ankles and push them up into a knee-chest position, then lower. Repeat several times. This stimulates the crawling reflex. In yet another exercise, you can lightly trace a finger over the baby's abdomen to stimulate a feeling sensation on the skin.

Here are some commonly used activities and exercises performed from birth to a developmental age of about six months. Usually, they are continued until the baby learns the specific skill.

In a darkened room, a pencil-flash beam is focused on a wall and arced around the room slowly enough for the baby's eyes to track the light. Light tracking exercises the eye muscles and teaches the baby to focus on a moving object.

A giant plastic ball (three-foot diameter) has numerous uses. It should be inflated to the point where it still "gives" a little. Placed and held securely on her back atop the ball and gently rocked, the baby is helped to develop a sense of balance. Being placed on her stomach and rocked, her hands and feet in contact with the ball, teaches precrawling reflexes. When the baby is a little older, the ball is used to encourage sitting-up skills by placing her in a sitting position on the ball and helping her balance.

Another early exercise to develop bodily awareness is to place the baby in a tub or a plastic wading pool filled with the large-size Styrofoam packing bubbles. The bubbles move when she moves. As she kicks or moves her arms in the featherweight bubbles, she is developing physical awareness of herself. One mom uses Rice Krispies for this, adding another sensation, that of bringing the Krispies to the mouth and experiencing the crunchy taste. (She doesn't use cereal too often, she adds; it gets expensive!)

Before the baby can sit by himself, he can be supported in a feeding table-infant seat and given various substances to aid his senses of taste and touch. A helping of colored gelatin placed within his reach makes an interesting tactile stimulator and tastes good, should any happen to get as far as his mouth. A dollop of nontoxic shaving cream also invites little hands and fingers to explore texture.

Mirrors are used at every age of infant training. Placed at floor level near the baby, a mirror gives her a chance to observe herself and eventually to relate herself to the image she sees.

As babies gain enough balance and control to sit unaided, more skills are added. (While babies without disabilities generally sit around the age of six months and walk at twelve months, these ages may have little to do with babies with handicapping conditions. Although a baby may be a year old, he may be at a developmental level about half that. When exercise books use the term *developmental age,* think in terms of what your baby is capable of, not how old he is.)

Tendencies of babies, such as drooling, are naturally thought by parents to be a necessary passing phase. With our special needs children, the drooling may come from weak jaw muscles. Without stimulation to make the baby aware that her mouth is open, this habit could continue indefinitely. A gentle pressure from the parent's finger pushing the chin back up to close the mouth, repeated patiently as often as needed, may stimulate the baby's muscles to hold her mouth closed. Many times this will eliminate the drooling, too.

Sometimes our children are prone to aimless arm and leg waving. In infant intervention classes, teachers will sometimes slip over each wrist and ankle a little elastic bracelet with bells sewn on to help them become aware of the waving members. Or sometimes elastic with a lead weight attached is used to help a baby remember to raise his arm or leg only when there is reason to.

About the age of six months babies, who are often able to grasp objects from birth, can learn to release objects purposely. In one game, one-inch blocks are piled beside an open coffee can. The baby is shown how to drop blocks in the can. The purpose of the game is to teach her to release a block over the can. Simple? Yes, but requiring coordination of hand, eye, and mind. Not so simple!

When some babies begin to crawl, they use a belly-wiggle or a side-roll motion to propel themselves. I noticed Mike doing that for months. Neither his brother nor his sister went through that phase. But it never occurred to me then, over two decades ago, to try to alter Mike's pattern of progress. (I can't recall that he ever did crawl properly.)

Now, in infant intervention classes, I see parents and other intervenors training children to use their arms and legs in a proper crawl. In one of these activities, the baby is strapped on her stomach to a padded shortened skateboard. The object is to lift her off the ground sufficiently to put her in the correct position to crawl on hands and knees. The baby's arms and legs are gently and consistently pulled down to touch the floor when she flails. Show her how to propel herself forward by taking her arms and legs and demonstrating the arm-pulling, knee-pushing motions used in crawling.

Another skill taught about this age and used throughout infant intervention class years involves a balance stool. A balance stool is nothing more than a flat board seat mounted on a six- to eight-inch length of two-by-four to form a T. Once the baby learns to sit unaided and to stand, he is taught to sit on the balance stool. Thus, he is not passively sitting but must be actively engaged, using his legs for support at all times.

Once he has mastered his balance stool, he can sit on it before a mirror for other games. In one exercise, a bit of masking tape is stuck on the mirror within the child's reach. He reaches out and pulls it off. This evolves into a more complicated version of eye-hand coordination: The masking tape is stuck on his nose or cheek or forehead. Then, looking in the mirror, he must locate the tape and remove it. This exercise also leads to awareness and recognition of body features.

Other games encourage a child's skill as she pulls herself to a standing position and takes a step or two. Toys placed on chairs encourage her to step and reach. A large cardboard box or sturdy light classroom-type chair is useful to the toddler as a steadying support as she pushes it across a bare floor.

A balance beam also has many uses. It is a wooden trough six inches wide on the inside and six inches deep; it can be several feet long. When the baby is able to walk, he is taught to walk down the center of the trough, which is placed on the floor, by putting one foot almost directly in front of the other. The purpose of this exercise is to intervene with the development of a bowlegged or flailing-type gait. When the balance beam is turned upside down, it becomes a beam for the more experienced walker to traverse.

These and many other skills can be adapted into games and family activities at home by the ingenious parent with the added benefit of bringing the baby into the family circle.

TOYS: SIMPLE IS BEST

When choosing toys, remember that simple is usually best. A large cardboard carton becomes a hiding place—or with both ends out a tunnel. A tablecloth over a card table creates a playhouse. Toys should require the baby to respond: a wooden puzzle rather than a picture, a picture book rather than a viewing tape, a ball rather than a wind-up toy, blocks or small canned goods to stack. (Creative Playthings manufactures many toys used in infant intervention and preschool programs. They are sturdy, well-thought-out toys.)

One immediate advantage of beginning an exercise program with your baby is the knowledge that you are taking positive steps to help him reach his highest potential. *Patient Care* magazine, a professional magazine for primary-care physicians, noted in a recent issue that parents have to guard against becoming overprotective. In their efforts to devote whatever possible energy, love, and care to the child with special needs, parents often do the child a disservice. Overprotection can prevent the child from developing motor, intellectual, and social skills—and independence—that he might otherwise develop.[3]

Your doctor, I hope, will approve your decision to begin an infant intervention program, will suggest exercises, or will work with a physical therapist to develop a program for you and the baby to follow. With their help you'll be off to a flying start.

If your doctor is hesitant or is unfamiliar with infant intervention programs, tell him of studies done in the field detailing the dramatic improvements that regular appropriate training has made in babies with disabilities. If he tends to dismiss it, obtain copies for him to study. You will not be the first layperson to contribute to a doctor's continuing education. A doctor is hard-pressed to keep up with new developments in the many branches of medicine and might welcome your new information.

Possibly, your doctor might know of other parents who are interested in forming an exercise group with you. (A strongly interested, time-generous, and sympathetic doctor might be willing to meet with several of you at once or to recommend a physical therapist to teach you simple routines that can be done with your babies at home.)

If, however, after reading about successful infant intervention programs, your doctor does not support the idea that anything you do can make a difference in the baby's growth and development, you may want to consider seeking a doctor more open to the truly exciting advances being made in the field.

Some parents would do anything rather than disagree with their doctor. Perhaps they feel that she won't like them or that she will withhold further help. Just remind yourself that you are not out to win a popularity contest. Your baby's ultimate well-being is at stake. It may be your first battle on her behalf, but it almost certainly won't be your last.

Being a parent doesn't mean you have no right to challenge your doctor's opinion or to seek other advice if he suggests that "nothing can be done" or that "one or two studies don't mean much." You have every right. You, not the doctor, live with this baby twenty-four hours a day and must train and nurture her. It is in your, as well as your child's, best interest to fight for her chances to approach normal development. Some doctors may truly believe that "exercises for babies with disabilities are good only as therapy for the parent—to keep her mind off her baby's irremediable condition."

It just isn't true. Miracles are being made every day by courageous, persevering parents who want no miracle but that their child have the best chance to live as capably as possible. The intensive daily skills and habit training given disabled babies and toddlers who are in infant intervention programs open paths to fuller independence for them.

The long-range effect of this sensorimotor training may depend in part on what happens to them next—when they graduate to preschool programs about the age of three.

CHAPTER 6

The Preschool Experience

I sat in the quiet office, listening to the distant shouts of little children at play. The secretary was a young woman. After telling me that the preschool director, Mrs. Betty Harris, would be free to see me very soon, she went about her work. The walls of the tiny office in the Baptist church were plastered with crinkly paintings done in poster paint on large sheets of newsprint. They were pictures of children with masses of curls and tepee-shaped dresses, stiff-legged dogs, and lollipop trees. My son was nowhere near able to produce anything so recognizable, although he was three. I began to lose my courage.

What right did I have to expect that this preschool, considered one of the best in our city, would even consider taking a child who was developmentally disabled and poorly coordinated, who still had "accidents," and whose speech was usually unintelligible? My palms perspired. I tried to assess our chances. The young woman hummed as she worked, smiled into the telephone as she accommodated mothers who wanted their children picked up at different times or who had forgotten their sweaters the evening before—so many little details. Then I heard her reassuring one parent that her diabetic daughter would indeed receive her nourishment promptly at ten. I felt a tiny flicker of hope. It seemed that the preschool believed in making things workable. Just maybe...

Yesterday and the days before I had visited many preschools, including a brief stop at this one to look over the premises and two that were run exclusively for children with developmental disabilities. I recalled walking into the fenced yard of one of the latter. Children were playing. One girl who might have been seven or eight ran up and threw her arms around me. An aide came forward, smiling. "This is Marcia," she told me. "Marcia just loves everyone."

It took a while to disengage from Marcia, who had tenaciously wrapped both arms and a leg around me. The aide, apparently used to her behavior, just waited. Then she took me on a tour of the facility. The children seemed happy and alert and the teachers and aides content to be there. They would welcome my son. He could enroll immediately. And I felt he would receive loving care. But something held me back.

It wasn't until the next day that I knew what it was. I didn't like children who are strangers running up and hugging me.

Prude was my first reaction. But then I thought, *No, it's not that. Seven-year-olds aren't supposed to behave that way. It's not socially acceptable.* If Marcia had not been developmentally disabled, her behavior would not have been permitted. Nor is it wise to allow children to believe it is safe to hug strangers. I did not want Mike receiving preschool training that allowed him to behave in a manner that would not be acceptable in nondisabled children. If he was to become socially well-behaving, he must begin when young.

So, there I sat, waiting to plead my case for enrolling Mike in a top preschool for nondisabled kids. Mentally, I began rehearsing all the reasons that might persuade Mrs. Harris to admit Mike. Yes, it would be more work for the teacher, and it would depend on her willingness to assume the extra tasks. And did I really have a right to "inflict" my son with special needs on other children? (Some people really did think that way not long ago. Awareness of civil rights has made a difference not only racially and sexually but in the ways families view the rights of their children with special needs.)

The door opened, and Mrs. Harris beckoned me into her office. "Mrs. Harris," I began, "I really would like my son Mike to go here. Maybe it wouldn't work, but..."

I didn't get any further. Mrs. Harris was smiling, nodding. Maybe she had forgotten I was the one with the disabled child.

"I was hoping you'd decide on us," she said. "It will be good for the other children to be around someone with a handicapping condition. I've already spoken to Mrs. Waters—she's wonderful with these little ones—and she feels excited about the challenge. She's felt for a long time we should be reaching more children who have special needs."

That was the beginning of two wonderful years, years of discovery for Mike, of great growth in social behavior and speech. For me, the experience brought eternal gratitude for the compassion and dedication of people who said yes when they could have just as easily said no.

Whether your child spends the first three years of her life at home as Mike did or is fortunate enough to be part of an infant intervention program, you have to make another decision when she approaches the age of three. Involved is your faith in yourselves and in what your child is capable of and what you expect for her future. Also, fortunately or unfortunately, where you live and what you can afford must also influence your decision.

For the moment, let's examine the choices.

She can stay home She has stayed home her first three years; the law does not insist she be sent to school yet, so why not? Keeping her at home may be fine for your circumstances if she has lots of opportunities for play with other children, if you are expecting and getting from her the most she is capable of, or if you are able to take periodic times away from her and she from you. Children who are not occasionally separated from their parents at a young age often find it increasingly hard to experience separation later.

She can go to a training center for children with special needs Increasingly, training centers for persons with disabilities paid for by state funds serve children from ages three to twenty-one. Many include door-to-door transportation and cost the parents little or nothing. Sounds like a deal you can't refuse, right? But is it?

How disabled is your child? Does she have severe physical problems, which mean that she needs the services of medical personnel during the day? Then of course you must choose a school that meets those needs. But if your child is merely a slow learner or a slow learner who has other physical conditions that are largely controlled, such as occasional seizures, please, dear fellow parent, don't stop at the first place that says, yes, she belongs here.

She can go to a preschool for nondisabled children Not all preschools may be willing to take youngsters with special needs. If you consider a preschool, your first task is to find one that is willing. If the director and the teacher are not enthusiastic about being able to make a difference, you're better off trying elsewhere. If they are willing, take time to observe the school for an hour or two at peak activity. How is discipline handled? What are the expectations for each child? Parents should assure the preschool director that their child is more like other children than different. Get them to agree to allow your child to attend one day so that the teacher can observe how she might fit in.

Accessibility is becoming increasingly commonplace, things such as extra-wide doors, ramps instead of steps, accessible bathrooms, and low, wide worktables. But evaluate the accessibility if your child has a physically handicapping condition.

Check that the school of your choice has insurance that does not exclude children with special needs.

A GOOD PRESCHOOL: WHERE THE TEACHER MAKES THINGS HAPPEN

Preschool experience is vital to the child who has no one to play with at home, nowhere else to gain the socialization skills so necessary to develop along with his physical development. A good preschool teacher sees that these things happen. She doesn't wait and say, "He'll pick up that skill when he's ready." She sees what he's ready for, what he needs, and provides the individual skills training to make it happen.

Seeking the best school for your child is easier if you know what to look for, easier still if you've been the route with your other children. Keep in mind what your child needs: a place where he feels protected because it may be his first time without Mother or Dad there to look to his needs; a place where the general feeling is easygoing and happy, yet where someone is always firmly in charge; and a place where there are plenty of other children his age.

Did you ever take a child's-eye view of the world? Sit or kneel so you are eye level with him. Look around. See how much bigger regular-size chairs seem? And how far away the water faucet is, how high the toilet seat? A preschool should look geared to its little charges.

As parents, of course, when you look at a preschool, you will be concerned that children are observing social skills, have opportunities for activities that require gross motor skills like tricycle riding as well as fine motor skills like using crayons and scissors. You will want to feel confidence in the competence of teachers and aides and know that there are enough of them to oversee all the activities and to encourage active participation from even the more passive children. There should be a clean, healthful atmosphere with lots of room to play outside and good lighting and heat inside.

PARENTS MUST MAKE THE FINAL CHOICE

Neither preschool directors nor the teachers of infant intervention programs are in agreement about which type of preschool furnishes the best learning environment for the youngster with special needs.

One infant intervention teacher believed strongly that her graduating three-year-olds should move right into regular preschools. She invited the directors of local preschools to an open house in her classroom. The directors observed the class in action for half a morning, then retired for coffee, cookies, and questions.

The teacher had been anticipating questions about the children's disabilities. But, no. The astounding response was, "But they use the same toys our children do! The same learning tools!"

"That's exactly the point," the teacher declared. "My children are not different in kind, only in degree." She had on hand studies showing that mixing children with and without disabilities enables children to mitigate one another's disabilities. Those with good speech help those with slow speech; the active children encourage those with motor problems; and so on.

Within that same year, several of those directors opened their preschools to disabled children for the first time.

Meanwhile, over the hill in the next town, several preschool directors were already sympathetic to admitting children with special needs, but few received requests from parents. The reason? The town's only infant intervention program director was vehemently opposed to sending her graduates to a regular preschool and so recommended against it to parents who asked her advice.

Her teachers worked intensively with the children in their care, often having the same children from shortly after birth to three years. She considered turning them over to a regular preschool a negation of all their intense training, fearing that the more relaxed atmosphere would allow the children to relax into passivity and they would be ignored by the teachers.

(When I visited this young director, she admitted that she had never visited either a regular preschool or the training school to which she was referring parents. She was basing her recommendation on educational beliefs inherited from her not-too-distant college days, where professors of rival theories inculcated their students to believe as they did.)

"So much depends on the teacher," she admitted. "The parent doesn't really know how much training her child will receive after she's dropped him off. If the child is in a room with nondisabled children and is just left to feel like he's 'part of it' without ever being actively involved, or if the teacher's attitude is that 'he'll get it eventually,' that child could lose some of the intensively trained skills he developed in infant intervention classes.

"But if you have a teacher with a small group who tells the other children that 'John will be in your class; he can do things just like the rest of you, but he's a little slower at it; he needs our help, and he needs all of you to be his friend,' you have an exceptional teacher who is really dedicated to the idea of mainstreaming. Too often, just as later in school, teachers are occupied with the majority of children in the class, and as long as your disabled child is content to observe and be a good boy (read: not behave in an attention-getting manner), they are content to leave him alone."

So, parents, it really *is* up to you. Don't just take another's word that a particular school is right for your child. Do your legwork. Visit several schools. Then make your decision.

Whatever preschool you select, remember that all will not run smoothly. There will be mishaps and setbacks and days when nothing seems to go right for him, but look at these occasions as minor growing incidents. On balance, the good experiences will almost surely outweigh the bad.

IS A REGULAR PRESCHOOL THE ANSWER?

Perhaps the learning programs at a school for preschoolers without disabilities are quite similar to those in a school for preschoolers with disabilities. Is it worth trying for that regular preschool? To be weighed against the obvious advantages of the state-supported special school is the fact that there your child will associate only with other youngsters who are disabled. This arrangement may work well if she has brothers and sisters at home who include her in their activities. But there are other considerations.

Studies indicate that when disabled children are included in classes with nondisabled children, they develop more socialization habits, learn to speak more clearly and with a larger vocabulary, and—perhaps most important of all—begin to see themselves as belonging in a world of nondisabled people. (Not that they are yet aware of anything other than their own world. None of us can live our lives and another one at the same time nor, when young, imagine any other life as "normal" but the one we are living.) But if your disabled child is always in a sheltered environment, her perception of the world will be skewed.

When children are allowed to learn in a supportive, safe environment like a good preschool, they continue to develop self-confidence and a positive attitude about themselves. That is even more true when the child concerned has special needs. Fear of not being able to perform a task or do it well, fear of being laughed at, can be paralyzing for a youngster with a handicapping condition. If he begins learning to be capable at a young age, before a self-conscious awareness of his disabilities sets in, he is more likely to develop a positive outlook toward new learning experiences. He is also more apt to assimilate the fact that other children are friendly and naturally curious rather than hostile.

Programs for children with severe, moderate, or multiple handicapping conditions are of necessity more structured, more geared to specific kinds of training, than the average preschool.

WHO WANTS TO BE A SQUEAKY WHEEL?

Few things are harder for parents than to stand apart from the crowd and demand rights for their child that other children in similar circumstances have been denied. Yet sometimes it is necessary. Sometimes, if you keep your sense of humor, you can learn to like it. Many times, when you see your efforts result in doors opening for others following, you experience the wonderful feeling of knowing it's worth it.

Take Marie Rose's parents, the Thorntons, who were both schoolteachers. They had worked closely with her teacher through Marie Rose's beginning years in an infant intervention class. When she was three, they sought an appropriate school to provide a link between that class and regular school. The district in which they lived had one school for all developmentally disabled children. Recent state law had mandated appropriate schooling for the children from the age of three. But when they went to visit the school prior to enrolling Marie Rose, they found no children younger than seven. After the three productive years of Marie Rose's early training, the parents could not see a place for her in this school that really had no provision—neither a separate room nor teacher—for preschool-age children. They feared that "schooling" would become little more than baby-sitting.

A sympathetic teacher at the school alerted them to a school in a neighboring district that would seem to fit her needs perfectly. The parents drove the twenty miles and found a program geared to three- and four-year-olds that employed many techniques from Marie Rose's early training. They were thrilled—until they applied for a transfer for Marie Rose.

School district administrators refused to transfer their daughter on the grounds that their district did provide a school that, on paper, served children of Marie Rose's age and disability. The fact that no children were within years of her age mattered not to them. What mattered was one thing: money.

Districts are paid for educating the children in their district by a system known as ADA. That is, funds are disbursed according to the Average Daily Attendance of each school-age child living in that district. Thus, if they allowed Marie Rose's parents to send her to school outside their district, they would lose money. Further, under the law governing education of disabled children, they would have to provide transportation. They balked.

Less determined parents would have given up. (And many had, they discovered later.) But they were not about to see all that good infant training get washed away. It took months of letters to school officials all the way to the state Department of Education, plus endless personal meetings—which frequently degenerated into confrontations—before Marie Rose's transfer was approved.

Ecstatic with their victory and with the program Marie Rose was now receiving, the Thorntons vowed not to let it end there. During their months of battle, they came in contact with other parents who had made similar requests for transfer but had been denied. Those parents came forward again, and Marie Rose's parents had the satisfaction of assisting four other couples to place their children in more appropriate schools outside the district.

Not all school districts are so contrary. Other parents faced with a similar situation likewise labored patiently to find an appropriate school for their child outside the home district. Then they approached their own district, requested the transfer, and calmly presented the facts to back up their request. The request was granted.

"It's amazing how easy it was by then," said the father. "The hard work was finding the right place. Once we had that, it seemed surprisingly easy to convince the home district. I guess people don't usually put in that kind of groundwork. They just go to the district and complain, without having anything better to suggest."

Back to Marie Rose. There is more to her story. When she was five, she had done so well in preschool that her teacher recommended placing her in a regular kindergarten in her home district. The kindergarten teacher and the principal, after interviewing the parents and child and observing Marie Rose in class, agreed it would be beneficial not only to continue Marie Rose's socialization with nondisabled children but the reverse, also.

It succeeded beyond their expectations. She was well accepted, due in part to the teacher's attitude in treating her as "just one of the children," to the parents' continuing interest and support of the teacher's efforts, and to Marie Rose herself.

It worked until the day a state school inspector learned that a developmentally disabled child was in the kindergarten class and ordered her transferred to the school for disabled children. His reasoning? The kindergarten personnel had not the proper training to teach disabled children. The inspector had the rules on his side. The principal was aghast. Marie Rose had fitted in beautifully! She had no specific disability other than a congenital one that left her a slow learner.

So Frank and Dora Thornton, knowing what squeaky wheels can accomplish, solicited letters from their doctors, a psychologist, the teacher, and the principal. Finally, a last-ditch call to their state senator resulted in a call to the superior of the inspector, who was told that rules are meant to serve people, not people to serve rules where common sense dictates otherwise. Marie Rose went happily back to her classmates in kindergarten.

Things can be changed. Pushing a little here, persuading a little there, parents can effect lasting and beneficial change for their children without acquiring too many gray hairs in the process.

Some years ago Mike, who is now a grown-up, and I revisited Cameron Christian Pre-School in West Covina, California, where so long ago the director had said, "Yes, we'd like to have Mike attend here." As we drove to the school, I explained to Mike that he had been the first youngster with a handicapping condition ever to attend Cameron. I told him that because he had gotten along well, learned to play, paint, wash his hands, stand in line, and wait his turn, maybe others like him had been given a chance to go to Cameron, too.

At the time of our visit in early 1981, Betty Harris was still the director, and his former teacher, Mildred Waters, still taught rambunctious three-year-olds. They remembered Mike. He was obviously flattered by their attention as he shook hands and answered questions about his school, his job at a training center, and his girlfriend. As Mike wandered off to inspect his old playground, Mrs. Harris turned to me with a smile: "You know, Mrs. Ross, in all the years since Mike went here, we've never turned down a child who was mentally retarded."

Yes, things change. And the bloom of Mrs. Harris's words made a few gray hairs worthwhile.

CHAPTER 7

...And Real School at Last

H i, Miz Ross, where you going?"

Our neighbor Billy caught up to us as Mike and I headed down the sidewalk one September morning in 1966. Billy was slicked up and combed down for the first day of second grade. I smiled at him.

"I'm taking Mike to school. He's starting kindergarten."

"Yeah?" Billy peered down at Mike with new interest, this sturdy little fellow who was also slicked and combed and being very serious. "Aren't you afraid he'll get lost?"

I laughed nervously. That's exactly what I had been thinking. *What if Mike just decided to go for a walk in the middle of school? What if—all sorts of things.*

"I'll keep an eye on him, Miz Ross," Billy said with a seriousness that showed the depth of his understanding. I thanked him, and he ran ahead to greet some friends, never dreaming that for me, the act of walking Mike to kindergarten was as close to a miracle as I ever expected.

I already knew the kindergarten teacher. She was an optimistic, outgoing person who had been my son Jim's teacher two years earlier. I suppose that is what had given me courage in the first place to dare think about kindergarten for Mike. His years at preschool had given me confidence that he could function in a program for young children without disabilities. I'd first mentioned it to the kindergarten teacher the previous spring when Mike had gone along to one of Jim's back-to-school nights. She considered a few minutes, then said she felt enrolling Mike would be a good experience for him and the other students, although no child with Down's syndrome had ever attended a regular kindergarten in our district. She promised to talk it over with the principal.

He had not been opposed. Trusting her judgment, he suggested we try it for a few weeks and see if it placed a strain on Mike. I was pleased that their emphasis from the beginning was on Mike, not on the rules, what other educators might think, or possible objections by other parents.

The children easily recognized that Mike was different, but that didn't stop them from liking him. In a way, because of the affection, Mike remained more babyish than he should have. The more mature five-year-olds treated him like a baby brother. The teacher was constantly reminding them to "let Mike do it for himself."

It was a very good year. So good, in fact, that the following September I approached the principal of the elementary school that hosted the primary class for educable mentally retarded (EMR) children in our district. The worst he could do was say no to what I had in mind. I knew a child with Down's syndrome had never attended the EMR class before. But I also had the assurance of Mike's kindergarten teacher that my request was not unreasonable, based on the growth Mike had exhibited that year. "But be prepared to be turned down," she cautioned me.

As I sat in the principal's office facing him, I felt that he was predisposed to turn me down. I don't know if it's the parenting or being a writer that develops these tenuous vibrations. But they are more often right than wrong. However, the principal listened courteously. He explained to me the purpose of the EMR class. Children who are considered educable—that is, able to receive and profit by academic instruction—are placed on regular school campuses in classes that "keep up" in outward appearance, at least, with their age mates. In this way, it is hoped, the stigma of being in a special class is lessened. Classes are smaller, and children are expected to progress academically but at their own rates. At the completion of his school years, the EMR student is expected to be able to go out and get a job of some sort, marry and have children if he desires, be self-supporting, and meld into the general population.

TMR children, those labeled trainable mentally retarded, are not expected to do any of the above. They are placed on a separate campus and taught social skills, how to follow directions, and how to do things with their hands, not their heads. The general consensus was that children with Down's syndrome belonged there.

71

After about twenty minutes, the principal asked if I would consent to bring Mike to his office for an interview. "He's here now," I said, "sitting outside your office."

"He's been sitting quietly all this time?"

I had to smile at his surprise. "Reading a book," I added. (It was a slight stretch of the truth. Mike couldn't read yet, but he loved books, turned pages carefully, and minutely scrutinized all the pictures. Certainly reading readiness, I'd call it.)

The principal got up, went outside, and invited Mike in. He asked him a few questions.

"He knows his colors and can count to twenty," I threw in. (Couldn't hurt!) The principal tried Mike on these points and turned to me with a shake of his head. "He's certainly higher than other children with Down's syndrome, isn't he?"

I shrugged, thinking but not saying that maybe other children just hadn't been given a chance to prove what they could do. Then and there the principal decided to give Mike a chance. I couldn't have been more pleased.

"DOES IT REALLY MATTER WHERE HE GETS HIS SCHOOLING?"

The answer is a resounding yes! As long as there are expectations based on groupings, *it matters.*

In an article written for *McCall's* when his mentally retarded son was young, Senator S. I. Hayakawa wrote, "Evaluations—value judgments—are built into many of the words we use to describe the world, and . . . these evaluations govern and sometimes distort our thinking. For example: 'ex-convict' (don't trust him); 'diplomat' (distinguished); 'blondes' (have more fun); and of course 'retarded child' (a tragedy—nothing to be done!)."[1]

Think of the labels that go with *trainable* and *educable,* with *elementary school* as opposed to *special school,* with *advanced placement (AP)* as opposed to *vocational training.*

Labeling is easy. Using labels is a convenient way of instantly pocketing people into understandable slots. And then, once slotted, people are expected to behave accordingly. When one understands this human tendency, it is easy to realize how important it is to fight for a child's placement in the school or program that best suits not just his present needs but also his potential. Wherever he is placed, the child will be expected by the teacher to perform as well as others in the class. The teacher's expectations and attitude can be big pluses in what the child achieves.

All through Mike's school years and as he began to move out in other directions, I felt so closely allied to him that I would view the success or failure of any particular experience according to how it related to his long-range chances for a successful, independent life. More so than with our other children.

When our other children experienced setbacks—didn't get the part in the play, didn't make first string—my husband and I saw it as our job to comfort the child, assure him or her that it was only a play or a game and that there would be other chances. With Mike, I didn't feel that way. I felt that not succeeding in each new situation was more than just losing one chance in a series of several; it was a step backward. (See chapter 12, "How to Help Your Child Experience Success.")

EVEN DANCING HAS A FEW BACKWARD STEPS

One of the most wrenching memories of Mike's early school years was a scene that happened after Mike had successfully completed a year in the EMR class.

We moved to a different town. Storm warnings went up when I attempted to sign him up for his new EMR class.

"Oh, ah, Mrs. Ross, you need to sign Michael up at the school he will be attending, the TMR school."

"Oh, no, he's completed first grade in an EMR class....He went to a regular kindergarten class before that," I added proudly.

"I see. Well, before we can take him you need to see the special education department at the district office. But I can tell you right now, we don't have any children with Down's syndrome in our district."

The red flag was being hoisted. Where were the warmth and accommodation found everywhere in our old district? The cold knot in the pit of my stomach that tightened before every crucial medical test, every psychological battery, every meeting with unfamiliar doctors or educators, returned.

I made the necessary appointment and showed up at the appointed time. They had been expecting me. We went into a small office. I was offered a chair. Two men sat on either side of me, and another one perched on the desk, his knee practically in my face. I had to tilt my head back to look him in the eye. None of them was smiling.

"Now, Mrs. Ross . . ."

My memory of that hour was of them telling me what my son could *not* be and could *not* do and they'd make sure he didn't.

"Now wouldn't you rather that he'd be a big fish in a little pond than a little fish in a big pond?"

My composure deserted me. My hand shook as I showed them the letters from his former teachers, his grades, and his latest IQ battery scores, which showed that he was currently functioning well above the cutoff that artificially separated EMR from TMR learners. Children who scored at 50 or below on a standard intelligence test were arbitrarily assigned to TMR classes.

"Oh, yes, I see. My, he certainly did well, didn't he? Of course children like yours always level off, and then they regress. Now you don't see any children like him on regular school campuses, do you? Do you?"

I stumbled out of that place blinded by angry tears, with a new level of abhorrence in my heart. The cruelty of those three men, their smug satisfaction that they had preserved the integrity of their little self-made barriers. They nearly destroyed me, my confidence in Mike, his future. How dare they take that away!

And so Mike was assigned to TMR school for "training."

Old habits are hard to break. Before long I was presenting myself to Mike's new teacher and offering to help in any way I could.

What I learned in the next two years convinced me how wrong it is to segregate children of differing abilities. Take the matter of reading. By definition, our TMR school was for training, not educating. Therefore, reading, as an academic subject, was not taught. TMR children could not read or be taught to read; therefore, one did not teach the skill. It sounded like Alice in Wonderland!

But I was determined that Mike not lose the primary reading skills gained the previous year. I asked Mike's teacher to allow me to teach reading.

With the bemused permission of her principal, she agreed, possibly because I possessed a valid elementary teaching credential. Twice a week I taught reading skills to six or eight children, including Mike, chosen from several classes. We met in the teachers' lounge. I was not to tell anyone what we were doing but merely to call it activities. (Other parents would want their children in on it, too, one teacher explained.)

I began the reading class with picture books from the local library. I made flash cards of each word in the book, using a broad felt-tipped pen to print the words on separate four-by-six cards. I read the story to the class, giving them plenty of time to scrutinize the pictures. Then I held up each word and asked the class to repeat the word after me. I would pin each word card to a bulletin board and move it from one side to the other when the class gave the correct answer.

After the children memorized the words, they would take turns "reading" the story to one another. At each reading, the children listened to one another with as much attention and suspense as if they'd never heard it before. Truly, they never had heard one another—and themselves—reading before!

At first, the cards were all nouns like *bird, house, baby,* and so on. Then we added words like *this, the,* and *when,* and a few verbs like *walks* and *smiles.* Soon most of them had a sight vocabulary of twenty-five words, then fifty. We talked about looking at the picture for clues to word meanings. They began to have fun and to gain confidence, guessing at meanings of the words below the picture. There were no put-downs for wrong guesses, only generous praise for courageous tries.

(One boy who had autism did not speak at all, but he was an instinctive cartoonist. Shown the word card *bird,* he would in a few deft, strong strokes produce a superior drawing of a bird. When shown the card *house,* he would draw a house with accurate three-dimensional perspective.)

I encouraged them to bring in pictures. We named things in their pictures. Thus, *football, ice hockey, hot dogs,* and other fun words entered their sight-reading vocabularies. I discovered they loved mastering big words like *elephant.* They were able to learn these words more easily than small words that looked alike, such as *this, that,* and *then.* In all we did, repetition and more repetition were the key to their learning.

Eventually, we progressed from picture books to preprimers and to I Can Read It Myself books, which are readily available in supermarkets. Books with lots of repetition, such as Dr. Seuss's *The Cat in the Hat,* were favorites.

I should stress that this reading was on a very basic level. Comprehension, which is the goal of reading, was barely touched upon. The children could and did follow directions suggested in little word games we played, like drawing a card and obeying what it said. ("Go stand by the window"; "Give the card to Sally.") But if I were to say, for instance, "Why did Jimmy run away from his mother?" only one or two would have been able to give a correct answer: "Because he had to look for his dog." Much of the time their guesses would be unrelated to the story content.

In spite of my keeping mum about the class, word did seep out. More than once a parent cornered me and asked if her child could be included. I would say lamely, "Well, it isn't exactly a reading class...," and end up advising her to talk to her child's teacher. The teachers had selected children for the class who had seemed to them most ready for reading readiness.

I did not always have the same children, but in the two years the class met, several children learned to read. My box of flash cards numbered over two hundred, and most of the children could identify them all. Then our family moved again. I heard later that the reading class was dropped.

Years later, I ran into Mike's former teacher. She brought up the reading class and expressed the astonishment she and the other teachers had felt when the children actually could and did read to them.

In all the schools Mike attended, his teachers never refused to allow me to bring my own brand of something special to do with the children. I consider teachers, by and large, among the most open of professionals. One might have been convinced a technique or a program would not work, but the attitude was always, "If you want to come in and try it, I'll make time for it."

I think one of the reasons for their attitude was that I always tried to have my schemes well thought out before approaching the teacher, and I had put in enough time with her and the class to convince her of my sincerity and that I could be trusted with the children.

Mike was eight when we moved a third time. Down I went to the new district's office, more wary this time, determined not to get tangled in lines like "big fish" and "little fish."

The new director of special education thought re-placing Mike in an EMR class was an interesting idea. I heard the familiar litany that there had never been a child with Down's syndrome in the EMR classes. Also, I was beginning to hear more frequently that Mike would probably be leveling off soon and I should not expect too much. Nevertheless, the director suggested having "some testing on Mike to see where he is now." I could scarcely control my elation.

AND THE WALLS CAME TUMBLING DOWN

They tested, Mike cooperated, and soon he was placed in a third-grade EMR class. Within one year, hearing of Mike's placement, three other parents were successful in having their children transferred from the TMR school to EMR classes. Another child with Down's syndrome was among them. Two had been in my reading class. I was as pleased as if they had been my own children.

I don't think the reading class did that much for the children. What it did accomplish was to reaffirm to parents that their children were capable of learning more than they had been led to believe. Parents gained confidence to step out and expect more.

A parent counselor with the state Department of Special Education recently said to me, "You parents don't demand enough. You don't demand enough of your children, and you don't demand enough of us."

If parents don't demand, who will?

Nationwide, the artificial barriers that separate educational programs for children at different levels of development are falling, although in some areas they are as rigid as ever. As long as barriers remain in place, bureaucracy has a way of interfering with common sense. Thus, a child placed in a TMR school is not taught to read. "If he were capable of learning to read, he'd be in an educable class, right?"

Few children with handicapping conditions are developed or undeveloped equally in all areas. Yet by forcing children to conform to this artificial distinction, school officials are saying—against their own good sense—"Of course he can't learn to read; he's in a training school, isn't he?"

Conversely, many skills taught in TMR classes, with their emphasis on physical training, gross and fine motor movement, and sports, would be of tremendous benefit to our children in EMR classes. In some high-school EMR classes, children are frequently denied physical education classes entirely because coaches plead they can't work with disabled children in classes where sixty or more boys or girls are already enrolled.

Common sense suggests combining all classes on a common campus where students have easy access to all classes they need. In places where that is being done, advantages are accruing to all the children. Placing severely disabled children on the same campus as nondisabled children, for instance, has also meant placing occupational and speech therapists there. Where formerly their services had been contracted only for children with handicapping conditions, now they are available to other children with special needs as well.

In the short term, students in special, segregated schools should be transported between campuses to access the best combination of specialty training and regular classes.

Feelings run high when one talks of integrating schools to include all ranges of ability and disability. This subject will be discussed in chapter 10 on mainstreaming.

It's always easier to gain cooperation from those whose lives touch yours or your children's when you understand their problems and empathize with them, as we all hope educators and other professionals will do with us.

HOW TO BE A TEAM PLAYER

When Mike's little sister, Laurie, entered kindergarten, the teacher had a registration table set up outside the door. Parents showed birth certificates, filled out forms, and were excused, while children filed into the gaping doorway beyond. In this way the teacher said to the parent, "This is as far as you come. This is the cutoff. Beyond this point your daughter is my responsibility. You will get her back in three hours."

Thus falls the first apron string. My daughter, a third child with two years of preschool under her sash, strode ahead without a backward glance. For me, it was the first time in five years I was returning home without a toddler in tow. I experienced a wonderful sense of elation and hurried home to enjoy a second cup of coffee and the entire morning newspaper.

This cutoff is symbolic. But for the parent of a child with disabilities, a complete cutoff is not desirable for several reasons. Throughout your child's growing-up years, you will almost certainly be more involved in her education and medical and social problems than in those of her brothers and sisters. Then there is the fact that you often feel powerless when your child is cut away from your sphere of influence. Having a disabled child is not so common that you are likely to have neighbors with similar problems to share. Alone, you try not to agonize over what could go wrong with you not present to buffer and interpret.

Studies done on preschool children with disabilities show that when parents participate fully in training programs, children do better than when parents are left out of the team. Today with school budgets hard-pressed to meet mandated needs, parents are being encouraged to volunteer their time and abilities to their children's schools in many capacities, from yard supervisor to schoolroom aide to tutor, to take up where budgets have slashed funds to pay others to do these important jobs.

This situation works to great advantage for us parents of children with disabilities. By our presence in the schoolroom, we can make a measurable difference in the amount of learning accomplished.

Some teachers consider the classroom a creative haven in which they are free to shape young lives to the best of their abilities. They are capable and enjoy working alone with the class. These teachers sometimes do not take kindly to aides or others helping out. They feel that taking time to train aides who, if they are unpaid, may be erratic in attendance is wasting time that could be better spent with the children.

The best way for a parent who really wants to be part of any child's classroom experience is to develop a personal-professional relationship with the teacher. Make an effort to see your child's education from her viewpoint. Really think about how you can help your child in a way that helps her, too. Maybe it begins with offering to bake cookies for parent night. Perhaps you can help with paperwork that can be done in your off hours, or you can construct needed math or reading aids.

In the classroom perhaps your abilities lie in tutoring, and you can help students with spelling or printing. Or if you are good in crafts, work on a project with the class while the teacher works singly with a child who needs more specialized help.

Ideally, parents should have time to offer their skills and services to the teachers of all their children. But many children come from families with two working parents, a single-parent family, or a foster family in which the parent cares for as many as six children with disabilities. Until flextime—the concept of work hours tailored to suit the convenience of the worker instead of nine-to-five schedules—is more wide-ranging, many parents are simply going to be unavailable to the teacher during school hours.

The point is, once the teacher discovers you are willing to work off-school hours or you can work efficiently and cooperatively, with a good relationship with the children (including being objective with your child), he will be more likely to depend on you. If you are discreet and sympathetic, you may find the teacher sharing views of issues concerning not only your child but the whole school experience.

WHY AREN'T MORE PARENTS INVOLVED
IN THEIR CHILDREN'S SCHOOLING?

Some educators claim that parents are just too lazy to get involved at school or they don't care. They are all involved with themselves these days, educators declare.

We're not involved because we're not wanted, parents retort.

How did it come about that schools and parents see one another as antagonists? That some teachers feel parents want to be in the classroom only to "catch them" at something. That some parents accuse principals and teachers of having "Watergate mentalities," hiding inadequate teaching practices under a cloak of secrecy.

Tempers flare and professionals clash with parents not because they are unfeeling or careless but often because in the fields of service to our children, each professional is so deeply involved, cares so deeply as a parent or a teacher or a doctor, and is so deeply dedicated to the betterment of the one child or the many like him that honest differences of opinion regarding training or treatment often meet on the sharp edge of hostility.

Others, even close relatives, often have difficulty understanding the depth of passion we parents develop for a child with a handicapping condition, the lengths to which we will go to help her achieve her best potential. If we are fighters, it's because we've had to be in order to be recognized as part of the professional team.

In classrooms where teachers have actively sought parent participation, the following reaction, as described by one teacher, has been typical: "They didn't seem to be very involved with their child's education. So I began writing a note to each parent every day, just a line or two about what Johnny did that was good that day and what we were working on now—maybe a social skill or an academic skill. Soon parents began to respond. They would write or take a moment when they dropped the child off to tell me what they were doing at home.

"Gradually, we began to reinforce each other's work. Then we would begin to get together and plan our program and goals jointly. Soon parents were saying, 'What can I do to help?' either in school or in school programs at home. It was no longer the 'You're here to teach him' and 'I'm at home to feed and clothe him' division. Parents are willing to come in, to learn, to work with you."

Behavior problems, this teacher found, minimized when parents were actively involved. Behavior problems often come out of children's inner confusion and their frustration about it. Working together, teacher and parent have a wonderful opportunity to defuse the situation.

The teacher reporting this finding has an outstandingly successful record in teaching autistic children.

No matter how little or how much time you are able to give physically to the classroom, stay in close touch with the teacher. Let her know you support her. Make it clear you consider yourself part of a team, not an adversary. As much as possible, bring the child into discussions of problems and solving them and goals. He, like you, will cooperate better when allowed to become an informed member of the team.

CHAPTER 8

Clap if You Love Jesus

C lap if you love Jesus!" cries the young priest.
Yeas, stomps, and whistles race through the audience.
"And does Jesus love you?"

Another chorus of shrieks and happy laughs. Is the Catholic church suddenly going in for old-time revivals? Not exactly. This priest is among the ranks of ministers and rabbis carrying the Word of God to people who are mentally retarded and live in institutions. This celebration happened at Lanterman State Hospital in southern California, and it shows something important: an increasing commitment by organized religion to the fact that since God meets people on their own levels, so must the churches.

"I teach a lot from the parable about the good Samaritan because these kids know what it is to be helped when you need it," said Father Francis Murphy, a local priest who divided his time between his parish and the state hospital. "And about planting seeds in good ground because some of them have gardens or help around here with the gardening. They may not understand all of it, but they sure know about love and happiness."

The word *Amen* isn't meaningful to some severely retarded people, but watching them the day Father Murphy preached, you knew that they knew how to make a joyful noise.

The vast majority of children with disabilities are capable of living outside an institution. For them, there are more varied opportunities to learn to know God.

HOW CAN WE TEACH CHILDREN
WITH DISABILITIES ABOUT GOD?

A strong church tie can help you teach your child about God. If you belong to a church or synagogue, you probably take your disabled youngster with you, along with your other children, when you worship. When she is a baby, there is little problem as long as her health permits leaving her in the church nursery during services.

For the next several years, finding a place she will fit in may be accomplished with grace and imagination. Many Sunday school classes have one or more teaching aides who can devote more time to a child with special needs. Or you can enroll her in a class with younger children.

This latter approach worked with Mike as long as he was relatively the same size as his classmates. But when he hit a growth spurt around twelve, his added inches made him self-conscious around much younger children. He seemed embarrassed that he still enjoyed coloring and pasting, circle dances and songs, and the same stories as the younger ones. His emerging awareness of his physical self also caused him to "feel funny" with them. He acted out these feelings with silliness and disruption, which only worsened the situation.

We didn't feel Mike was ready to join us in worship in the sanctuary yet, and a wise Sunday school teacher came up with the idea of asking Mike to help in the prekindergarten class. It was a beautiful solution. For the next year he worked as a teacher's aide, serving juice at nutrition time, reading Bible stories to them, helping get out and put away the building blocks, and moving furniture. We discovered that he had a knack for getting along with four-year-olds. The children recognized the specialness of the relationship and returned his friendship.

When children attend worship in the sanctuary, another facet of learning takes over. When Mike did join in regular worship services a year later, we realized again how he thrives on routine. He found security in knowing what came next in the service, in rising to sing the familiar passage "Praise God from whom all blessings flow." And if he didn't understand much of the sermon, he appreciated the unchanging beauty of our stained-glass windows, the sanctuary bursting with song, and the reverence of the silences. And he knew God loved him when familiar friends clapped his shoulder after service and said, "Well, how's my buddy Mike this morning?"

There is a kind of Sunday morning psychology at work at

worship services. People feel good about themselves. They forget to be afraid of the "strange one" in their midst. Mike isn't subject to the curious stares that sometimes embarrass him when he's out of familiar surroundings.

Church can provide an active social center in a setting that gives persons who are disabled plenty of emotional security. This aspect is especially important for teenagers because on school campuses, problems of adolescence are rampant, and children with obvious disabilities are easy targets of scapegoating. Church offers them an opportunity to enjoy themselves, to be useful, and to be at ease, too.

Mike hasn't the voice for choir, but he made a fine spear carrier in pageants. At potlucks he bused tables with a flourish. In summer he enjoyed being part of the unstructured field trips to beaches and zoos with the high-school department. He loved the adventure each Thanksgiving of teaming to collect canned goods for needy families.

I think Christ told us to love and help one another because it does so much for us to be helpers. What a tremendous lift it is for anyone to be able to help once in a while rather than always be the "helpee"! How wonderful to have a skill that someone else needs! What a special glow comes from being useful!

THE PHYSICAL FACILITIES

If your child has a physical disability, look over your church's accommodations for persons with handicapping conditions before he is old enough to need them.

Are doors to church schoolrooms and bathrooms wide enough to permit easy passage for wheelchairs? Is there a toilet stall designed for persons with disabilities? Are the door sills tapered so that they are easy to roll over? Are there ramps as well as steps into the sanctuary, and at least one aisle wide enough to take a wheelchair all the way to the altar?

More often than not, the answer to these questions is no. For some time, many churches have provided pews with hearing aids for hearing impaired worshipers, probably because hearing loss happens to most of us as we grow older. But disabled worshipers form a distinct minority—until recently not a very vocal minority.

For years, a catch-22 argument has gone on in budget sessions at churches as well as further up the hierarchical ladder: "Shouldn't we provide better facilities for people with handicapping conditions?"

"Why? There aren't any in our church."

"Maybe they are not coming here because we don't offer the facilities. Maybe they don't feel wanted."

If you have a child who will use a wheelchair, you have a strong reason to advocate her rights, and that includes the right to partake of worship as others do in church.

The same argument, "There aren't any here," has been given for not extending the church ministry to developmentally disabled people: "Well, I know Mr. and Mrs. So-and-So have a girl who is mentally retarded, but they are the only ones. How can we justify using one of our rooms and one of our teachers for only one person? We never have enough rooms or teachers!"

Although many major denominations have issued statements in response to the problems of persons with handicapping conditions, most of the proposed changes remain in the planning stages. But change is coming. Some congregations regularly interpret their services through sign language to help persons who are deaf. Most religious denominations now urge that any new buildings be barrier free. The American Lutheran church denied low-cost loans to new churches whose building plans did not meet the needs of disabled persons. The Catholic church, with a good history of educating persons with handicapping conditions in isolated settings, is moving toward special support services in the regular classroom.

WHAT YOU CAN DO

If your church has no facilities or for some reason seems unable to adapt to your child's special needs for religious instruction, you can do several things. Call the local ministerial association and ask for suggestions. If you get no help, ask if you might attend a meeting of the association and solicit their help directly in meeting your needs.

School districts often pool resources to provide education for disabled children. One school may house a class for the area's deaf children; another has classes for blind children; a third offers classes for neurologically or developmentally disabled children. Why can't neighboring churches pool resources to form community classes in religious instruction for disabled children? We love the same God. Surely a path through various denominational curricula can be found. The disadvantage, of course, is that your child may be going to a different church on Sunday morning, creating a time crunch. But you may find the advantages in spiritual growth and socialization to be worth the effort. Perhaps a community bus pickup could be instituted. Perhaps Bible classes can be offered on a day other than Sunday. Another possibility might be to volunteer to organize and teach a class yourself (if your church is willing but unorganized). Or if you do not feel gifted to teach, volunteer to organize a class, find a teacher, or be an aide. Or organize a Bible learning time in your home. Invite children from your child's special education class at school to attend.

Many good programs, in church as well as in the community, have begun because one parent refused to take no for an answer. Can you be that parent?

When you think about it, teaching mentally retarded persons about God would seem to be about the hardest thing there is. You can't pick up God and hug Him. You can't teach theory and Christian ethics. You can't even teach your child about God by asking that so reasonable question, If God didn't make us, who did?

The greatest thing you have going for you as a teacher is your faith. If faith in God is an active force in your life, it will show. It would be almost impossible not to teach because your heart knows why you love God even if your brain can't articulate it. And when your child sees you leaning on God for help, appreciating Him through the beauty of His world, sharing Him with others in times of worship, he will accept God as part of your family even as you do.

It's like getting letters from Grandma, even though she may live far away. No one doubts she exists. And there are even birthday presents sometimes.

Our letters from God are in the Bible. Our presents from Him are all around us—in a day free of pain, an hour shared with special friends, a particularly glorious April day, the turning of the leaves in fall.

And "family" may not be the television family of one dad, one mom, 2½ kids, and a dog. It may be just you and your child and God. It may be you and your spouse caring for six disabled children in a family care home. Whoever the nurturing unit consists of, with God in its midst, it will be a family.

I asked Mike which day he liked better, his birthday or Christmas. He answered Christmas "because we give presents to each other." That made it easy to ask what present God gave us on the first Christmas. "Baby Jesus" came the ready answer.

But why select Christmas over a birthday? Both have equal value as far as "loot"; a birthday would seem to be more special because all attention is focused on one person. Mike's answer lay in the special joy he finds in participating in a holy celebration that draws all of us together. He never tires of the ageless beauty of the carols and the story they tell. He loves each year to arrange the manger scene on its bed of cotton snow. (We could put it on a bed of desert sand, but no one's asked and I'm not offering!) Mike may never verbalize the importance of Christmas, but he recognizes its transcendence over birthdays.

With each Easter, Hanukkah, or other holiday celebrated by different faiths comes a special opportunity to relate the present reality to God's endless love. The holy traditions you build in your child year by year will be hers after she has moved beyond your daily care.

Helping children to know and love God begins early. With our children with special needs the focus is slightly different. Most children can be relied upon to ask where clouds come from, why all caterpillars aren't fuzzy, or who made them. If you wait for a lead-in from your disabled child to teach him about God, you may have a long wait. So, create your own leads when the opportunity arises. Here's one way it happened in our family.

We lived at the base of the San Gabriel Mountains. Often in December, though it was sunny in the valley, the hills were already wearing sparkling caps of snow. I used to say, "Oh, Mike, aren't those mountains beautiful!"

Yes, he'd say, but he'd not be looking in the right direction. I'd urge him to look more up and away, and he'd stare at the nearby orange globe on the Union 76 sign.

Only gradually did I realize that "mountain" was an abstract for Mike. It took a few trips to the mountains before he could positively associate the blue distant peaks with the shallow rocky streambeds, the live oaks and chaparral of the canyons, and the pines. You couldn't see any of those things when you saw mountains from our house in the valley! How could *that* mountain be *this* mountain? If he couldn't relate mountain close to mountain far, how could he relate to God, an even farther look?

We really had to get to basics. On numerous trips we'd say, "Okay, Mike, here we go up into the mountains!" as the road climbed higher and narrowed. Then, "Look, now the trees are coming closer, and look how big these rocks really are!" The colder air, the skittering chipmunks, and occasional patches of snow—each thing that was found in the mountains was associated with "mountain."

Conversely, we'd pull off the road to look back at the valley. We'd say, "If we were closer, we could see our house, but we are so far away, our eyes can't see it." Mike knows by faith that our house is there, even though he can't see it.

As I said, I couldn't wait for him to ask, "Who made me?" That question isn't in his imagination. He needs to understand God concretely, through his own senses. Back to the mountains. We stomped through leaves. They made a great crunchy sound.

"Didn't God do a great job on these leaves? And look at the gorgeous colors!" With no other encouragement Mike would find especially beautiful leaves for us to admire together.

His dad would break away a bit of bark on an old pine and tell Mike to put his nose against the tree and sniff. The newly exposed bark of a certain species of pine has the fragrance of vanilla. And what a great time to point out that here's this scraggly old tree, kind of ugly, too, and you just get inside a bit and it has this wonderful aroma, like cookie dough. What an analogy can be made! Things that are rugged on the outside can still have a beautiful fragrance (be nice inside). Mike could never make that connection verbally by himself, but he did with help.

With enough examples in enough ways, our children can grasp that although they may have a handicapping condition, God has gifted them with a special beauty, even if it's the single beauty of innocence.

Jesus said, "Assuredly, I say to you, unless you are converted and become as little children, you will by no means enter the kingdom of heaven" (Matt. 18:3). When Jesus said that to the disciples, was He thinking of our children whose faith, when won, remains imperturbably childlike?

Gradually, Mike learned to know by faith that all the things he saw on the mountain are always there, even though from home he can see only shining peaks against a blue sky.

Because we can see God's handiwork "up close," we know He is "there"—just like the mountain is "there." We can image the mountain when we are away from it. We can image God through His works even as we worship Him in the abstract. Mike may never make the conscious leap to know that individual trees and rocks recede to form a mountainous mass, re-forming at a distance into a blue silhouette, but he knows that both images are "the mountains." He knows that Jesus is in our lives and that the kingdom of heaven is there, too, only farther.

With Mike, as with many of his friends with disabilities, memory is a highly developed function. Bible stories he heard years ago in church crop up in his conversation sometimes, the ark animals two by two or a rainbow reminding us of God's promise not to flood the earth again. Once in a church play about Daniel, he played a centurion. Do you think he will ever forget the names of Shadrach, Meshach, and Abed-Nego who were thrown into the furnace? Hardly! They are such delicious tongue twisters that once learned they are learned forever.

At home I can think of no better way to begin building your child's love for God than at prayer. Through the years, through impromptu graces and Bible readings or written meditations, Mike heard daily our thanks for food, our laying of problems before God, our thanks for prayers answered, and our prayerful concern for others. He says the grace himself at times. Usually, though, he prefers to tack on a P.S. after the "Amen." His P.S.'s usually ask God to take care of some member of the family we've overlooked, but sometimes his concerns widen enough to cause the rest of us to exchange glances of wonder. He'll pray for rain during a drought, for a friend who had an accident at school, or for the safety of a relative on a trip.

It's important for children to feel God as a personal experience. Prayers can help. Prayers about schoolwork, cut fingers, fears about an upcoming hospital trip, hurt feelings—confided as in a trusted friend—can make God more real.

So what if a person's understanding of God is no greater than swelling with happy feelings and shouting approval when a priest cries, "Does Jesus love you?"

What more can any of us claim to know about God's love?

CHAPTER 9

Parents as Central Data Banks

*P*arents are such sitting ducks. Did you ever take your child to catch the bus for camp and discover you've forgotten her vaccination certificate? (While 900 stricken children hang their necks out the bus window and 900 sleeping bags teeter on top.)

When our children are grown, we reap laurels or scorn for the way they turned out. One way or another we are credited or blamed for much that is beyond our control. Consider the parents of the child with special needs. Parents are the only path linking the fragmented services, the physicians, schools, and therapies needed at one time or another by their child. Do the various agencies make that job easy for them?

Surely, the orthopedist is familiar with and takes time to inform the new parents about available community services and special programs for the child with an orthopedically handicapping condition. No? Then the psychologist who has just tested the child gives the parents a clearly written report, devoid of psychological jargon, to share with the child's teacher. What, again no?

Then how are the parents to be the links or, to change metaphors, the grease between the gears so that all agencies serving the child mesh smoothly in his best interest?

The parents are the child's central data bank, the one continuing factor in the progression through doctors, pediatricians, diagnosticians, early intervention specialists, school directors, teachers, and social services. They must maintain a complete record.

It sounds like a sensible truth, but it is one fraught with irony, writes Kathryn A. Gorham in "A Lost Generation of Parents." She adds, "Professionals, especially doctors, assume parents can't possibly understand the complexities of their trade."[1] The more specialized the diagnostician, the less concerned he is about giving information to parents. On the other hand, parents are expected to sign releases to permit a multitude of others access to records they are denied!

Withholding information from parents has the effect of making parents feel helpless and powerless, in awe of specialists and intimidated by their expertise. "It has made us," says Gorham, "unduly grateful to principals or school directors for merely accepting our children." The idea of twenty-four-hour, seven-days-a-week care at home has made us humbly grateful for any help.

Chronically being excluded from those "in the know" about our children has made parents at times indifferent to the latest "bandwagon on which the mental retardation experts are riding. We tend to listen politely, then do what we think is best for our children. For this we are accused of apathy," Gorham believes.

HOW PROFESSIONALS CAN HELP PARENTS

Gorham offers several positive suggestions for parents who want to help professionals recognize the necessity for correcting this imbalance. Parents should insist upon being part of the team at every step. They should have access to all information related to tests and diagnoses, written in language they can understand. (If reports go from doctors to schools in medical jargon, school personnel may not be able to read them, either.)

Parents might ask for suggestions for managing on a day-to-day basis considering needs of the child, capacities of the parents, and resources of the community. Keep in mind that parents must live with the child from day to day, help her along, shop for services to meet her needs, and support her ego. The professional can't be there to do it for her, so parents must be as well informed as possible. Information they don't understand isn't useful to them. The goal is parents who understand their child well enough to help her handle her problems. Parents need to understand the child's abilities as well as disabilities. What she can do is more important than what she can't.

These issues are compounded for families who live in the United States but whose first language is not English. For parents who do not read or speak English well enough to manage the inflow of information about their child, some sort of written translation service is needed to help them maintain up-to-date records.

Parents should be aware that there will be service insufficiencies. Helping agencies won't always be helpful. Their child has a right to services; parents have a right to be part of all decisions about their child. Some people down the line—teachers, nurses, professionals of any kind, and other parents—may emphasize the negative. Parents need to think positively and to teach others in their child's life to do so.

PARENTS IN CHARGE

"Learn to keep records," Kathryn Gorham advises. fellow parents. As soon as you learn your child has a problem, start a notebook. List everyone he sees; get copies of clinical reports. Record telephone calls you make and receive by date, subject, and the name of the person you spoke to. A thorough documentation of every step may help you obtain needed services more quickly or back up your claim for insufficient services.

Never leave the office of a doctor or other professional without understanding exactly what she means. If necessary ask her to illustrate what she means by giving you an example. Knowing the correct terminology is helpful, too, so that you can use it to explain to your child's teacher, for example, when discussing his needs. Talk freely and openly with professionals, teachers, and other parents.

Obtain records of results of all testing from schools, whether psychological, intelligence, behavioral, or vision and hearing screenings. And take snapshots as you go along. (On days when you feel discouraged, flip through his file. You'll probably make the pleasurable discovery that he has progressed much further than you had believed.)

When you change residences, schools, or doctors, a complete and up-to-date file is your best assurance that services for your child will flow smoothly without needless delays. Persuasion, not anger, is your best tool when faced with the task of convincing educators or medical personnel to see things your way. And with documented facts to back up your position, you are certain to be taken seriously.

Keeping good records has many advantages:

- To give yourself satisfaction in discovering progress that may be slow but is there

- To back up your right to be considered part of the professional team
- To be an effective link in keeping all helping agencies abreast of actions in each of the other agencies, including schools
- To press convincingly for services or education needed but not provided
- To help secure needed legislation.

NEW BILLS OF RIGHTS

Parents are no longer without clout as they fight for services for their child. Every state and school district has many laws and rules that apply. At the federal level, three laws stand as landmarks.

The Rehabilitation Act of 1973 This bill secured the rights of persons with handicapping conditions to work and gain acceptance as useful members of the labor force. Among the provisions of the law is one that prohibits discrimination in federally funded programs on the basis of a handicapping condition.

PL 94-142 Equally far-reaching is PL 94-142, the Education for All Handicapped Children Act of 1975. This law requires that all children with handicapping conditions in the United States be identified, evaluated, and provided free, appropriate public education in the least restrictive environment possible. The bill advises physicians to advise parents to notify the school district as soon as diagnosis is made, even in infancy, so that an evaluation of projected educational needs can be made. It requires that parents be involved in the planning and placement process; parents may appeal a placement decision if they are dissatisfied.

You may be familiar with the Individual Education Program (IEP) if your child with special needs is already in school. Teachers of students with handicapping conditions are required to set up a plan, in cooperation with the parents, for each student under the provisions of PL 94-142. When a child is first placed in special classes, all those who will be taking part in his educational program are called together to evaluate him. They decide on long-range goals, short-term objectives (which are skills developed to meet the long-range goals), and specific activities that will be carried out in the classroom to meet the instructional objectives.

After your child is in class, IEP meetings continue twice a year thereafter, once at the beginning of the school year to formulate new objectives and again at the end of the year to evaluate progress. Those involved in each IEP meeting are the parents, the teacher, the child's school counselor and frequently his social worker, and also any speech, audio, or physical therapists working with the child.

Periodically, teams of state inspectors visit each school to ascertain that the federal regulations are being complied with. They spot-check the IEPs on file. They talk with teachers, students, therapists, and parents. They go into classrooms to verify that the specific instructional activities listed on the IEP are being carried out. The state inspectors then file reports with the federal bureau, which in turn releases the additional money to each state's schools for implementing the program.

Is it all worth it? PL 94-142 came about in the first place because children with mentally handicapping conditions in certain states were denied admission to school. Yes, it was parents again—fighting for the rights of their children to be educated regardless of handicapping condition—who were responsible for the passage of this law.

Detractors of IEPs (as the local expression of PL 94-142) claim the time teachers spend filling out IEPs on each child and the time highly paid specialists must set aside to add their input, to say nothing of the meetings that are also mandated, add up to a monumental waste of time and money.

The IEP forces teachers and parents to sit down and think about where they want the child to go and how they are going to get her there. Writing these objectives is a good educational tool. Some teachers are just not that goal-oriented as far as individual children go. Other experienced teachers, given a few days with a child at the beginning of the year, know exactly what the child needs and have in their heads strategies to achieve those needs.

Unfortunately, when a law is mandated, certain procedures are also mandated to make sure the law is carried out. Therefore, the sometimes irritating provision of the law, in this case the IEP and the time consumed, must be applied equally to programs that left alone would still be outstanding and to those that need shoring up.

Parents may get information on the availability of special education services and on the applications of PL 94-142 in their area by contacting their local school district or state Department of Special Education.

Another piece of legislation of great import is the *Buckley-Pell Amendment,* making it possible for parents to examine their children's school records if the school receives federal assistance. (The Buckley-Pell Amendment is part of PL 93-380, Education Amendments of 1974.) H. Rutherford Turnbull III, who is a parent and lawyer specializing in mental health and mental retardation law, insists that "access [to records] is not only invaluable to parents and professionals, it is imperative as a course of decent conduct between people and as a weapon against charlatanry."[2]

The underlying concepts of Buckley-Pell include accountability by schools, parent rights to control children, school-home dialogue and teamwork, due process, and avoidance of misclassification.

PL 99-457 In 1990, a new federal bill, the Americans with Disabilities Act (U.S. Justice Dept. et al., 1990), was signed into law. It carries the intent of PL 94-142 into broader arenas, acknowledging the needs and civil rights of adults with handicapping conditions as well. Key elements of this law include the following:

- Public accommodations must be accessible, including stores, restaurants, hotels, and other public places.
- Transportation, including bus and train systems and privately operated van services, must be made accessible.
- Government services are barred from discriminating against disabled employees or disabled consumers seeking government services.
- Employers may not discriminate against qualified disabled job applicants or employees.

This legislation is important to parents because it affirms that their children's futures are protected beyond their school years. It gives added resonance to their quest for education, which will empower their children when they grow up to function to the maximum of their capabilities.

Additional sources of information about these and other laws include special education departments of colleges and universities, and national organizations with state and local affiliates such as the National Association for Retarded Citizens and Closer Look Information Center, a government-sponsored information and referral service for mentally retarded persons.

It would be comforting to believe that because these laws exist, they are being spiritedly complied with. Then parents would be spared ever having to shake fists in the air and cry, "I know my rights!" Unfortunately, that is exactly what you may have to do.

Let's go back to Marie Rose, the three-year-old whose parents, the Thorntons, did not believe she belonged in a class in which the youngest child was seven. The parents were facing school officials who realized that they were being asked to institute a separate class for the benefit of one child. Naturally, from their point of view, they balked. Their reasoning was, Why create a class that will cost as much to maintain for one as it would for a dozen when we can place the child in another class for one-twelfth the cost?

I can see their point. But it's like going to a dress sale and finding an exquisite dress a size too small. It's marked down to a ridiculously low price. Try as you might, it doesn't fit. You can buy it, but it still won't fit. Is it a bargain then? You can let school administrators, psychologists, and the rest persuade you that your child will "fit in" a class they have available. They will be happy to have such an accommodating parent.

The Thorntons, faced with this situation, successfully argued that PL 94-142, giving Marie Rose the right to education in the least restrictive environment possible, meant that she had a right to education among children her own age. Being only among children more than twice her age was not a "least restrictive environment."

Going to a placement meeting armed with the knowledge of what the law mandates for your child and with records to prove your child's abilities and assets, you are in a position to insist that the child's needs be met. In the case of school placement, that means if the home district can't provide that environment for the child, it must, at its own cost, send your child to the nearest district that does.

TESTING, TESTING, 1-2-3...

As Mike went through school, I was dimly aware that from time to time other parents complained about biased tests or the way they were interpreted. When I began to collect copies of Mike's tests from schools and psychologists, I realized they had a legitimate complaint.

Sometimes schools don't want to give you copies of tests or their written evaluations because "you won't understand them." Knowing you have the right to something and actually insisting upon receiving it are two different things. Before I became "so independent," as Guy, my husband, says, I found it easier to fabricate a convincing story. If the school said I wouldn't be able to understand it, I'd say, "That's okay. My brother is a psychologist." (Well, if I did have a brother, maybe he would be a psychologist.) Today, I'd just say, "I want to make an appointment with you to go over this test." The law is on my side. This, of course, is far better strategy. It tells the psychologist or teacher or administrator that you are genuinely interested in what the test results show and that you are willing to give your time, too.

Intelligence tests are notoriously faulty. To begin with, the makers of IQ tests admit that test results are subject to a 15 percent error in either direction. That could be especially important for children with mentally handicapping conditions. For example, a score of 58 on a standard IQ test could actually be as high as 66. For another thing, an IQ test measures *not ability but only achievement at that particular time*. If your child had a seizure a day or two earlier, if she was recovering from a bout of flu, the score could be wildly inaccurate. A lesser-known fact is that most standardized tests were developed based on knowledge that would be most common to white males living in middle-class circumstances. These are just some of the reasons why no one can accurately predict, based on a so-called IQ test, how your child or any child will perform when given an opportunity to reach beyond the present level of achievement.

In 1985, Howard Gardner wrote a book called *Frame of Mind: A Theory of Multiple Intelligences*. The book defined many kinds of intelligence. Among them are artistic, musical, and other creative abilities; the ability to adapt to new situations, to think logically, to get along with others, to build a strong internal personality; academic ability in science, math, or linguistics; and kinesthetic and spatial ability.

In the years since Gardner's work, other studies have affirmed his findings. Change is slow. Schools in the United States and elsewhere continue to measure only one kind of intelligence when they decide how high on the ladder to place students, and that is academic intelligence (despite the fact that having a high academic IQ is not a predictor of success later in life).

In the past, test evaluations that reflect personal biases have been used to keep a child out of his correct placement. This will happen less as more parents insist upon access to all records and test results. Looking back in Mike's records, I discovered reference on one evaluation to the time when Mike was taken out of EMR and put into TMR because the school district refused to place a child with Down's syndrome in the EMR program. (I didn't acquire this record until years later when Mike's high-school district made it available to me.)

Quoting from the record: "Dec. 14, 1972. This Down's syndrome child's intelligence makes placement in a class for Educable Mentally Retarded appropriate. He was formerly in the Trainable

Program. This committee unanimously recommends placement in a class for the Educable Mentally Retarded."

Under the section for background information was this paragraph: "Michael was admitted to the ___ TMR Program on 12-1-69. A review of the medical history indicates that Michael has a diagnosis of Down's syndrome. Michael had previously attended the EMR Program in his district, however *his progress was slow and he was referred to the County TMR Program*" (italics mine). This was simply untrue. At the time I was too uneducated to demand to be shown those records that proved he was too slow to continue in EMR. Even in the years he attended the TMR school, he consistently tested well within the academic level for EMR.

If I had not pursued, back in December of 1972, a trial placement for Mike in an EMR class, and if sympathetic school administrators in the district had not been confident enough of their program to agree, Mike would never have received the education he has. What if those administrators had been afraid to look beyond the Down's syndrome label!

It's comfortable to pigeonhole people. It's human nature to want to know what to expect. It's how we learn to "face facts," to accommodate ourselves to reality. That creates a problem because human beings have the interesting capacity to outdo themselves—to confound the prognosticators.

All through their lives people are tested to find out what they know, from infancy through school, on the job, and in the armed forces. Tests may measure intellectual abilities, motor skills, social behavior, or a thousand other things. But people sometimes forget that tests measure only skills someone has at the time.

The danger comes in two areas: (1) when tests are used to predict what that person will be capable of learning in the future, and (2) when they are used to predict capabilities in areas that actually were not tested.

I suppose people who devise tests are as much in pursuit of the perfect test that accurately measures exactly what it is supposed to measure as is the surfer in search of the perfect wave.

On a test Mike took in high school, he scored very low in the math portion. The test results were summarized thus: "He has fairly good analytical ability but is unable to calculate past simple addition. He does not apply the math he knows." That was what was shown by his answers to the test questions in math. From that, plus his responses to the rest of the test questions, the testers also inferred that "his short-term memory and sequencing appear to limit his math skills. He would be able to work in jobs not requiring academic skills but would need supervision of independent living skills." All from one test!

I strongly object to this type of projection. How can a test given today rate a person's chances for independent living five—or twelve—years from now? But the most devastating result of such prognosticating is that too often it becomes a self-fulfilling prophecy.

Future teachers and placement specialists, supervisors of sheltered workshops, and parents who read these test evaluations come to expect certain future performance because of them. Then, because they "know what to expect," they decide where or how to place or steer that individual.

Thus, based on what someone concluded from specific test results a year or three years ago, decisions are made that limit an individual's progress to what someone else expects of her! So, instead of continually challenging a person to exceed her present levels of function, tests encourage those who rely on them to place individuals comfortably within their present capabilities—perhaps again on the notion that it is better to be a big fish in a little pond.

I am not advocating deliberately placing someone out of his depth. But I am saying, By your personal observation as a parent or a teacher, are you expecting enough of the child?

I have met some very wise people in education. One was the principal where I had my first teaching assignment. She said to me, "Don't even open the children's 'cum' folders [accumulated progress files that pass from teacher to teacher as the child progresses through school] until the end of the semester." She did not want her teachers to be influenced by what that child did, or how he performed, in previous years. She felt each child had the right to a fresh slate—a new year, a new teacher, a new start.

Mike's high-school teacher had the same sort of common sense. Rather than say Mike's math was so bad he wouldn't be able to function independently (he read the same test evaluation I did), he told me, "Look here, Mrs. Ross, Mike's been on a plateau for several months in math, so we're backing off. We're concentrating on his strong areas for a while, to build up his confidence. I've seen this happen before. He knows it; he just can't use it. There will probably be a breakthrough before long."

Before the conference had ended, he had decided to have one of his aides work with Mike counting change as a way of trying to bridge the gap between learning new skills and learning to apply them to practical situations. And at home we were to work with Mike a few minutes each night on the same thing.

Then one Saturday a week or two later, I was going to be gone all day. Mike would be home alone. I didn't want him to watch TV all day or listen to tapes, so I gave him a list of jobs that needed doing around the house with the price I would pay him for each. The prices varied between twenty-five and fifty cents.

Mike had been saving money to buy a new tape deck (his was running slow—have you ever been a captive listener to four hours of Donny Osmond on slow?). I expected him to pick one or two jobs from the list (I left it up to him). When I returned, Mike had done every job on the list, checked it off, and then added up all the money I owed him—plus the amount of his weekly allowance, lest I forget! He had correctly added a column of five two-digit figures, "carried," changed cents into dollars, and correctly placed the decimal point. I was so proud of him I hugged him breathless.

My expectation was that as he grew closer to living independently, he would be motivated to transfer classroom skills from abstract to practical usefulness.

So, when it comes to reliance on today's test results as I look to Mike's future tomorrow, I think of the words of Elizabeth Cleghorn Gaskell: "I'll not listen to reason. Reason always means what someone else has to say."

You are the primary helper, monitor, coordinator, observer, record keeper, placement specialist, and decision maker for your child. Insist that you be treated as such. No change in treatment or education should take place without your involvement. Any school that receives any public funds may not refuse to show you your child's records. If you encounter resistance to being included, your best tool, again, is persuasion, not anger. Be confident and cool about your abilities and intuitions. You know your child better than anyone else.

You are a vital member on the team of experts.

CHAPTER 10

Mainstreaming
the Little Red Schoolhouse

*I*n school the terms *mainstreaming* and *normalization* are used almost interchangeably to mean allowing disabled children to become part of regular classes for their age group wherever possible.

Twelve-year-old Roberto, his head full of dreams, rode along the heavily traveled street toward his house. Roberto was in an advanced class for gifted children, often remaining at school until late afternoon. Now, in heavy commuter traffic, he did not see the car making a left turn in the path of his bicycle.

It was two years before Roberto saw the outside of a hospital again. He was unable to use his legs; he had to use a wheelchair and depend on a portable respirator and a breathing tube in his throat for permanent life support. Many times he had nearly given up. The prospect of life as a disabled person was almost unbearable.

"You want to go back to your own school, don't you?" One doctor, recognizing the boy's brilliance, had found the carrot to entice him to struggle on. He had seen the boy, in the hospital's classroom for children with orthopedically handicapping conditions, gradually succumb to hopelessness. He had seen his IQ tests drop from near-genius scores to dull-normal. But the doctor knew Roberto's mind had not been physically damaged by the accident. He also knew his handicapping condition was more or less permanent; any future achievements or contributions Roberto made in his lifetime would have to come about through exercise of his mental capacity. And the doctor was determined that Roberto have the chance he so desperately needed and deserved to attain that potential.

So now it was, two years later, that he, Roberto, the parents, Roberto's former teacher and principal, the school district director for special education, and therapists sat around a large table to decide Roberto's future. Roberto's father had approached his old teacher to plead for Roberto to be allowed to return to his former school. The school district had planned to enter Roberto in a special class for children with orthopedically handicapping conditions where trained personnel were on hand to cope with Roberto's special needs.

The medical case history was presented. It was clear that failure to understand his needs or an absence of personnel trained to respond quickly to an emergency, could result in a life-threatening situation. School personnel were quick to point out the benefits of the OH class. Roberto, his doctor, and his parents felt that with so much of his physical life gone, he would surely die unless his mental capacity was challenged as far as possible.

Around the table the discussion went, with each specialist presenting his or her view of the problems entailed and how they could be solved. It was generally agreed that success at his old school would depend on the willingness of others to be trained to act for him in emergencies. He was subject to accumulation of mucus in the bronchial airways, which, when it occurred, had to be aspirated by hand through the tube in his throat. At least one person who was trained to perform the service must be around him at all times.

At the conclusion of the meeting, the vote was to give the boy a chance to return to his old school. Ironically, the only dissenting voice came from the principal, who had initially encouraged the boy and his parents to request a transfer from the special school. Until the conference, the principal said, he had not really understood the magnitude of the problem or of the cooperation that would be mandatory.

Much of the credit for influencing the decision is due the teacher, a man who has always believed that all children belonged on one campus, regardless of disabilities, sharing regular classes whenever possible. He and several others were willing to receive training to manipulate the boy's throat tube and perform whatever else was necessary to keep him on the main school campus.

Roberto's reintegration on campus was an outstanding success. In a note to the director of special education for his district, the principal affirmed the wisdom of their decision and offered to accept any other children with disabilities who needed placement.

This is but one dramatic example of mainstreaming working at its best, with all concerned parties sharing in the placement decision and the related responsibilities.

In 1970, one child in twelve in the United States was in some kind of special training program for persons with handicapping conditions. Doesn't this statistic suggest that we were overcompartmentalized?

Picture a giant conveyor belt carrying all the nation's children in all the rich diversity of backgrounds and skills, special talents, the dreamers and the doers, those motivated by lives made hard by disability or adversity together with those children who seem magically beautiful, strong, and bright. Now see the vibrations of the conveyor belt gently shake and nudge those who are different into separate compartments, cut off forever from the mainstream of fashion, slang talk, food fads, variety, and gregariousness.

Suddenly, the world for those in their tight little compartments has become very circumscribed, very monotone. People they know during that important school time when they are with others of their age are like them—the same disabling conditions, the same problems with pain and braces, struggling to learn what is hard for them, to walk when it hurts, to speak through signing, or to "see" through fingertips.

All the while the mainstream of children has swept past them, caught up in their own passions and delights, able to forget that such things as mental retardation and sightlessness exist. The children forget it to the point that when persons with disabilities do appear, they excite much curiosity.

They have been so completely and effectively removed from the general stream of American life that when one suddenly notices step-off curbs being converted to ramps and doorways in restaurants and public bathrooms being widened to accommodate wheelchairs, one realizes with a shock that this is why one has seen so few people with physically handicapping conditions—they had been so blocked from public consciousness, it was as if they did not exist.

We are at last coming to realize how limited has been a vision that blocks 8 percent of our citizens from enjoying mainstream American living. And with suddenly sharpened acuity, we realize why more public passenger buses have hydraulic lifts for people who use wheelchairs, why some traffic lights are equipped with bells that ding when lights turn red, and why the poles for street signs now have printing in Braille at hand level. And ballots, which are bilingual in almost every state, are becoming available in Braille, too. Now we need voting booths wide and low enough so citizens who use wheel-chairs can vote unhampered.

These monstrous inequities went on so long that some public thinking ossified into a complete reversal of reality: Why should we spend money on ramps, sheltered workshops, bus routes posted in Braille, and so on, when most of us don't need them? A welfare state, that's what it is! Never considering that it was public ignorance in the first place that began the systematic exclusion of persons with disabilities from image-conscious America.

How to make it right? Little children lead again. For it is in the schools where full recognition and appreciation of all our citizens have begun.

In the past fifty years, billions of dollars across the country were spent building special institutions to care for persons with handicapping conditions, literally from the cradle to the grave. Gradually, communities accepted the institutionalized approach as the norm.

Now, with the belated discovery that children with disabilities have more in common with children without disabilities than was once thought, there is a massive shift to reverse the emphasis. Studies have been springing up around the country, affirming such amazing facts as "separate but equal education is no more fair to the disabled than separate but equal education based on ethnic minorities."

MAINSTREAMING IN ACTION

When you see a developmentally disabled young person painstakingly reading street signs, then walking to catch the correct bus; when a woman in a wheelchair expertly maneuvers about on a school campus; when a sightless man with his guide dog orders food and exchanges money correctly at McDonald's and makes his way to a booth unaided, you are being treated to mainstreaming in the community. Mainstreaming means converging. It embodies the ideal that every person, disabled or not, has the right to be brought up in a caring environment, to be trained or educated, and to have a job that will allow him or her to function in the community as a worthwhile person to the highest level of capability.

Teachers are often divided in their opinions about the desirability of mainstreaming. Just as one infant intervention director feared that enrolling children in a regular preschool would cause them to lose their skills, so some teachers of TMR classes, children with orthopedically handicapping conditions, and others who are taught on special campuses advise parents not to try to mainstream their children.

THE NATURE OF HUMAN BEINGS

People tend to fear what they do not know. Parents sometimes fear allowing their disabled children to venture beyond their known boundaries, their known capabilities. More than most parents, those who have children with handicapping conditions have to fight themselves first. Even if they believe in mainstream education, they have to convince themselves that children and teachers on that "foreign" campus will understand and be helpful and kind to their children.

What always pushed me on was this fear: *And if I don't let him go, how will he fare when I'm gone?* I needed to do everything I could to help Mike function in a grown-up world filled with nondisabled persons. That meant begin right then to help him, before he became afraid, to become accustomed to going places by himself, to learn how to ask directions, how to sit and learn in a class, how to ask the teacher questions, how to study.

Teachers in special day-classes often say they don't want to let their kids go into other classes because they don't think they'll get the attention they need. Just like parents, teachers develop protective attitudes toward their students.

Their fear is often reciprocated by targeted regular classroom teachers who have not been trained to teach children with special needs. How can they add children with special needs to a class that is already full, with more requirements than one teacher can possibly meet?

"What they learn is how to be disabled" Gay L. Parrish is Chief of Community Development at North Los Angeles Regional Center. She believes in the appropriateness of educating children with special needs in the mainstream classroom: "If they see and interact with only disabled kids all day long, they are learning how to act disabled. We want them to learn to live in everyone else's world."[1]

The need exists to educate the child's future teachers and classmates about what it means to have a mentally or physically handicapping condition. Teachers who have not experienced children with special needs in their classrooms can request in-servicing or seek out other resources that will enable them to see the person the parent and special day teacher know, the young person who is more like their other students than different. These teachers may need special coaching to understand how they can make a positive impact on the futures of their students with special needs.

Advantages of having one or two disabled kids in the class   Large strides in social growth, greater peripheral learning, more confidence, and increased vocabulary use are some of the benefits most frequently reported by teachers or parents of incoming students.

The child who early on becomes comfortable associating with children with special needs will eventually learn to see beyond the disability to the person. She will become more tolerant of differences and more able to see similarities between herself and the student with special needs. How soon this learning takes place and how insightful it is depend largely on the attitudes projected by the teacher.

Extra funds are available for educating children with special needs. The classroom that contains these students also inherits extra time from a teacher's aide and possibly extra technological equipment. In some cases, these expenditures are designated (wrongfully, in my opinion) only for the use of the child with special needs.

The long view   In California in 1990, the cost of educating a nondisabled child in K-12 was roughly $2,500 a year. As a productive adult, the child pays a return on this investment through income and various other taxes and social security tax. The cost to educate a child with special needs is estimated at $17,600 a year. Can our burdened educational system afford to educate these kids? We can't afford not to!

The long view in education is concerned for, among other things, what kinds of citizens students will be when they graduate from high school. Will they become productive members of society? Our children with special needs will be if we continue to focus on the long view, making our kids as capable and independent as possible through optimum education and training while they are young.

There is another consideration. By the time they reach high school, most children with special needs are living in the homes of foster parents. Many foster parents are caring, concerned people. They turn out for open house at school, keep counseling appointments, and are proud of their children's achievements. But they seldom feel it is part of the bargain to try to change society. That's no easy task. Only a dedicated parent, who is perhaps extremely devoted to the idea of seeing that the child obtains the best education possible, is willing to attempt it.

The planning in California and elsewhere is now toward moving children from segregated special schools to education in integrated schools that, I hope, will eventually do away with the artificial partitioning off of children like radishes and onions in different parts of the garden.

HOW ONE SCHOOL DISTRICT INTEGRATED

Three years ago, Huntington Beach Union High School District housed students with special needs on separate well-equipped campuses with competent teachers and cooperative parents. It was felt, however, by a cadre of leaders from the Guidance Center school for disabled students and Edison High School, a major high school in the district, that Guidance Center students were at a disadvantage by being cut off from their peers.

Leaders from those schools and the district office formed a Nuts and Bolts Committee to explore the feasibility of merging the two schools. The overriding issues, all agreed, were the safety of the students and the necessity of keeping their transition as uncomplicated as possible.

Issues they were concerned about included the following:

- Lunch and curriculum schedules
- Getting schedules into a computer data base for easy access by all
- Easing apprehension of Guidance Center parents
- Getting Guidance Center parents into existing Edison High organizations
- Guidance Center teachers observing Edison classes to see where their students would fit in
- Room facility for assaultive students
- Ratios of students to teacher
- Elective courses
- Solutions to toileting and feeding issues
- All-staff visitation from Guidance Center to Edison

Remodeling was both extensive and expensive. When it was completed, parents of the students coming onto the Edison campus filled out surveys to identify what they felt were their students' areas of greatest need upon entering. Priorities were in the following areas: "To be with nondisabled kids" was seen as the biggest bene-fit their children would derive from merging with Edison High; in the curricular area most parents identified basic living skills, vocational training, and physical education as major concerns; and assemblies and lunch were the areas they felt the students could best integrate into. Of eighty-three surveys sent out, parents returned forty.

Former Guidance Center students now participate in as wide a variety of classes as they are capable of. Curricula available to the students are grouped under vocational training, academic classes, daily living classes, and computer classes. Nearly all the girls are integrated in homemaking class and the boys in shop class. Nearly all students are in basic English, math, physical education, music, and computers. Some are in the adaptive computer program, which offers peripheral devices enabling them to interact with the computers even with physical disabilities including blindness, deafness, and major paralysis.

Integrated Edison High is also concerned now about transition services from school to post-school activities for students with special needs. Present classes include training for post-secondary education, vocational training, and integrated employment (including supported employment, continuing and adult education, adult services, independent living, or community participation): "The coordinated set of activities shall be based upon the individual student's needs, taking into account the student's preferences and interests" (*Transition Services Language Survival Guide for California*).

All students now have individual transition plans. Together with school counselors and parents, they identify their goals for employment, further training and education, financial or economic needs, recreation, social relationships, and independent living. These are the goals they will work toward and train for during their years at Edison.

Edison High School teacher Tami Yamaga, who formerly taught at the Guidance Center, is one of the leaders whose initial vision of an integrated high-school system shaped it into reality two years later. The first year of integration is now over. "Initially, we had to overcome lots of fear," Yamaga confesses. "Teachers on both campuses and the parents were afraid. . . . Most of the students wanted to come. They were enthusiastic."[2]

Teachers from both campuses have become increasingly more supportive of the integrated program and the combined student body is contagiously enthusiastic. The new Edison students exceeded the hopes of their teachers and parents in the rate and extent to which they adapted to what was asked of them on their new campus. Plans are under way to survey parents again. Mrs. Yamaga hopes some will be raising their sights as they envision a broader future for their children.

Thanks to careful and thoughtful planning done by the Nuts and Bolts Committee and much hard work by all, it has been a very good first year at Edison High School.

COMPUTERS!

One hundred years ago, the word *computer* meant "someone who computes." If your child is approaching school age, you may already be wondering what computers can do for her. The ability to use a computer can bring to your child an unparalleled experience, a sense of empowerment, a link with the world that may have been impossible previously because she cannot talk or move her fingers or control her body the way she and you would like.

Being able to access a computer will enable your child to focus all his abilities and senses. The computer can give the child its undivided attention. It proceeds only as fast as the learner can go. It provides immediate feedback and reinforcement, thus raising the learner's self-esteem. It offers visual and auditory support as well as inventive ways to interact with the screen.

If a person with special needs cannot manage a regular keyboard, there are adaptive attachments he can manage. Touch-sensitive screens or graphic tablets that lie flat on a wheelchair tray allow the use of one's finger or a stylus on a special pad to either draw lines or input commands. Pressure from a finger, the side of a head, a wrinkled eyebrow, or a toe can move a program on the screen forward. We're not quite to the level of sophistication of "Star Trek: The Next Generation," but computers that operate by voice command do exist. They currently have limited capability and are very expensive but will become increasingly more accessible.

Graphics and game-playing situations make basic drill and practice more interesting and improve eye-hand coordination. Students benefit from the patience and repetitiveness possible with the computer. In Berkeley, California, there is even a computer-user group for disabled children. There might be an appropriate computer-user group in your area. I would start with the community education department of your city, the public library, the computer and technology department of your school or community college, or a store that sells computer software. At least one of these sources will be able to put you in touch with a computer club, which might be able to provide you with more specific information.

If you have a modem (a computer and telephone attachment that enables your computer signal to be carried over telephone lines), your child could belong to a user group without leaving home. It's an education in itself! But then, the way information is growing, if we as adults are not learning, we're falling behind, too.

Become familiar with computers. They will become lifelong friends to you and your child. The Macintosh and the Apple GS are especially good choices for several reasons:

- They are the easiest to learn on and to use.
- A wide variety of educational programs (software) is available by mail from Educational Resources and other software companies. (You can send for the Educational Resources catalog by calling 800-624-2926.)
- It is exceptionally easy to plug in peripheral devices to the Macintosh for the learner who needs some way other than a keyboard to tell the computer what to do.

HOW ONE TEACHER USES COMPUTERS IN HER CLASSROOM

This year I observed a master teacher with her class of twelve hearing impaired students who have multiple handicapping conditions. The class is part of the elementary school system of Newport Mesa Unified School District in California. The classroom is wired for extensive use of electronic media. Funds were made available through one of the federal programs for educating children with special needs.

The students observe the same recess and lunch hours and attend all the assemblies as the rest of the seven hundred students on campus. They use all the facilities such as library, lunchroom, bathrooms, and playground equipment.

Because of the special auditory equipment available to them in their room, most students do not mainstream into classes elsewhere with the exception of arithmetic. Their teacher feels very strongly that their work is so holistically integrated with the electronic multimedia that for them to go to other classes would mean weaker, not stronger, education.

She has turned her class into a microcosm of advanced, integrated learning opportunities in which the children are bombarded with multisensory learning from the time they enter. To the observer, so much is going on simultaneously that it is hard to track.

The television monitor is connected to the videocam. The children's behavior is constantly revealed on the monitor screen. Watch

Us Learn proclaims a sign over the monitor. The teacher is a believer in peer coaching: "The videocam is on during the day so we see ourselves learn. Kids observe what's happening on the screen, go to the computer, and type in positive comments about what they see. They may write about an individual or a group once a week per child."

A portable microphone pack sits on the floor, and four Franklin audiovisual Wordmasters are on a table. Stories on cassette are available in another center for use with earphones.

At another monitor and keyboard in front of the class, the students are composing a group report based on a trip to the San Juan Capistrano Mission made the day before. (Before going on a field trip, the teacher types on the computer questions her students ask about what they want to learn. After the field trip, she plays back their questions and uses them to lead the review discussion.) Each student has notes made following the trip. The teacher inputs their information in no particular order. The students attend closely, totally involved. The program they use for most of their group reports and stories is Children's Writing and Publishing, a popular software program for the elementary level produced by the Learning Company.

"When the author uses these words, what is he doing?" she asked about a child's input.

"Putting pictures in your mind," several respond.

Then they start the editing process. Unself-consciously, they discuss what grammatical changes to make or perhaps how to rearrange sentences. When they are satisfied, the teacher chooses a reader. The student sets up the portable microphone pack (terrific stage presence while doing this) and reads the work.

A blank tape is placed in the camera, and another student films two students reading their report. (The teacher records three children at various times each day on their individual tapes. It becomes part of their work, which she shares with parents.) Following the taping and working in teams, the students prepare reports of their trip, incorporating the information on the monitor. Some students in the teams prepare to work on illustrations, others on writing.

Nearly all the students have learned how to use the videocamera, rewind, change tapes, and use the videocam as a VCR. They are able to change cables at will to link their equipment in different ways. They are comfortable using the computer as an editor. The teacher frequently lends some of her older students to other teachers to help with multimedia productions. She has given them a technological edge enjoyed by few other students their age.

The students are immersed in multimedia learning in a way I've never seen. Every sensory ability is engaged. They move with confidence. All around them are student-created books, reports, drawings, files of cassette tapes, and experiments. For the most part, they are professionally courteous with each other. Some sign language is used but not a lot, I believe, possibly because they are surrounded with electronic and written print.

This is a different type of mainstreaming. Technology as employed in this class gives children a powerful tool, granting them access to the best in technological education and making full use of their capabilities. I am sure that they have a valued (not to say envied!) position on campus. They are the technology authorities among peers in other classes. Their knowledge gives them a way of breaking through intergroup barriers. The curriculum as employed by this outstanding teacher is used to help them develop marvelous communication skills.

INTEGRATION WORKS

The first state to fully integrate all children in its schools was Kansas. Many doubted how well integration would work. Would the children who needed special services such as physical and speech therapy still receive it? A study of the Kansas program found that far from depriving severely retarded children from needed services, integration also made those services available to nondisabled children who needed them. Because special services were available on campuses, teachers were quick to take advantage of them for their other students.

Would aberrant behavior by disabled children "rub off" on their children? That worry was expressed by parents of nondisabled children. Again, those fears proved unfounded in Kansas schools. Conversely, parents of disabled children worried that their children would suffer abuse at the hands of the other children. Some ridicule, aping, and harassment did occur, but such behavior was short-lived. It seemed to result less from the fact that the newcomers were disabled than that they were the "new kids on the school ground."

Would nondisabled children shy away from the newcomers? Again, after an initial period, nondisabled students became involved as aides and occasionally as friends of their disabled peers. Peers have become an important component of the success of the Kansas integration.

Social interaction between disabled and nondisabled children of a similar age doesn't often happen by itself but needs sensitive structuring. One way it is happening with good results is in adaptive physical education classes. Nondisabled youngsters pick disabled youngsters their age and work one on one at a particular skill. As a result, the disabled child gains social confidence and skill, and the nondisabled child gains increased understanding and tolerance.

New teachers tend to be in favor of educating children with special needs in the same rooms with children without special needs. Having recently graduated from universities and teaching colleges where they have been introduced to the ideal and the practical desirability of mainstreaming as an educational goal, they may be more aware of the positive effects than are long-time teachers.

They know, for example, that the great majority of mentally and physically disabled children fall into the mild range and that they have many skills in normal or near normal ranges. One child may consistently bowl games of 165. Another may swim competitively on her high-school swim team. Many girls and boys who are retarded are extremely capable cooks. I know one young man who, though aphasic and moderately retarded, is a superlative cartoonist.

Gardner's studies, mentioned earlier, have shown that social behavior rather than academic intelligence is the crucial index to how well people can fit in with peers, whether at school or on the job. Disabled children make astonishing gains in self-help skills, social behavior, personal confidence, and correct responses to social pressures when they regularly interact with nondisabled children—even more so than when they receive intensive training by a highly skilled teacher where interaction with nondisabled peers is lacking.

Today's administrators and teachers deserve parents' support during this period of change. Mainstreaming works best in an atmosphere of mutual support and commitment. Teachers must be given in-service training to develop their skills in working with children with special needs, and their confidence in dealing with parents and others. They must be given classroom help in two ways: smaller numbers of children per class, and more help in the form of aides. Active parent participation as aides can help a willing teacher tremendously.

Some teachers have to be convinced that mainstreaming is worth the effort, that it is better not only for our children with special needs but for the humanizing of nondisabled children.

Teachers will learn, even as we parents have learned, that bringing a child with special needs into a group can make the entire group closer and more understanding. Little children are not the only ones afraid of what they don't understand. Only in the schools is there such a rich opportunity for all children to confront and explore the nature of children of all ethnic backgrounds and all degrees of ability.

If children are provided examples by teachers who show by attitude that there is something good and something to appreciate in all people, they will likely develop these attitudes, too.

And as adults, because they understand something of the worth of all people, they will be more likely to vote approval for extra money needed for specially equipped buses and parking and street ramps for persons with physical disabilities and for subsidized workshops in which developmentally disabled persons can work. Also, I hope, they will be citizens who fight back when fearful neighbors want to rezone their residential area to keep out family care homes where disabled adults live.

HOW PARENTS CAN HELP

With conflicting attitudes by teachers concerning mainstreaming, how do parents decide what is the best way for their child? Yes, he needs to be educated in the least restrictive environment, but he also must be safe.

Parents must look at both sides. Mike's TMR teacher tried to dissuade me from attempting to transfer him to an EMR class on the regular elementary school campus. She said, "Here he's accepted, right? All of the kids have handicapping conditions. Mike is one of the brighter ones. Why put him where he will be one of the lower functioning—and get a lot of the wrong kind of attention?" She was speaking out of love, trying to protect Mike from hurt and rejection.

But on the other hand, I wanted to prepare Mike to live in a world that belongs to people without handicapping conditions. I wanted him to acquire the chance to observe and imitate acceptable social behavior. I wanted him to be challenged by real academic and other learning—to learn whatever he could. So we kept hammering at the gates until we were accepted.

Mike attended high school and also spent a half day in a sheltered workshop. There he learned the important work training skills of staying at a task until it's done correctly, not wandering away from his work area, listening to his supervisor's instructions, getting to work on time, and returning on time after lunch. These skills are necessary for any young person who wants to make a go of it in the job market. The actual task Mike worked at during that time— pasting labels on cans and similar rote tasks—was secondary.

After six months, Mike seemed bored with his routine. I wondered if he needed something more to challenge him. He had always been interested in food service (or at least since his older brother became manager of a pizza restaurant). In our district there was a high-school training program in which youngsters worked to prepare, serve, and clean up after a noon meal. The lunchroom was open to everyone so there were also the jobs of handling money correctly and meeting the public. I discussed the program with Mike's teacher. He had placed other young people in the program but didn't feel Mike was ready to handle it.

IT'S NOT EXACTLY BLACKMAIL, BUT...

When Mike's teacher did not recommend placing Mike in food service, I followed my intuition and looked elsewhere. A neighboring district had a food service program similar to ours as a part of the adult education program. Since Mike was then eighteen, he was eligible to participate. We went to visit the program. We toured and asked questions. Mike grew excited about the prospect of working there. They agreed to take him on a trial basis if we decided to apply for a transfer from our home district.

Armed with this knowledge, I went back to Mike's teacher to discuss transferring Mike. He replied, "Well, if he could work there, he might be able to work in our district, too." Together we visited the training supervisor at the food service facilities in our district. We tried to give her an idea of Mike's strengths and weaknesses, and she suggested bringing him to the lunchroom as the next step.

They got along fine. Mike was able to communicate well enough to give her an idea of his receptivity to training. She was willing to give him a chance to try out as a food service trainee. It was agreed that the first week would be a probationary period. I would provide Mike's transportation. It did not make sense to rearrange his bus schedules until the supervisor, the teacher, and Mike felt comfortable with the new program.

At the end of the week the supervisor called his teacher. "Mike's doing fine," she said. He was welcome to continue. What beautiful words! Bus schedules were changed accordingly, and then Mike spent two hours a day in his EMR class keeping up his reading and arithmetic skills, two hours at workshop where he still received work habit training, and two hours at food service training, all in different locations.

Had the program not worked out, we would have gone back to

his former schedule and tried again the following year. Mike was the first person with Down's syndrome to be placed in the program.

Today, young people with Down's and other disabilities may be seen serving in McDonald's and other fast-food places. As long as children with special needs were "protected" on special campuses, out of sight, I doubt we would have seen their acceptance in the community as widespread as it is today. How wonderful when a restaurant or chain that takes a humane, spiritual view of God's children gives children with special needs the chance they deserve!

WHAT IS YOUR CQ?

Maybe you have experienced difficulty getting cooperation from your school. What is your personal "Cooperation Quotient"? Are you a reasonable person? Have you convinced your child's teacher and the other people at school of this fact?

Our district broke some of its rules to make food service training possible for Mike. For one thing, we changed programs in the middle of the semester. The administrators would have been within their rights to say, "We can't transfer him now; you'll have to wait until a new semester starts," which would have meant six months' delay.

It is of inestimable help if you have resided in the district long enough to be familiar with the workings of the school administration and have built a reputation for cooperating with the school's and the teacher's objectives for your child (as far as you believe they are correct). Be willing to help out as and when you are needed. Also, be clear in your mind about what you believe your child is capable of and have cogent reasons for it. Knowing what alternate programs are available in neighboring districts is important. Most significant of all, I like to think, is that the teacher, the supervisor, and the district special education director were willing to help Mike because we had always tried to cooperate with them.

Whenever Mike was having problems at school, whether in skills or discipline or whatever, all the teacher needed to do was to call to be assured of cooperation from our family. Whenever I suggested alternate programming, the teacher—though not always in agreement—was generally willing to give it a try. If my suggestions didn't work, we pulled back. I never insisted that Mike be placed in one certain class or training program; I only wanted my views to be considered as part of the team approach and Mike to be given the chance to try new things on his own merit.

The right programs for each of our children are not always available. Our local teachers, principals, and facilitators, by and large, would like nothing better than to announce to all parents the beginnings of stimulating new programs to meet each child's needs. Money, money, money—it becomes pick and choose, and often a battle for the programs that will meet the greatest need and for those that receive the loudest demands from parents.

By understanding the nature of existing programs and the new ones being considered, you are in a better position to ask for changes. It does little good to demand changes without having something better in mind. You'll be more effective when you can show educators you've given enough thought and done enough investigating to show you really understand what you are asking of them.

If your child's class is located on the campus of a regular school, try to win acceptance for her in at least one regular classroom or in an extracurricular activity guided by a sympathetic instructor. If the situation in your local school is such that you can find no support for mainstreaming, look for other ways to go. Can she join an after-school or weekend craft or art class? How about folk dancing or a city-sponsored recreation program? Churches and synagogues traditionally are accepting of people with handicapping conditions. Are there activities in your church in which she can take part?

As for our family, at every level of Mike's development we ran into people who gave us the tired line, "Wouldn't he do better with his own kind?"

Charitably, I will regard such persons as well-meaning. But you cannot foster growth by constantly protecting a child from situations where he won't always be on top. What good would it do Mike to associate with no one to whom he could look as a role model?

Although you might never say it to your child, the attitude comes through so clearly. If you say, "I am protecting you from a situation because you might be hurt, or your feelings hurt, or because you can't possibly keep up," don't be surprised if your child develops the same attitude toward himself.

Wheelchairs or braces or mental disabilities will not create nearly the gulf that your attitude does. Children who are told often enough they are incapable of doing something eventually will believe just that and stop trying.

This is not to say that you would tell a child with no use of his legs to get up and walk. Nor would you tell a developmentally disabled child, "If you try hard enough, you can go to college." It is to say, be aware of what your child might be capable of; then give him plenty of opportunities that will challenge him to live up to that potential.

Parents have a selfish interest, in the best sense of the word, to do everything possible to secure for their disabled children as complete an education as they can handle. Again, the goal is for your child to live as fully, as much in the mainstream of life, as she is capable of. Once our children become adults, many of these opportunities are lost to them. And once they are adults between the ages of eighteen and twenty-one, you probably want to see them out of the nest. This is a positive, healthy outlook.

Every effort you make now will be repaid a hundredfold as your child steps out, as responsible for herself as possible, just as you expect of your other children.

PART

3

THE GROWING-UP
YEARS

CHAPTER 11

You Can't Be Nine Until You Can Tie Your Shoelaces— On Setting Goals

S ometimes, after a few years of being so tuned in to the special needs of a disabled child, treating him as "one of the gang" may come a little hard.

Mike was approaching his ninth birthday when I suddenly decided I was fed up with his not being able to tie his own laces. In a fit of impatience I said, "Mike, you can't be nine until you can do your own shoelaces." I was sick of his fiddling around and then wailing, "I can't do-o-o it!" (Rule 1: Never make rash threats. Rule 2: At least don't do it when your other kids are around to hear.)

Sure enough, his brother and sister picked up on it. Suddenly, no one in the family would help Mike with his laces without throwing in a free sermon: "You're never going to be nine until you can do it all by yourself!"

Did you know there are twenty-seven steps to tying your laces? (More if you start with the pair that just broke and a new pair has to be threaded in.)

The days rolled by. Soon only a week was left before Mike's birthday. Mike was worried. God had decreed he couldn't be nine unless he could tie his laces. Pronouncements from heaven were immutable. Day after day, he'd sit in the middle of the kitchen floor after school, trying to get that tiny loop to hold still while he pushed the other loop around and through. He didn't have enough fingers for the job. There seemed to be six strings at once. We all sensed his desperation. Jim even said, "Mike, don't you know your birthday will come even if you can't tie them?"

No way. He'd been shocked into believing otherwise. As the days ticked by, everyone in the family began taking a few spare minutes to hunker down and give Mike a hand. "You'll make it, Mike!" became the watchword.

The day before his birthday, he finally did it successfully. The crowning glory of his ninth birthday was not candles glowing on a cake; it was Mike performing the act of tying both shoelaces for the whole family, including grandparents. For months afterward, whenever a sufficient crowd of the uninitiated was around, Mike would suddenly give a sigh of impatience, plunk himself down, untie his shoelaces, look around, and retie them. Was he proud? Does cheddar cheese go with apple pie?

Tying his laces represented a gigantic achievement for Mike. But just as important, he learned that by trying patiently over and over to accomplish a task, he could do it. (Although never again did I go out on a limb with such an arbitrary demand. How could I know that he was even capable of managing to tie his laces? Oh, well, live and learn.) Since Mike did it, he evidently did have the skills. I just hadn't recognized that he did until my impatience forced the issue.

How do you know when your child is capable of accomplishing more than she's doing? It's safe to say almost any child is capable of doing more than she does. (Aren't we all?) With our disabled children, it's a matter of setting reasonable goals. Children being like snowflakes, no two alike, there is no single right way to help them achieve goals; it's a matter of trying different approaches until you find one that succeeds.

For instance, can your child reach into a cupboard and get a glass and carry it without breaking it? If she can, maybe she's capable of setting the table. If she has sufficient coordination and understanding to separate large items such as spoons and forks, she can not only set the table but put the silver away after it's dried. Soon she will become dexterous enough to dry dishes, too. Then wash them. Who knows? Today the dishes, tomorrow the world!

Getting back to the glass and the cupboard: Can she also turn on the water faucet? If so, she can reasonably be expected to be able to get a glass of water when she is thirsty.

Let's say she comes in from playing, hot and thirsty, and would love a drink of cool water. You are busy with something else. Do you

- drop what you are doing to wipe her face with a cool cloth and give her a drink?
- smile at her, comment that she looks hot and thirsty—and then wait?
- wait for her to communicate her needs, then suggest she get herself a drink?
- watch critically as she tries to help herself, then get up and do it "the right way"?

If you are doing the first or last, you may be unconsciously denying her a chance to show how capable she is. Let's say she wants water but is waiting for your help. In a calm, confident voice you tell her to help herself. If you simply can't stand to watch her fumbling or awkwardness, leave the room. (We always imagine the worst happening—it's better not to look.) Find work to do. Be "too busy" to help her. In this way you help her begin to assume responsibility for her own needs.

How did it happen that she pulls this helpless act anyway? (If that is what it is.) Take a minute to observe her and to think about your reactions: Is she being made to feel she can't perform up to some standard that she's not even aware of? Or is someone always around to respond to her needs—or even anticipate them—so that she never feels motivated to act independently? Is that someone you by any chance? Why? Don't you have anything else to do?

What would happen if you purposely did nothing for your child until she asked for help? If your household is like ours, other duties don't cease because you have the added care of a person with a handicapping condition. Sometimes there truly doesn't seem to be enough of you to take care of all the jobs needing to be done.

PARENTS HAVE RIGHTS, TOO

"Don't you want to be able to do things for yourself?" you may say to your child during a particularly harried time. I have (as if it were perfectly natural to expect my child to consider my rights, too). Well, no, you find out from the child's blank stare, he isn't especially interested in doing things for himself.

Why isn't he interested? Because your personal goals aren't his. My goal—perhaps yours, too—was to do everything possible to help my disabled youngster be independent in as many areas as possible. I wanted all my children to become independent so my husband and I could eventually move out of the parenting phase of our lives into what I hope will be lifelong love and friendship with our children as adults.

Mike's immediate goals, on the other hand, might include staying up late, having his own TV, being waited on by a bevy of servants, or getting dessert with every meal. Come to think of it, those are pretty nifty goals. I could use a bevy of servants.

A baby's goals of being warm, dry, and fed are identical with his needs. As he grows older, his goals not only may not be in line with his needs, they may be just the opposite. Mike's need for sleep may be in direct opposition to his goal of staying up late. Or his need may be for more exercise while his desire is to watch TV for hours on end.

This is a roundabout way of saying that it isn't good for children to get their own way all the time. Of course, all parents know that! But knowing that, some parents still accept actions or demands they would not dream of putting up with from their other children.

How can we change this? The fact that we have the child's best interests at heart carries no weight with most children. Telling my son something is "for your own good" is about as big a turnoff as saying, "Eat your liver."

BEHAVIOR MOD—IT WORKS!

Behavior modification is a phrase that's been big among psychologists and educators. It means persuading people to modify objectionable behavior in favor of behavior that is more acceptable. Knowing that good social behavior rather than intelligence is actually more important in how well a child is accepted in the community, we parents should become familiar with behavior modification. Here is how it works.

Dana Smith believes Brittany, age nine, should take on household responsibilities. Brittany agrees with her mother that she will accept the responsibility of setting the table for dinner each night.

The first night, Dana calls her daughter. Brittany comes running. Dana takes time to show her how to place the paper napkin beside the fork. When Brittany is finished, both are proud of the job she has done. Her father and her brother praise her, too.

But Brittany's pride in her new job wears down. When she is not praised every night, she loses interest. Soon Dana is calling to remind her, and still she dawdles. Sometimes Dana is running on a tight schedule. She can't wait for Brittany and does the job herself. Angrily, she reminds Brittany, "Mommy had to do your job tonight."

If that happens a few more times, what has Brittany learned? That if she doesn't feel like doing her job, Mommy will do it.

How can the situation be handled? Here are two suggestions that will allow Brittany to suffer the logical and natural consequences of failing to do her job. Dana can finish cooking dinner, then go to the living room. Prewarned, her husband is part of the game. Brittany is ready to eat. "None of us can eat yet because a certain young lady hasn't set the table," Dana might remind Brittany. A second way to go would be for Brittany's father or brother to take over her job and set places for everyone in the family except her. She will probably be outraged, but she will grasp the connection between her failure to perform and her failure to receive dinner like everyone else, even if she doesn't understand the logic behind your acts.

Allowing a child to suffer the consequences of his own acts, within reason, is sensible. The boy who hasn't done his yard work hasn't earned his allowance and therefore cannot go to the show Friday night. The only one he can blame is himself. The only behavior that will have to change to alter the end result is his. The girl who doesn't get her clothes in the hamper for Mother to wash has no clean skirt for school the next day. She has no one but herself to blame when she must wash out a skirt the night before.

The value of this kind of training can't be stressed too often. If your goal as parents is to rear a child who can take her place in society to the fullest extent she is capable of, that child must be allowed to suffer the consequences of wrong behavior. There is no reason to depart from this goal when rearing a child with special needs. Sure, parents can expect too much, but 90 percent of the time parents expect too little.

Parents who do not expend the time and energy to make their child understand the importance of his behavior are often uncomfortably made aware of it as the child grows older.

NOBODY LOVES AN OBNOXIOUS CHILD

Years of being required to do nothing for himself, of being waited on unnecessarily, can result in a child no one enjoys being around. Other parents, relatives, and friends may tolerate obnoxious behavior in your disabled youngster for your sake. But when you are not around, look out! Your child will be deservedly unpopular. Who wants to be around a complainer, a lazy person, or an overaggressive child? You may blame your woes on the child's handicapping condition or his teacher or the other kids in the class, but all too often his behavior developed because you were not quick enough to see that this behavior would be the natural and logical consequence of overindulging your child, doing for him what he could have done for himself, and having failed to teach him respect for the rights and needs of others.

Paul was a handsome lad who lost the use of his legs as a result of a bicycle accident when he was eight. He whizzed his chair up and down the ramps at school. But few people actually liked him (except his parents, who idolized him). Now in high school, he was thoroughly conceited. In every group he entered, he turned the conversation to himself. He was honorary this and that, including manager of the football team, but away from the appointed jobs he was alone. Was his friendlessness due to his handicapping condition? Probably not. He was a spoiled child turned spoiled teenager, and his peers knew it.

Parents often do not realize what they are doing until a day when the child is completely unmanageable, and they lament, "I have no control whatsoever over this child! Someone will have to take him off my hands!" Emotional problems are no less a problem for our disabled children than for our others.

"YOU CAN DO IT!"

All children bloom in the sun of their parents' approval. For children with disabilities, approval is special. It floods their lives with sunshine and gives them courage to grow on, to attempt new tasks, to develop faith in their abilities. Parents who encourage their child by attitude and action reaffirm that he is a capable human being.

One day when Mike was fifteen, his teacher called me. "Mrs. Ross," he said, "Mike just missed the bus again. Shall I tell him you'll pick him up?"

Was I aggravated! That was the third time in two weeks. "Let him walk home," I told Dave Golden. As soon as I hung up, my mind rasped with fear. I wasn't even sure he knew the way home! Buses seldom take direct routes to school. And the school was two miles away. Mike would have to cross several boulevards with signal lights and use the freeway underpass to reach home. Hastily, I called back. "Mr. Golden, has Mike left yet?" Assured he hadn't, I asked the teacher to delay him for ten minutes, time for me to reach the school by car and follow him home.

Mike reached home without incident. I was so proud of him! But rather than tell him, I gave him my sympathy, agreeing it was too bad he had to walk home because he had missed the bus. He never knew, of course, I'd followed him home, but it made a delicious story to share with the family when Mike wasn't around.

Two noteworthy events followed that incident, both of which made my life a little easier. They also eased the three-o'clock-in-the-morning fears that find you suddenly awake and starkly worrying what will become of your child with special needs.

The first was a nonevent: Mike never missed the bus again, although he did occasionally choose to walk home. His teacher always called and let me know when he was starting so I'd know when to look for him.

The second event still makes me laugh. Mike bowled on Friday afternoons. Usually, he came home from school, changed clothes, and had a bite to eat. Then it was time to be dropped off. This particular Friday I slipped up. I had been out and reached home about fifteen minutes late to take Mike bowling.

No one was home. My daughter had been home—her schoolbooks were as usual scattered across the dining room table—but she and Mike and his bowling bag were gone. I assumed she had driven him, so I took off again to buy groceries for dinner. I returned home at the same time as my daughter—alone—and my husband from work—alone. We all looked at each other. "Where's Mike?" said everyone at once.

Right on cue, Mike came puffing up the driveway, bowling bag nearly dragging the ground. He was outraged, his chin quivering with righteous anger.

"Where were you?" he demanded.

We burst out laughing. Not a very nice response. But he looked so funny, still clutching the fourteen-pound bowling ball in the bag that was causing him to grow more lopsided by the minute, shirttail out, sweat pouring down his face. The fact that I was hugging him tightly and laughing at the same time made no sense to him at all. "Where were you?" he repeated.

It was a comedy of errors. After school, Mike had confidently waited for someone to appear to drop him off at the bowling lanes, nearly a mile distant. When no one came, he made up his mind to walk. When he had finished bowling and still no one was there for him, he realized he'd have to walk home. He even told the parent who collects the two dollars from each child on the team each week that he'd have to pay her next week.

That time we really lavished praise on Mike. Realizing something had gone wrong, he had acted independently and responsibly for himself. He had not panicked or become helpless in self-pity. All our hearts were full of love and pride for Mike that night.

Oh wad some power the giftie gie us to see ourselves as others see us.

—Robert Burns

CHAPTER 12

How to Help Your Child Experience Success

K ids who are mentally retarded can be disheartened by too many failures. We must plan ways they can experience some successes. Knowing your child well, you can become adept at evaluating her chance for success at the outset of many situations.

One Saturday morning I was typing at my desk when I saw the United Parcel Service delivery truck stopping in front of our house. I asked Mike to answer the door when the driver rang, and I automatically began wondering if Mike could handle it. By the time he came back to tell me the man had a package for Daddy, I knew he could take care of it. My instant evaluation went something like this: Mike can speak well enough to be understood, and he can sign his name on a line. I knew that because by then I had been letting him fill out his own applications— permission slips from school and workshop and the like— and I had seen him write small enough to fit the tiny space allotted on a UPS form.

To Mike, I said, "A package for Daddy? Mike, the driver will have a sign-up sheet. If you sign your name on his sheet, he will give you the package. Can you do that?"

"I sign my name?"

"That's right. The driver will show you where."

"And he gives me the package?"

"Yep."

Off he went to sign for the package and receive the added gift of a lift in self-esteem, another task to which he'd proved equal.

When you have the chance to help your child in a similar situation, don't forget to ask for feedback. Saying something like, "Can you do that?" gives him a chance to think about it. If you add, "Tell me how you're going to do it," he has the chance to rephrase your directions and show that he understands.

In addition to unplanned successes that come your way, you can set up experiences for success. One of the best and easiest ways is in cooking. Cooking is a skill every person needs. It is a perfect skill and success builder because it comes with a built-in reward: eating the profits. Beginning with measuring water for gelatin desserts, your child can move on to helping bake cookies, chop vegetables, shape meat patties, or cut biscuits.

The child without reading skills can memorize recipes. The child without much skill in numbers can identify one-quarter cup with the proper measure; perhaps you can coordinate them by color—the blue cup in the recipe means the blue cup measure, for example. The child can also memorize directions on the backs of prepared frozen dinners. You can rewrite recipes or put them on computer substituting graphic icons for products and measurements. It is easy and fun to teach the child to access the recipe from the computer and print herself a copy.

The key is knowing she has acquired the separate skills necessary, even though she may not have strung them together to accomplish the task you have in mind.

As a toddler, for instance, if she loves to sit on the floor and work her socks off, let her help undress herself when it's time for bed. Play games. Race with her. (I'll take this sock off and you take that one off and we'll see which one comes off first.) Of course, you always manage to lose! Later you lay out her pajamas, seeing that buttons, zippers, and knots are unfastened, and suddenly become very busy elsewhere. If she grows tired waiting for you, she's likely to start undressing herself and struggling into her pajamas.

SUCCESS: "A-ONE AND A-TWO AND A-THREE..."

"Why is it," a social worker asked me, "that parents don't think to give their disabled daughters ballet lessons?"

Even parents who do everything imaginable to make life more pleasant for a child with special needs often overlook the popular activities we use to help our other children develop grace, agility, or just plain confidence.

"You see children with disabilities from obviously well-off families," she mused, "and where the other children in the family are well dressed, have nice haircuts, and wear braces on their teeth if they need them, these children are not given these benefits related to appearance."

How can we expect them to act self-assured, she asked, if we "forget" them when passing out lessons and braces and chances to become involved in sports and hobbies? We all recognize that the more varied activities our children are involved in, the more well-rounded their social development is likely to be.

I had never thought about it before. Are we unconsciously telling our disabled children that these extra goodies won't do them any good?

Ballet gives any child a sense of grace, a sense of being beautiful, a chance to appreciate beautiful music and develop a sense of rhythm. In the same way, music or yoga or swimming or square dance lessons do so much more than train a child in a particular skill. We recognize this advantage for our other children. Are we overlooking it as one more way to help our disabled children enjoy success?

SUCCESS: IT'S THE LITTLE THINGS THAT COUNT

Parents may become so accustomed to the sight of their child drooling or with his mouth hanging slightly agape that after a while they no longer see it. We need to be aware of unlovely personal habits and do our best to help the child change the habit. Infant interventionists who teach babies and toddlers to keep their mouths closed by frequent gentle boosts under the child's chin with their finger stimulate the child's muscles to get to work.

Untended nasal discharge is another unlovely sight. If he continually forgets to blow properly, show him how he looks in the mirror. Remind him that other people do not look like that and that they won't like to look at him, either. For parents of older children, it's not too late to begin correcting these habits, but it will take more time and patience.

We all have little irritating personal habits, and we usually appreciate caring reminders if the habits are potentially offensive. Care enough for your child to help him realize which of his habits could offend other people, friends or strangers. Zipping up pants or rearranging clothing in public after using the bathroom is socially offensive. It should be completed before the door is opened. Many of our children rock back and forth to relieve tension. It isn't harmful or particularly embarrassing, but it's annoying. Teach them to rock when they are alone—on their beds or in a special place in their room.

Masturbation is another habit that makes other people uncomfortable. Therefore, we need to teach our boys and girls that it is courteous not to touch their genitals when other people are present. Parents who are uncomfortable with their child's masturbating might want to talk it over with their doctor. She will probably tell them that unless it is practiced to excess, it is an acceptable means of relieving tension and is not harmful to the child or adult.

Other behaviors involve learned social graces. Just a little training can make such a difference in how well your child is accepted! When two people talk at the same time, the courteous thing is for one to say something like, "Excuse me. Go ahead." Parents and brothers and sisters can have fun role-playing this. Two talk at the same time. First one, then the other, practices saying, "Excuse me," then listening attentively. Practice the technique of listening for a pause in the conversation before speaking out.

Role playing is also effective—and fun—in teaching our children what to do, for instance, when one inadvertently bumps into another. "Oh! Excuse me!" you say and take an exaggerated step away from the other person. Exchange roles. Let him be the bumper and you be the "bumpee."

Teach respect for others' property and persons. You (as the one whose property is taken) show how sad it makes you feel when people take things without asking. Stress the "without asking." Teach her the magic words "may I borrow," "please," and "thank you." And, of course, that one always takes good care of others' property and returns it when promised.

On another day take up the idea of being touched: "Do you always like it when people touch you?" If he seems not to understand what you are getting at, ask him how he likes it when someone puts his arms around him or gets too close and has bad breath. Then he will probably say, "Eeuw! I wouldn't like that!" You say, "What if he wants to anyway?"

Whatever method seems to make sense to your child, you are trying to help him understand that people should not touch other people unless they want to be touched. Teach it now, when he is in your protection. Later when he's on his own, the appropriate response will come more easily. Perhaps it will help in a potentially threatening situation in which he would have felt helpless if he hadn't been taught the simple defense of being able to say, "Don't touch me. I don't like it."

The other side of the coin, of course, is that he will not touch anyone unless that person is willing.

Disabled children often lack the ability to pick up by observation the nuances of social behavior, says one experienced teacher of a high-school EMR class. We must teach them—and parents should, too—such things as not to comb their hair while they are being interviewed for a job, not to lean on the wall when the boss is talking to them, and where to put their hands so they look natural. They want to learn because they do not want to be laughed at if they exhibit adverse social habits.

Often overlooked is the importance of eye contact. We as parents may out of habit pay no attention to whether or not our children look us in the eye during conversation. Asking your child to look you in the eye doesn't have to be an admonishment. Make a game of it. It's important for all your children, just as are the other skills that make up social awareness. Show them how much more important they feel when you talk directly to them, meeting their gaze, than if you talk at a point past their shoulder or look at someone or something else. (Not that one would stare another down—it's not a power play we're after but friendly communication!)

Eye contact tells the other person you are paying attention to her words, that you are genuinely interested in what she is telling you, in short, that you are aware.

If you were a critical observer (or an army sergeant) rather than a loving parent, how would you rate your child's grooming? Are her fingernails clean and trimmed? Face and hands scrubbed? Hair shining clean and neat? Teeth clean and professionally cared for? Clothing neat, clean, and appropriate?

Other skills and habits, equally obvious, are also overlooked sometimes. How does your child appear from a distance? Is he hard to distinguish in a crowd? Our children are so eager to be like children without disabilities. Does something about him, his walk, for instance, make him distinctive? Love can blind your vision!

Mike's teacher called to my attention one day that when Mike was feeling especially jaunty, he walked with a weird flailing gait, almost as if he were rapping to a hidden beat. His arms sailed out, and he twisted from side to side at the hips. "Other kids at high school make fun of his walk," the teacher told me bluntly.

I hadn't even noticed. The peculiar gait was in no way connected with his disability, so it became something to work on. I started dragging him along with me on my evening walks—over his protests, he'd have rather been watching TV. We experimented with what a good masculine walk looked like. Arms arcing in a straight line, at an angle that brings the loosely coiled fist slightly in front of the body, body balanced on the ball of the foot, torso at a slight forward angle with little side-to-side motion. Mike practiced, but protestingly, or else he mimicked me mimicking him and made fun of the whole experience. We really must have looked like a couple of coconuts alternately mincing and prancing down the street. However, with patience as well as practice, I was confident that if we kept at it, at least until Mike recognized the difference, he would gradually correct himself.

The greatest thing we ever did to raise Mike's consciousness about his appearance was an accident. We installed mirror doors on our daughter's bedroom closet. When Mike's older brother Jim moved away, Laurie inherited Jim's bedroom. Mike fell heir to Laurie's room and the mirror doors.

"Mike, did you see how you look?" I asked one morning when he came out for breakfast wearing his Sunday school pants and vest with a plaid flannel shirt shoved into the front of the pants. Back we went into his room and stood together before the mirror. I was no prize, bleary-eyed and in a rumpled housecoat, but Mike was kind enough not to notice.

I pulled out a couple of plain-colored shirts. One by one I held them in front of him. "Wouldn't one of these look better with your suit?" I asked. "Or else, if you really want to wear that plaid shirt, how about your dark corduroy pants?" I held them out so he could examine the effect in the mirror.

It did not take too many sessions before Mike's critical eye began to discriminate. Rather than put down his first selection, I would try to offer him a variety of choices where he could reach a semi-independent decision and still be confident that he looked nice. After a while he would occasionally come to the kitchen in his robe holding out a couple of shirts, wanting an opinion. His own taste developed nicely. And we always complimented him when his clothes looked especially well put together.

A few weeks before school began one year, Laurie took him shopping for a new school outfit. Together they selected blue slacks, a two-tone blue terry top, and matching socks. Mike was confident he looked handsome because Laurie can do no wrong as far as he's concerned, and as he pointed out, everything matched. Laurie confided that Mike had made the final selection.

SUCCESS: I WAS HOLDING THE CAMERA RIGHT (THEY WERE STANDING SIDEWAYS)

Ever notice how your children want to do just what you are doing? Usually at the same time you are doing it. People in our family are camera buffs. One Saturday morning Laurie sped down to the local shopping center where a circus was going up. Armed with her camera, she persuaded them to allow her inside the barriers to photograph the elephants at work, the zebras and tigers being unloaded, and the big top ballooning into the sky.

Mike hasn't photographed a circus, but the gift of a simply operated camera that uses a 35mm drop-in cartridge has given him hours of pleasure. It has also given him a socially successful inroad to acceptance, one that continues into adulthood.

Frequently while living at home, Mike took his camera to the Little League field and improved his skill with the camera capturing base slides and outs. At school he was fascinated by the cute cheerleaders. None of them was his personal friend, but they were obliging when he asked them to pose for him on rally days.

He has grown from capturing people who were standing sideways and people whose heads were missing above the eyes to getting well-composed shots. While he was in high school, I glued a three-foot-square section of fine-grained cork on his bedroom wall and bought a package of thumb tacks that have a knob instead of a flat plate to grasp. As his collection grew, we all enjoyed the snapshots, and Mike was never at a loss for something to talk about to visitors.

Mike recently purchased a Polaroid camera. He discovered to his dismay that it was a more expensive way to shoot, but the lure of seeing his shots instantly was too strong.

Many other activities can produce similar beneficial results for your child with special needs.

Stamp collecting This hobby sparks interest in receiving letters, writing letters, reading, reading postmarks, finding places on maps, and discovering a connectedness between one's own community and distant places.

Sports trading cards Trading cards are especially fascinating to young adolescents. They are a good lead-in to conversation with adults as well as peers because acquiring any knowledge about a national pastime and spectator sport gives one a link, a common area

135

of interest with others, that has nothing to do with having a handicapping condition. Mike collects wrestling cards.

Knitting, needlepoint, and other types of needlework   These fine skills should not be confined to occupational therapy. Handwork is an excellent attention-getter of the right sort, sure to create a good impression because a carryover feeling about people who do handwork is that they are steady and capable persons. It is valuable for both sexes in that it is excellent therapy as well as a pleasant pastime. Another advantage is that the worker has a product to show for the effort.

Woodwork   Again, work with the hands produces satisfaction and pride of a special quality. With a skilled people-person instructor, people with some handicapping conditions can attend community craft classes, learning skills as diverse as cake decorating and leatherwork, macramé and cooking, and meeting fine people at the same time.

Computer   Computers are accessible to nearly everyone, and software programs are available for nearly every level of mental skill and physical capability. Programs from the merely entertaining game format to educational to sophisticated virtual reality programs are within reach.

A computer is a complex companion. Too much time before a computer may have the unintended effect of reenforcing tendencies to withdraw or be alone. It's easy to forget you still need physical exercise and companionship with real people! On the other hand, the computer offers an incomparable, dazzling link with the entire globe.

Having a hobby that she enjoys can do much to draw your child out of herself, to forget self-consciousness. The satisfaction of participating in a universally recognized hobby says, "I am like you. We both enjoy the same things."

SUCCESS: SPORTS

The Special Olympics, sponsored by the Joseph P. Kennedy Jr. Foundation, gave children with special needs a new vista: the world of sports. Perhaps the finest contribution of the Special Olympics has been to make nondisabled people realize that having a handicapping condition doesn't mean you don't love to win or that you can't participate in sports.

"We can learn so much about living from these kids," a volunteer Special Olympics coach said recently. He told of two youngsters who were racing in the forefront of their heat. Suddenly, one fell. The other ran on a few paces, realized he was running alone, and stopped. He looked around. When he saw what had happened, he ran back and helped his competitor to his feet. Then they both started running again.

"Not a bad set of values, is it?" said the coach.

This same attitude imbues a successful ski program for developmentally disabled children in Park City, Utah.

For Cindy, success was something which only happened in the lives of other people. An epileptic since birth, she was accustomed to the role of a clumsy observer in a world which rewards those who achieve. Now, with the approval of an understanding doctor she stands at the top of the beginners' ski run, along with other special education junior high school students. Awkward, uncertain and frightened, she begins that first reluctant slide downhill. . . . For Cindy, success is about to become more than a word.[1]

This is the introduction by Bev Carhart to the Park West Special Education program brochure, describing a sports program developed by Park West Resort in Park City, Utah. In 1975, they added to Park West's ski instruction program for junior and senior high-school students a section for special education students. Cindy was a member of the first class. She is now a competent and frequent skier.

Success is habit forming. For many of the Cindys of the world, a noncompetitive outdoor experience opens that magic door. Similar programs have been developed in other parts of the skiing country. Parents and teachers universally praise this program and others like it, citing the changes in behavior, the improvement in habits in other areas of children's lives, in short, the difference that success in a sport has meant to disabled children.

Depending on your child's levels of capability, he can become part of a specially designed sports program for children with handicapping conditions in bowling, swimming, horseback riding, dancing, or many other things. Camping is another favorite and beneficial activity, including both day and overnight camping experiences.

More and more disabled children are being included in regular Girl and Boy Scout troops, Indian Guides, and Camp Fire Girls. At the same time, there are youth clubs tailored especially for children with handicapping conditions.

Helping your children—all of them—to experience success is not, as you can see, a one-time or single-direction thing. A combination of age-appropriate experiences, including unplanned opportunities and planned experiences at home, training in social habits and personal grooming, and taking advantage of hobbies, sports, and clubs, can help your child with special needs become a confident, well-rounded person.

Being a part of planning your child's successful living experiences grants you immense satisfaction. You are providing him yet another avenue toward happy independence.

CHAPTER 13

One Big Happy Family—
Siblings Have Needs, Too

When Mike was only a year or two old, we began receiving predictions of dire consequences if he were reared in the home. "Your older child will probably have repressed guilt feelings." (Guilt was a big seller then.) "Your new baby could suffer from neglect. Younger siblings are affected more by a mentally retarded child." (Is there a worse guilt trip for parents than neglect?) "You risk damaging your other children psychologically if you elect to rear a disabled child at home" was a common professional attitude.

It is easy now to write with flippant humor of those days when as a young couple we agonized over whether we were doing irreparable damage to Jim and Laurie by keeping Mike home. But in the intervening years the whole field of psychology has done a flip.

Predicting how people will feel or behave in the future based on today's circumstances is not nearly so popular a pastime. The approach now, a much more healthy and positive one, is to admit, "This is what we got, folks. Where do we go from here?"

In terms of your disabled child and the rest of the family, it means parents no longer are told to worry about the effect one person has on the rest of the family just because that person happens to have a handicapping condition. We all affect each other, everyone who lives together. Our attitudes toward our children, the way we treat them, and the way they treat us and each other contribute much more to how any of them "turn out" than a simple fact of a handicapping condition.

Children with siblings who have special physical or mental needs do face unusual problems. Feeling ashamed of their brother, resenting the time the parents spend with that child, being embarrassed because people are always gawking at them, having to "stick up for him" sometimes when he's the subject of cruel ridicule—these are tough grown-up-size problems. It's asking a lot of kids to cope with them. And the children have no more choice in facing them than do their parents. The only choice they have—and, thank God, parents and other professionals can truly help here—is how well they will manage it.

"When I was eleven years old I can remember being acutely embarrassed by the stares our family received as we entered pushing Robin in his wheelchair. I was certain that everyone was looking at my brother . . . and then wondering what was wrong with the rest of us. I began to refuse to go out to dinner with my family and took precautions to avoid being seen on the street or in the yard with Robin," Marge Helsel wrote in *Parents Speak Out.*[1]

Marge's actions were accompanied by guilt. Looking back, Marge believes she would have benefited from counseling during that period if only to help her realize that others felt the same way: "Most children growing up in a society which places a great deal of emphasis on so-called normalcy come to a point where they are ashamed or even outright rejecting of a disabled sibling. It's then they need guidance in problem-solving skills and coping."

Next, Marge entered a period of false pretenses. She would take her brother out only when she was dressed to the teeth, inviting the comparison that if people were going to stare, at least they wouldn't find anything wrong with *her*. On reflection, Marge feels that she must have also wanted to encourage people to think, *Oh, look at that sweet young girl pushing her poor crippled brother. How wonderful!* That period lasted until she was in college and her brother had a seizure that left him comatose. She visited him in the hospital and called his name over and over until he finally responded with a squeeze of her hand. Marge was so grateful. She realized the strength of her love for him, just as he was.

SOMETIMES IT'S THE ADULTS WHO NEED THE EDUCATION

When Mike was four, Jim six, and Laurie two, a favorite family friend came to visit. He lived out of state and had never met the two younger children. Having children of his own, he felt overwhelming sympathy for Mike's Down's syndrome.

Soon, to their great delight, he was roughhousing with all three on the living room rug. It was near their bedtime, and the children were getting out of hand, especially Mike, whose self-control was limited. I moved to stop the play. The friend misunderstood.

"It's okay," he insisted. And he persisted in the jostling and tickling.

Within a few minutes Mike was out of control—rocking, shouting, flailing—and releasing his emotions in tears before he could be calmed down. Our friend was stunned. He hadn't foreseen such consequences.

It's hard for parents to sidetrack scenes like that. Since you can't very well remove the offending adult, it would be wise to remove the child before he reaches his point of loss of control. "Come on, Mike, let's plunk you in the tub" would have been a good exit line, swooping up the child and disappearing. As it was, I exited with Mike squirming and crying in my arms, leaving my husband to explain to our guest and to calm Jim and Laurie.

Scolding Jim and Laurie for prolonging the roughhousing would have been unfair. It could have caused justifiable resentment. Not much perhaps, but a seed. If you adopt the attitude of treating your disabled child as much like the other children as possible and consistently refuse to blame others for her shortcomings, you will be ahead of the game in terms of rearing an unspoiled child and well-adjusted siblings who do not resent their sister who is special in a different way.

Relatives and friends, especially those you don't see often, are sometimes unwitting perpetrators of the myth that your disabled child is more important than your others. With great goodwill they engage him in conversations or play. Often these are the very adults who would never dream of being so congenial to a nondisabled child.

If this adult is likely to be around a few years, I've sometimes suggested in a light vein that Mike doesn't need all that extra attention; he thinks he's pretty great already. When my other kids pick up on this type of behavior, I tell them frankly that some adults act this way because they've never learned to treat disabled people like everyone else.

It is not always easy, maybe not even possible, to treat children equally. Parents with disabled children have a particularly prickly situation because very often the disabled child requires more time and encouragement and at the same time causes more worry and greater expense in medical care than his brothers and sisters.

No wonder, then, that we must give great care to noting how our other children respond to this inequality and take steps to reassure them that our love and concern for them are no less than for the child with a handicapping condition.

I have gone even further with my daughter Laurie. When she grew old enough to talk thoughtfully about Mike's condition, I shared with her our sorrow for Mike when we first learned he was disabled, and I told her frankly how blessed we felt when she was born.

There are times when favored treatment isn't needed, when your disabled child should be allowed to fend for himself. He shouldn't grow up always expecting that you or someone will intercede for him. He needs to develop his own cooperative give-and-take.

One day our family was visiting my aunt and uncle, who had bought a used electric mail delivery cart. The kids, all preteens at the time, were fascinated with it. Laurie and Jim outraced Mike to the cart, and he was frustrated to find there was no room for him, too.

"Well, aren't you lucky," I told Mike. "Nobody's using Uncle Lee's hammock right now."

"I want to play mailman," Mike answered.

"Yes, but when it's your turn, you'll get it all to yourself. Jim and Laurie have to share it."

"Yeah!" Mike agreed. "Boy, am I lucky!" Off he sped to the hammock.

"I was wondering how you were going to handle that," my aunt said. "I thought you'd tell Jim to let Mike play, too."

"He doesn't have to have his turn right now," I remember telling her.

The thing is, I wanted Laurie and Jim to enjoy having Mike around rather than to feel they must always include him. And like other children, Mike needed to learn that taking turns sometimes meant postponing immediate gratification. Also, it was no big deal. I wasn't about to reprimand the others for "selfish" behavior or cause Mike to feel left out by overreacting.

Later when the adults were having coffee in the kitchen, I looked out to see Mike happily occupying the mail cart by himself. Soon Laurie trotted over, and he obligingly moved over so she could play, too.

"I WISH I WAS MIKE SOMETIMES"

Once Laurie said wistfully, "I wish I was Mike sometimes."
I was shocked. "Why, honey?"

"Oh, everybody always says, 'How's Mike?' like he's so important."

"He's not any more important than you or Jim," I replied. Nevertheless, her innocuous words set me thinking. Were we acting as if Mike was first in importance because of his more obvious needs? Was I doing more for him or with him than with the others? (Guilty as charged!) Talking more about Mike than Jim or Laurie in conversations with relatives and friends—making them feel I considered Mike more interesting, more important?

From that time on, I began trying to keep Mike's disability in perspective. I've discovered that when your child confides such feelings, you encourage her to enlarge on her feelings if your response is mild and nondefensive.

Sometimes if you react to a child's accusation of favoritism with anger, it might mean he has struck a nerve. If so, just knowing that gives you the first step to correcting it—either the situation or the child's view of it. But what if the child really doesn't understand the situation?

How can you help a child to be more accepting of a disabled sibling? If your disabled child must wear braces or use a wheelchair, I can tell you what a friend did. She rented a wheelchair so her son Ricky, age seven, could spend the day in a wheelchair, too, along with five-year-old Bobby who had cerebral palsy. Ricky thought it was great. (So did Bobby!) But then Ricky wanted to go to the bathroom. His mother refused to let him out of the wheelchair to go by himself. As he endured the embarrassment (after all, he was seven years old, nearly grown up!) of being helped to go to the bathroom the way his mother had to help Bobby, she could see that Ricky was having second thoughts. Maybe using a wheelchair wasn't so much fun after all.

When a friend came over later and wanted to play, Ricky was ready to call the game off. But his mother was adamant. They had agreed he would get to be like Bobby for the whole day. By suppertime, he was eagerly volunteering for all sorts of helping chores, anything to take him out of the confining chair. His mother sympathetically refused.

That night she lifted him tenderly into bed. As his arms wound around her neck, she thought she heard a sob. But Ricky merely whispered a very small good night. The mother came out of the bedroom and threw herself into a chair.

"What I need now," she told her husband, "is to slip out of these clothes and into a hot tub."

He grinned. "Think it did the trick?"

"Think so."

Right she was. From that day on, Ricky never complained about how much time his mother spent to help Bobby. He also became, in time, a willing helper himself, treating Bobby with increasing kindness and sympathy.

Ricky was ready to be told more about Bobby's disability. And a week later it was a far different Ricky who announced, "When I grow up, I'm going to invent a cure for cerebral palsy!"

Sometimes the behavior parents notice from siblings is a strange absence of any reaction to their disabled brother or sister. One girl, age seven, has a three-year-old brother with CP with fairly constant small seizures and an occasional grand mal. Despite his behavior during these episodes, which the girl has often observed, she has never commented about it to either parent. They are understandably concerned. They feel their daughter must be afraid of such violent and unpredictable episodes, must notice the inordinate number of medications her little brother takes while she takes none and the sudden drop-everything trips to the doctor.

Should the parents say anything or nothing?

Another sibling may react at the opposite end of the scale, indulging in outrageous behavior in such a manner or at such times as to cause the parent to suspect the behavior is somehow tied to his feelings about his brother or sister.

Again, what should the parents do?

"IF ONLY I KNEW WHY THEY ACT THAT WAY!"

Howard Chudler, who was a family counselor with San Gabriel Valley Regional Center in Covina, California, had a few suggestions. First, he said, don't overconcern yourselves with why. There will be as many explanations of why siblings act out their feelings the way they do as there are different theories of psychology. The important thing is to help the child now to modify behavior.

Parents concerned about actions by nondisabled siblings should be very observant. Notice what the behavior is, when and where it occurs, and how other family members react when he does whatever he is doing. What does the child do when he sees the rest of the family reacting to him?

Sometimes a parent saying, "It bothers me when you do that," is enough to curb the child's behavior.

Sometimes a child will say, "You're always nicer to Mike than you are to me." It may be an honest attempt to make you pay more attention to him or an attempt at manipulation. One way to defuse it is to agree: "You know something, you're right. And I feel bad that I don't have more time to give you."

Chudler suggested behavior modification techniques. Praising good behavior reinforces it: "I really like the way you played with Mike this afternoon while I was busy." This technique rewards good behavior. Changing a person's behavior ultimately changes attitudes, behavior modification psychologists believe.

A companion technique, often used with a younger child, is to remove something or someone that the child desires when she misbehaves. The key is to let her know ahead of time what privilege will be removed if she misbehaves, and then follow through.

Modeling A technique that is especially good with siblings of disabled children is called modeling: practicing the behavior beforehand you want your children to emulate. For instance, you are all going to a restaurant for dinner. You realize that some people might be rude and stare at your disabled child. The children may or may not be aware of it.

Discuss ahead of time how people might act and what you should do. "I think we should tell them it's rude!" says one child. "I think we should punch their lights out," says another. "They are rude, for sure. Maybe we should just ignore them." You come to an agreement. You will ignore them. At the restaurant, you all ignore those people, catch each other's eye—in on the game!—keep conversation going, and are extra courteous to each other. What a family of winners!

You have just given all your children invaluable help not only in achieving positive public behavior but in coping with such situations, which will confront them their whole lives, whenever they are out with a person who has a handicapping condition.

Another behavior you may want to model is how you attend to your disabled child's special needs in public, unobtrusively and matter-of-factly, so that others will do the same. This approach will help him and everyone else be at ease. Eating out is a good time to practice conversation skills that include everyone. By drawing each of the children into the table talk, you are showing your other children a way to help their disabled sibling learn to respond well socially, too.

A desirable technique to use with all children is education: What do you know about your brother's disability? Knowledge of the disability, including how children who had it in the past used to be treated, can ease any guilt your other children may be harboring. Emphasize that no one was in any way responsible for the disability. Share what you know of how people get such disabilities.

Another thing you can do is to put yourself in your child's shoes: How would I feel if I had a brother with Down's syndrome?

UNDERSTANDING IS BENEFICIAL

By being aware of some of the conflicts felt by brothers and sisters of youngsters with handicapping conditions, you can help them become more accepting and more understanding. You can

- have special times with each child separately, to do or talk about whatever he wants. Make it clear you two share something unique.
- realize that to each child, her own life is the most important. That's why she can't in all honesty always share the depths of your despair or the heights of your happiness over the accomplishments of the disabled child. Are you as dizzy over her achievements?
- not saddle siblings with responsibility for baby-sitting their disabled brother or sister all the time, but let them share the care.

As you develop your own positive habits, you may want to

- gently encourage questions about the child's disability if the siblings are old enough but not asking.
- try to be aware that in plunging wholeheartedly into helping your disabled child, you aren't forgetting needs of others.
- share as much information about the disability as the siblings can comprehend.
- spread around your activities to include those important to the other children, too.
- frequently show your appreciation of the brothers and sisters for their help and their understanding.

Parents who have a good perspective on their children and can view the disability of one in proper relation to the whole of family life need worry little about adverse effects on other children. From stories read and told to me by brothers and sisters of mentally retarded adults reared at home, the happy truth is that growing up with a person who has a handicapping condition can bring rewards of deeper maturity, greater compassion toward all disabled persons, and an almost spiritual affinity for them—in sum, a deeper, richer personality for the siblings.

CHAPTER 14

Communication

*H*elping your child achieve good communication skills begins when he is a baby. Is there a mother anywhere on the globe who has never played some version of peek-a-boo with her children? Her smiles and cooing sounds, her attentiveness to him when he returns the cooing noises, are vital. "Now we put your little arm in here...boo! Look what comes out the sleeve—fingers! My, my!"

She is giving him his later vocabulary. Although he may be far too young to understand the words, he hears the sequences and patterns of sounds and the high and low inflections of her voice. He sees her mouth shaping in different ways to make those sounds, and he sees or is a part of the actions she takes with the words.

"Come to Mommy" is not just words. It's loving tone quality, it's arms outstretched, it's the smile on her face that all say, "Yes, you! I love you!"

RUNNING INTERFERENCE

Robert is a darling little boy. He is brain injured; but until he tries to talk, no one knows he is mentally disabled. With his dark curling hair and snapping brown eyes, he is the personification of the bright, mischievous child. His adoring parents and older sister, age six, make sure that three-year-old Robert gets everything he wants. His sister has become expert at anticipating his wishes. Robert has only to grunt and point, and Susie knows what he means. Feeling very motherly and responsible, she has given herself the role of protector and interpreter.

What happens when Susie tires of the role? When she wants to go off and play with her own friends once in a while without Robert? Will her mother say, "But, darling, you know just how to handle him. Why, you can understand him better than any of us." Susie will be in a bind. She put herself in this role, a very commendable one, and now must get out of it. And is Robert better able to cope for himself? Of course not! As always happens, the one who has been running interference has grown stronger and the protected one even more dependent.

In families of more than one child, it's an accepted fact that the oldest child is likely to be the most verbal. She is often better able to understand the baby's gibberish than the parent. The question is, Is the older child more verbal because she takes over the talking and interpreting chores for the younger, or is she more verbal because the parents communicate more directly with her—just like the military chain of command, orders get passed down one rung at a time?

If that is so, the child on the bottom rung (either in age or in ability) is responsible for communicating with no one under him, which possibly causes his communication skills to develop more slowly.

How does this tendency relate to our children with handicapping conditions?

Studies report that the degree to which a child can communicate successfully with others may not give a true picture of how bright he is. A child who is only mildly retarded, with good learning potential, may be almost totally nonverbal if he has not been required to express himself to get what he wants.

I suspect that this is one of the chief reasons why studies done of institutionalized developmentally disabled children have failed to give an accurate picture of positive development potential. Attendants in institutions or large community care facilities simply haven't patience or time or interest to wait for children to express wants and needs in understandable language.

Families do. Look at it as an investment. The more time you give now to the painstaking process of helping your child become communicative, the less time anyone will have to spend later as the child's interpreter, and the more outreaching the child will grow.

One thing you can do is teach yourself to slow down. Speaking slowly and enunciating clearly when you converse with developmentally disabled people help them understand you better.

A few years ago I was teaching ESL (English as a Second Language) to some Vietnamese women and an Egyptian family. "It's so much easier to understand you than most Americans," they told me.

I realized later they were not just being polite. I did speak more understandably because my son had trained me that way! Most Americans speak in rushes and slurs. Without realizing it, many parents of children with mental disabilities acquire a habit of speaking slowly and distinctly as a method of improving their children's understanding.

That's half the battle. The other half is getting the child to slow down! Sometimes the thoughts rush ahead of the ability to form words, resulting in a mud slide of conversation that can be understood only by context. Ask—insist—that she repeat herself until her words are understandable (providing that she is capable of speaking more clearly).

Does your disabled child jump into conversations with inappropriate remarks? Take the inappropriateness as a cue that he needs help developing the skill of conversing. It is a social skill; it can be learned. Make a game of it. Involve your other children. (They can probably use the practice, too.) Have them practice looking at each other as they talk. Tell them, "Listen hard to what the other person says. Make your answer fit what the person says."

"NOW TELL ME WHAT I SAID"

Another habit you can develop when talking with your child is to ask for feedback to be sure you are being understood. I can't think of another tool in our communication with our son that has been more important. Here is how it works.

"Mike, I'm going to the store. If Daddy comes before I get home, tell him I'll be back soon."

Mike is watching TV and gives no appearance of hearing me—a trait common to all ten-year-olds.

"Mike?"

"Okay."

"What are you going to tell Daddy?"

"You'll be back soon."

"And where am I going?"

"Oh, Mom! To the store."

It may seem tedious to go through this process each time to be sure you are understood. (It certainly results in a well-trained mother.) For your child, it's a must. It is forcing him to use the vocal cords well enough to produce meaning to another and to restate questions in a way that tells you that what you said has meaning for him.

"Can I have another... uh..."

"Glass of milk? Coming up."

"And how about another... uh..."

"Piece of toast? Okay."

Does this routine ever go on at your house? We are so busy sometimes that we can't wait for each other to complete sentences. Living together and knowing family members so well, we know what they are going to say anyway! And so we "help" the child, who may have difficulty forming speech as well as enunciating, by supplying the word she is groping for or by allowing her to use grunts and gestures to tell us what she means.

Natural sympathy and occasional impatience are at fault. But imagine your child on a street corner asking directions. Will busy strangers take time to understand her? So it is to help her communicate successfully with others that you are there, smiling and patient. Knowing how hard and frustrating it is for her, pulling for her because you realize how essential it is that she be able to communicate effectively, you wait for her answers as though you had all the time in the world. (And the expression she sees on your face has a lot to do with how encouraged she is about ever getting out the words she wants to say in an understandable form and in a meaningful sequence.)

Eventually, your communication will go from the simplest questions that can be answered by mere actions or by yes or no to ones that require the child to make her own choice of words. Get in the habit of phrasing questions so that they cannot be answered by a gesture or by yes or no. Instead of saying, "It's cold outside; put on your sweater," say, "It's cold outside. Which sweater are you going to wear?" Instead of saying, "Wash your hands before you sit down," try saying, "How clean are your hands? Hm. What do you think you'd better do about it?"

Think up games to push your child into more active verbalization. Instead of saying, "We're having soup for dinner; doesn't that sound good?" you say, "Guess what we're having for dinner?"

If you say, "Is your room cleaned up yet?" a nod or a grunt may be the child's response. By asking, "When are you planning to clean up your room?" you require the child to think about what you asked and to specify a time and therefore a commitment. Ask him if he would like to watch "Sesame Street" on television, and again he can get by with a nonverbal answer. Change your question to a choice of three programs (even though you know he always watches one in particular) and you require a verbal response.

Children love a game called Rumor. You sit in a circle and whisper something into the ear of the person next to you. (It can be something as simple as "I love hot dogs, don't you?") He must listen closely, then whisper what he has heard into the ear of the person next to him, and on around the circle. The last person whispers into your ear the sentence as it has come to him. Sometimes the sentence gets around intact. More often it's completely different. It's a good game for a rainy day.

Another game involving clear speech is Grocery Store. Play it on a long automobile trip when everybody begins to twist and twitch. It's played like Twenty Questions. A person will say, "I'm thinking of something at the grocery store." Or to make it easier, specify which department. The others take turns asking, "Is it a _____?" (When we played this game with Mike, we learned to make him write down his choices so he wouldn't be tempted to switch choices when someone got too "hot.")

Your other children probably know dozens of similar games that can be adapted to help your disabled child acquire clearer speech.

HERE'S TALKIN' AT YA, BABY

In some communities, children begin speech therapy as soon as they are able to talk. It was not made available to Mike in his early years in school, although he could have benefited from it.

If your child is in school, needs speech therapy, and will benefit from it, ask his teacher if it is available. If it is, try to get it included in his Individual Education Program. If you feel it will support your request, ask your child's doctor to provide you with a written recommendation for therapy. You might tape-record your child's voice in conversation, reading, or reciting and play it for your doctor to reinforce your claim of need.

What if the school district does provide speech therapy, agrees your child needs it, but has no money to include him? Your child may qualify for funding from another source. Call or write to one of the sources listed in this book in the Appendix to find out which government or private agencies fund such services.

A dozen years ago I wasn't informed enough to do these things. I have no idea if speech therapy was available in our district at that time, and no one ever suggested that Mike could—and should—learn to speak more clearly through specific exercises and concentrated practice.

"How important is it?" Johnny Carson's audience used to shout when he fed them the line that something is important. Well, being understood when you talk is so important you can hardly get by without it. Picture a foreigner with no English coming to live in the United States. He needs to find a place to live, learn how to use transportation, seek out doctors—and for all of this he totally depends on someone else's tongue and ears until he can make his own way in our language.

Our children who are mentally retarded share the same problem, coupled with limited intelligence. Few things are more important to them than being able to ask questions, to take in and understand information, and to make their wants known. Children who are severely retarded may have difficulty making their wants known in sentences or understanding even simple conversational sentences directed at them, even when they become adults.

Years ago when I was a volunteer helper in Mike's class, my attention was drawn to two other thirteen-year-olds, both girls, who seemed total opposites. They had similar IQs, in the mildly retarded range. Yet one was happy and outgoing, talked a lot, produced messy papers, but labored hard to make letters correctly and sound out words phonetically.

The other child said not more than ten words the whole year I was there. Though capable of talking and answering questions, Opal understood and obeyed directions only nonverbally. Later I had a chance to observe Opal at home. According to her mother, the father, principal of a private boys' school, never accepted his daughter's disability and never spoke to her directly at all. He treated her as a nonperson. The mother, perhaps in an effort to make it up to her, indulged the child. Her bedroom was filled with hundreds of dollars' worth of antique dolls, Barbie dolls, and doll costumes that young girls frequently collect. Her clothing would make a free-spending teenager drool. The mother talked incessantly at her daughter but never paused for answers. When I asked her what she saw for Opal after she was out of school, the mother gave me a blank look. Then she laughed, "That's five years away!"

The other girl, Tracie, is a middle child of a large close-knit family. Her brothers and sisters, ever on the lookout for equal rights, make certain she does not get any favors. Thus, she has to do her share of work around the house, keep her side of her bedroom clean, and feed the dogs. In addition, because it was the pattern set by the parents, they all talk to her as a person—expecting and getting answers. And she shares all her ups and downs with whomever is handy.

"Guess what's on TV tonight, Ted!"

"The Dallas Cowboy Cheerleaders?"

"No! Teenage Mutant Ninja Turtles!"

"Wow! You gonna watch them?"

"I sure am."

Guess which one of these girls will be better prepared to join the mainstream?

I don't want to leave the area of communication without stressing again the importance of a computer to school-age children. Children with Down's syndrome and other disabilities sometimes are able to learn to communicate through the computer before they can verbalize. The computer has a unique ability to ask questions verbally as well as on screen, to focus a child's attention on a word or icon or sentence on screen while the child uses a pointer or other device as highlighter, and to reward correct interactive responses with voice, music, and/or colorful screen animation.

WOULD YOU REPEAT THAT, PLEASE?

Training your child to give you feedback will show you that she understands you. Often it benefits her in another way, too. She learns to ask questions. Many, many children never learn to speak up in school, despite their parents' urging. The night before a big test, a child cries, "I don't understand!" The frustrated parent says, "Well, why didn't you tell someone!" The child may reveal shamefacedly that she was too embarrassed to say anything in class because the others would laugh at her.

Such fears keep many children from getting help when they need it. If you have brought your children up on feedback, they will more likely ask questions, without embarrassment, when they don't understand. Always providing, of course, that the person owning the information encourages questions and treats them with respect.

Have you ever seen a young child absorbed in his own play suddenly interrupted by an adult who fires a direction at him? The child looks blank for a moment, then begins playing again. The adult sometimes gets angry at what she perceives as willful disobedience. The child may have simply not processed the request or processed it too slowly to answer the adult.

The adult could break down her request into steps: first, getting the child's attention by calling his name or touching him; second, when his attention is received, speaking the request slowly and clearly; and third, waiting for a response. If an appropriate response isn't forthcoming, the adult may ask the child if he understood the request. A sympathetic tone will tell the child that the adult's concern is more for him than the fact that he ignored what was asked of him.

If a child seems confused when you ask him questions, consider whether the directions were too complicated. Did you ask more than one thing at a time? If he's playing trucks outside in the dirt and you ask him to come inside for a jacket but first knock the dirt off his shoes, and would he mind bringing in your watering can, too, you've given him three separate orders!

Here's another example, not confusing because the child was asked to do too many things but because he lacked the necessary skill. Ray, a young teenager, is visiting his grandfather. Ray has always lived in an apartment. Grandpa lives in a house. Grandpa asks him to mow the lawn. Ray is willing, but he's never had a personal acquaintance with a lawn mower. Rather than confess he hasn't the slightest idea how to begin, he acts embarrassed, maybe cuts up a bit, and makes a hash of the job. Watching his grandson, Grandpa mumbles dire thoughts about the future of the country. If Ray had been able to level with his grandfather, teaching and learning and companionable closeness might have taken place.

Encourage children to admit it when they don't understand something Grandpa, had he thought a moment, would have realized that Ray had had absolutely no chance to learn about mowing lawns and said so. He might have added that Ray probably knew how to do many things that Grandpa didn't; then he could have shown Ray, without any implied criticism, how to mow the lawn. Ray would have felt good mastering a new skill and understood that Grandpa didn't think he was either stupid or lazy. That would have made it easy for Ray to admit his ignorance without feeling put down.

Parents, teachers, and employers are not always sensitive to the reasons why mentally disabled children fail to perform skills within their grasp. We can help them by breaking down requests into easy steps, making sure they understand exactly what is wanted, making sure they have the necessary skills, and being open and confident with our children so that they feel safe admitting ignorance.

All of us need to constantly encourage questions and to praise each small step of accomplishment—not only for our children but for each other! Fear of failure keeps many a woman and man from achieving their potential. Think what it can do to a person with a handicapping condition.

Making the child responsible for being understood, developing habits of feedback, and teaching him to be comfortable asking questions are all important communication techniques. They can be combined and furthered by adding telephone skills to his capabilities.

"I'LL GET IT!"

"Hello?"

[*Sound of breathing*]

"Hello, this is Uncle Bob. Who am I talking to? [*More breathing*] Susie?"

"Ah dub du gee do."

"Oh. This is Ronnie, isn't it? Ronnie, get someone else. Put the telephone down and call someone."

[*Click*]

If you've ever been through this, you know what an irritation it is. It's excusable in two-year-olds but hardly in older children who are expected to be able to carry on intelligible conversation. And that includes most of our children with handicapping conditions.

As soon as your child is able to talk well enough to carry on a conversation, he should be allowed the opportunity of answering the telephone when you are around. Perhaps parents ignore telephone training because they believe the call won't be for the child anyway. But a child does not really have to understand much to be able to successfully receive and relay telephone messages.

If your home has two telephones, use them to make a game of teaching him to answer the telephone. (If not, employ a neighbor or friend to help you.)

"Hello, Ronnie? [*You, from the extension*] This is Mommy calling."

[*Breathing*]

"Ronnie, say, 'Hi, Mommy!'"

"Hi, Mommy."

"Well, hello there, Ronnie! What a nice surprise!"

[*Giggles*]

"I just called up to ask you if you would like to go for ice cream after lunch."

"Yes!"

"Okay. Good-bye. [*Waiting for click*] Good-bye means you say good-bye, too, and hang up the phone."

"Good-bye." [*Click*]

After a few sessions, you will develop in Ronnie a sense of confidence and fun in answering the telephone. Then as he learns to make letters and numerals you can teach him to add dialing and writing down numbers to his skills. The joy in all this is that it won't be long at all before you find yourself saying, "Ronnie, honey, I have to run to the store. Listen for the phone and take messages, will you?"

The first time I said that to my son Mike, I experienced a thrill, a sudden pretaste of freedom. I was actually depending on him. And it becomes a repeatable success story for him when you return to find a carefully lettered note of someone's name and number. The praise you give him for this service is real and deserved. (Don't we all have nondisabled kids who have never in their busy young lives delivered an unscrambled telephone message?)

I was working at my desk one day—on the first edition of this book, as a matter of fact—when I answered the telephone and a woman's voice began talking at me in a slow, nonstop drawl. It took a few seconds to figure out who was speaking. Ah, yes! It was Beverly, a young woman I'd met a few months ago.

Beverly was brought up in a board-and-care home, a private home housing six young women and their foster parents. A year before, she had joined others from the home in a bowling league that Mike belonged to. There she met a young man also in his twenties. The attraction was mutual. Soon they fell in love and wanted to marry. The young man's parents were at first opposed but then agreed. His mother took Beverly into her home so that she could teach her some homemaking skills. Among the things his mother taught Beverly was how to use the telephone.

At the time she called me, Beverly had just learned to dial by herself. She had a long way to go—asking for a person by name, introducing herself when someone picked up the receiver, and limiting her conversations to a moderate time—but she was so enthusiastic with her newfound ability that I was happy to celebrate with her. (It took her a much longer time to be adventurous enough to pick up a ringing telephone.)

Beverly is capable now in many areas. The sad thing is, she was also capable fifteen years ago, but no one bothered to teach her.

Allan, Beverly's husband, is much more able to deal with life situations. But he, too, has to find the courage to make full use of services like the telephone. He refuses to call the bus company anymore because "they talk too fast." Instead of saying, "Please talk slower, I can't understand you," Allan merely hung up in frustration the one time he called. He is a stubborn young man with pride. He wants to be accepted like any other young man, apparently believing that other people never have problems understanding each other over the phone.

If you teach your disabled child to keep hands off the phone, she may develop a block that will be even harder to retrain as an adult. Thinking ahead again to your goal of wanting your child to become the most independent person possible, encourage her to answer the telephone and take messages. And as she is able, expand the telephone's role so that she can successfully call friends and call for services, including bus companies, and ask them to talk more slowly.

The greatest benefit of helping your child develop her communication skills comes, of course, in the years she steps out into the community—to school, to church, to the grocery store—first with someone, later by herself. We know, no matter how much we love our children, that they will probably outlive us. It is imperative that a lack of communication skills, which could and should have been theirs, not become an additional handicapping condition.

PART

4

TOWARD INDEPENDENCE

CHAPTER 15

Not Made of Stone

T he young couple came out of the theater holding hands, like many of the kids around them. It was Friday night, the feature had been *Creature from the Black Lagoon*, and the air was full of nervously excited laughter. The couple moved a little closer together, smiling but not taking part in the general horseplay that usually goes with Friday night at the movies. They were careful to step out of the way of anyone charging their path.

I could see Mike look over the row of cars swinging slowly through the circle drive in front of the marquee. I'd arrived early and was already parked. Not seeing the car, he walked Sharon toward the ice-cream parlor next door. Through the glass front, I saw them choose ice cream, saw Mike give Sharon his cone to hold while he fished out his allowance. All in slow time. Transaction painstakingly completed, he took back his cone, and they sauntered outside. Mike's step was jaunty. I knew he was pleased by being able to do just what everyone else does on Friday night. I honked to attract their attention.

The night was a triumph for Mike—well, maybe not a triumph, but one of life's better showings. Behind the single night lay years of groundwork. From going to the show Saturday afternoon with his sister or brother and their friends, Mike had graduated to double-dating with his brother, who was old enough to drive.

Before his first double date, I called the girl's mother. I had no idea how she felt about her daughter going out with other young people. I didn't want Mike to be rebuffed through no fault of his own. Her mother was in favor of it, so when Mike came home from school, he called the girl and made the date. He was elated when she accepted.

I'd also asked Jim ahead of time if he would mind going out with Mike a few times. Jim said, "No, of course not." And I asked him to check with his date also.

Going out with Jim and his date helped Mike to see in action and therefore imitate what we felt were sound social habits, such as calling for his date at the door and letting her precede him, and opening the car door for her.

One golden day Mike brought a girlfriend to the beach with the family. They took a long stroll along the edge of lapping waves, tiny shimmering figures blending in the distance with others. They squashed through hot sand to try out the playground equipment. *Was that really my son, who loves to swing himself so high, sedately pushing his girl back and forth, back and forth?*

When Mike moves away from home, I thought, *he will probably have few nondisabled friends aside from those with a responsibility for or interest in his welfare. Yet he will be living in a world of nondisabled people.* I was happy to see him learning to feel ever more comfortable among them when he was alone or with other mentally disabled people. Just the very fact that he was comfortable made him fit in better.

That such an idyllic relationship could go on forever! It didn't, of course. Eventually, Mike wanted more out of personal relationships than strolls on the beach. "More" might and probably will include sex as part of the flowering of a permanent relationship.

Parents are not always as fortunate in having such warm memories of their child's adolescence as we were. Following are two actual examples where parents' failure to deal realistically with their children has produced or is likely to produce unhappy results.

FANTASY "I" LAND

"When Kenny's all grown up, he's going to marry a beautiful girl with long blonde hair like on 'The Dating Game' and drive a Cadillac and have his own swimming pool, aren't you, honey?" Alice brushed back Kenny's shock of pale hair as she repeated for the rest of us what Kenneth had just told her. Her eyes shone with love. She appreciated the breadth of her son's imagination.

But twenty-year-old Kenneth believed it. And he told any and all who listened greater and greater tales of heroic and girl-centered adventures. Then one day Kenneth was in the house alone, watching a rerun of a police show.

Outside, his younger brother, Harper, was working in the yard. Suddenly, a line of police cars, sirens screaming, roared down the street and cordoned the house. Men jumped out with shotguns. Harper was frightened. An officer ran to his side. "Are you all right?"

"Yes."

"Have you seen him?"

"No. Who?"

The officers had received a call that a man brandishing a long knife was threatening people in the neighborhood.

His heart sinking, Harper felt immediately that he knew what had happened. He led the officers inside. Kenneth was standing rigidly before the TV watching the action in fascination. Kenneth's words came at Harper in a rush. The television story had become Kenneth's reality. Of course, he had called the police! Wasn't Harper proud of him?

When Harper had straightened out the situation and given the police his embarrassed apologies, he knew he'd still have to face his mother.

Alice scolded Harper for not watching Kenneth better and praised Kenneth for knowing how to use the telephone to call the police. Alice often repeated this "cute" story for her friends' entertainment.

And what if Kenneth one day sees a seduction scene in which a man overpowers a woman, and Kenneth believes that is how a man treats a woman with whom he wants to have sex?

Allowing Kenneth to dwell in a fantasy world may warp his concepts of male-female relationships. Assuming he eventually attracts a girlfriend, how satisfied will he be with someone unlike the women in his fantasies—women his mother always agreed that he would date?

There is a sad sequel to this anecdote. Kenneth's mother had always taken complete responsibility for rearing both boys. Kenneth is thirty-four now. As far as I was able to learn, no preparations were ever made for him to live away from home, although he did attend a sheltered workshop for two years. In the classic "things you fear most" vein, Kenneth and his mother were in an auto accident, and Alice was killed. In the months following, we occasionally saw Kenneth around town. He lost his job at a local car wash (which his mother had campaigned valiantly to secure), his brother canceled his marriage plans indefinitely, and his father withdrew for a time into a noncoping state.

Once in a while after that, Kenneth would stop in to ask about Mike and tell us stories about the beautiful women he dated. He'd stay for milk and cookies, he and Guy would talk about cars and football, and eventually, he'd say he guessed he'd go home.

Were the father and younger son ever able to pull Kenneth's life into focus so that he, too, could have a promising future? Or did he become another disabled adult out of school with no planned activities, with nothing to do but walk the streets and dream fantasies?

Television is so powerful. Parents should remind their children occasionally that what they are seeing on television is not real. Encourage discussion about it—about the actors' real lives or how stuntmen and stuntwomen do the car tricks. The nondisabled child has difficulty sometimes separating the fantasies of television from reality. How much more difficulty do our children with disabilities have! We need to give children realistic and positive direction to achieve their own "someday" expectations. We need to sensitively help them separate their myths from their realities.

For me, it meant that pretending with Mike that he would actually date those cheerleaders from high school would have been cruel. What young woman who is emotionally stable and intellectually capable would be content to date a young man whose mental age is only half that of hers? Unlike persons who just have physically handicapping conditions ("just!" I know), children like Mike can never provide the caliber of sharing and caring that a nondisabled person needs.

Nothing angers me more than hearing parents—more often it's well-meaning relatives—whine, "It can't hurt, my goodness, when they have so little." True, they have little compared to a nondisabled person. But providing dreams instead of building vigorously on their talents and good traits certainly *can* hurt.

The second example involves a loving, overly protecting mother and her daughter Beth.

"Sex education? Look, I know what's going to happen out there. Beth is friendly to everybody. The minute someone came along and said, 'C'mon, sweetie, get in the car,' she'd do it."

Hazel C., the speaker, is a well-to-do highly vocal woman from San Francisco. Beth, twenty-six, is her eldest child, the only one still living at home. The words *institution, family care home, independent living,* and even *summer camp* are scare words to her.

Beth has never been separated, even for a night, from her family.

"I sent her to camp one year," Hazel recalled. "The first night she called for me to come and get her. Same thing happened to me when I was a kid. Who wants to sleep on the ground when you have a comfortable bed at home? Why should I subject her to an inferior type of living? She has everything she wants right here."

"And when you are gone?" she is asked.

"Her sister and brother will take her in. She will never have to go to an institution. *Institution* is a dirty word. Beth has said to me, 'Don't ever put me in one of those places.'"

Is Beth, then, one of the few profoundly retarded persons who would probably have to go to a maximum care facility if she did not live at home? Hardly! According to her workshop supervisor at the time, Beth functioned well in the mild-to-moderate range. He tried repeatedly to discuss with Hazel training Beth for more independent living in the future.

That was ten years ago. Beth was never alone outside the walls of her parents' home. A workshop bus picked her up at the door and delivered her there at day's end. She accompanied her mother shopping and on errands but was not permitted out by herself on any occasion. Hazel had herself appointed Beth's guardian by the court, a move that she believed (erroneously) gave her total control over Beth's future.

Beth is fortunate to be part of a caring, closely knit family. That she has benefited from it shows in her stable, outgoing attitude toward others. But having done the best a parent could for her child, bringing her to the brink of maturity, Hazel was afraid to let go.

Beth's doctor, a well-known specialist in mental retardation, did persuade her to bring Beth to the first of a series of lectures on sexuality and birth control. "Your daughter has sexual drives just like most people," the doctor told her. "The best thing you can do is help her understand and deal with them."

"Not my daughter!" Hazel insisted. "We went to one lecture," she said later. "All she got out of it is dirty words. We never went back." The "dirty words" used in the lecture were actually only the clinically correct words for parts of the anatomy.

Perhaps it is fear of something dreadful happening to her daughter that prompts such fierce protectiveness in Hazel. The idea that her daughter also has rights is foreign to her and provokes a rush of anger.

What will happen if Beth takes a liking to someone in workshop—or he to her? What if they want to marry, or if Beth decides to move away from home? Hazel cannot legally stop her. And although

Beth is well-groomed and can cook and keep a tidy house, she has so far been denied the education and training needed to make any sensible move toward semi-independence.

I saw Beth and her mother a couple of years ago. Beth does not seem to be a sad young woman. Neither does she exude happiness. She is docile and possesses beautiful manners. She carries on a conversation better than most people who work beside her in the training workshop. She was eager to tell me about her workshop's bowling team and square dance group, both of which she partici-pates in. Beth's mother's only regret is that she and her husband never have any time to themselves.

If Beth remains home until Hazel dies or can no longer care for her, what is in store for her? Studies indicate that very few developmentally disabled adults who have been cared for by aged parents are taken in by relatives after the deaths of the parents—even though parents may have wrung promises from their other children to "always care for Beth." So Beth's future may not be as secure as her mother believes. At some point she will be at risk of losing all at once her parents, her home, her familiar surroundings, her routines. She will be cut adrift and expected to adapt to an entirely new life pattern. How many of us could do that without some severe adjust-ment problems?

Many parents are aware of these problems while still refusing to consider alternatives. One father said to me recently, "I hope and pray my daughter dies before I do." The daughter is thirty-one, in good health, and only mild-to-moderately retarded. How realistic is this parent being?

How widespread are attitudes like these: parental fantasizing with the child about his future, and parental refusal to look at the child's future beyond a protective home environment? What effect do these attitudes then have on the suddenly-set-adrift adult retarded person?

An astounding figure surfaced in a study released in late 1979 by Jerome R. Evans, Ph.D., who investigated mental health problems among clients of the California Regional Centers. Regional Centers serve approximately fifty thousand people, most of the develop-mentally disabled citizens living in that state. Dr. Evans and mem-bers of his task force found that 41 percent of all Regional Center clients are in need of psychiatric assistance. What you have, accord-ing to Dr. Evans, is mental illness developing on top of developmen-tal disability. Some of the mental illness is the result of organic brain damage, but the rest of it—probably the larger part of it—can be attributed to familial, societal, and environmental factors:

Developmentally disabled individuals face a lifetime of coping with their physical handicaps in a world which both pushes them to accomplish their best while reminding them of their limitations. Such conflicting forces generate tension which often leads to symptoms of emotional disturbance. In addition to this special form of stress the developmentally disabled are exposed to the same psychological, social and economic pressures which burden the nonhandicapped; thus, some will live with faulty parenting, face family breakup or encounter failure in their school or occupation. These experiences too can lead to disturbed thoughts, feelings and behavior. Regional Center clients often live with a double burden of psychopathology producing pressures while at the same time they have a more limited capacity to adequately defend themselves.[1]

Dr. Evans observed, "The five problems which most commonly caused serious impairment . . . are Immaturity in Socialization, Uncooperative-Rebellious, Hostile-Threatening, Anxiety, and Disturbances in Mood."[2] Counselors questioning their clients for Dr. Evans's study found, however, that two causes of mental disturbance frequently mentioned by clients were not on his list of problems to be surveyed. They were client or family conflict in accepting a disability and parental marital problems. This finding suggests that parental attitudes toward their disabled child and their ability to create a successful, stable family life have a strong influence on the child's ability to cope successfully with his own problems, which is exactly what one would expect about any child.

Just as among the general population, social immaturity was found to be the most common mental health problem.

Yet 80 percent of developmentally disabled adults are able to develop friendships and engage in social activities within their own group. It is only the remaining 20 percent who as adults have difficulty moving away from dependency-clinging relationships—attachments formed usually with a member of the family—that, Dr. Evans's counselors found, prove exhausting to the family.

Acting-out behavior was the second most prominent form of mental disturbance. Behavior ranging from irritability and hostility to destructive or assaultive occurred among both boys and girls, although a little more frequently and severely in the less bright adult male. Here again, Dr. Evans found that "there is little in their disturbances of emotion, thought and feeling that distinguishes the developmentally disabled person from others with mental illness."[3]

This information seems to suggest that parents should not expect behavior described as mental illness to occur any more often in their disabled child than in her brothers or sisters. And yet, if statistics gathered in California can be taken as fairly representative, 41 percent of the developmentally disabled population has some form of mental illness serious enough to require attention.

Why? Obviously, follow-up studies are needed to discover why developmentally disabled people should have a far greater percentage of mental illness than the general population. I think it is rooted in the fact that until recently the attitude toward persons born with disabilities was "care for them and love them as long as you have them." Totally left out of the picture was a plan for the individual's social, spiritual, and emotional future. It was as if he were a plant. Fed, watered, and vitamined, he'd do all right until he died.

Is it any wonder then, when confronted by the range of experiences necessary to become a well-functioning member of society, this person experiences terrible adjustment problems?

Before discussing parents' roles in preventing mental illness, let's look at treatment. Can mentally ill children who are also developmentally disabled be treated in community mental health centers like the rest of the population? They can. But apparently they and their families seldom consider this resource when emotional problems develop. Evans's study found that even when a recommendation is made to a family to take their child to a community mental health center, one-third of the time they fail to keep the first appointment. Another problem also exists: Mental health centers are geared toward working with clients who are verbal. Their methods may not be attuned to the needs of persons who are very mentally retarded.

Another problem involves priorities given by community mental health centers to different forms of mental illness:

> Most administrators and clinicians believe that these programs are intended for care of the psychotic patient and for time-limited, crisis intervention to others. On-going treatment of neuroses, personality disorders and behavior problems, while available in most areas, is not emphasized. Where such treatment is provided it is most often directed toward children and adolescents. The mental health needs of many developmentally disabled [adults] will not, therefore, be met by agencies with these treatment prerequisites.[4]

Community health centers are beginning to emphasize prevention and early intervention in their client services. To take advantage of this trend, family members could be on the lookout for warning signals of excessive psychological stress and seek treatment. Early treatment can limit or in some cases prevent emotional illness.

Like recommendations of other experts in the field, Dr. Evans's study makes a strong case for treating developmentally disabled children like same-age peers as far as possible. Severe mental problems do not develop overnight. Nor do they mean parents are necessarily "at fault" if they develop. But for the child at each age, parents have the opportunity to encourage positive attitudes and outgoing living skills. Using these opportunities may be parents' strongest weapon against emotional illness in the child.

Thus, knowing that keeping a young person dependent past the age of natural dependency will throw her into confusion when thrust out upon an uncaring world helps parents encourage new relationships and new activities, even though a part of them wants to protect the child forever.

Good mental health for parents as well as their disabled children would seem to involve the following concerns.

In infancy When a baby is diagnosed as disabled, parents should seek confirmation of the diagnosis if there is any doubt and then accept it. They should seek all available information about the disability, what it is and—where possible—what they can reasonably expect to happen in their baby's future. From the beginning, they should plan times together without their disabled baby, times to enjoy each other. They should also begin accommodating themselves to the fact that ideally, children are ready to leave home between the ages of eighteen and twenty-one, and that this applies to their disabled baby, too.

Training Seeking early training to minimize the baby's disabilities brings parents into contact with parents of other disabled babies, one of the strongest support networks. Parents frequently act as each other's therapists, talking out problems before they become major. Seeing the child in relation to his peers also helps parents and teachers spot problems in early, more easily treatable stages.

Schooling Wise parents develop strong ties of cooperation with their child's teacher. The child who knows that his parents and teacher respect each other and work together for his goodwill feels more secure in his environment.

Parents naturally teach their school-age children that "you are going to have to learn to get along with others" when they begin having problems with schoolmates or brothers and sisters. Thinking of our disabled children, too, as being eventually independent adults, we will also insist on good social behavior from them—common courtesies, good grooming, good table manners, "hands-off-others" policy, and so on.

I sometimes have the feeling that when parents see their developmentally disabled child suddenly exhibit outrageous or anti-social behavior at the age of eleven or thirteen, they are stunned. They ask themselves, Is this when it starts? Is this when he becomes impossible to control? If the child were not disabled, the same parents would probably say, "Look here, young man, you're not going to be permitted to behave that way!" and make it stick. Parents know that such behavior will stand in the way of their son's becoming a first-rate member of society.

Living in a family is, after all, a microcosm of living in the world. And beneath it all is the fact that to survive, we must get along. And so must our developmentally disabled children.

Adolescence These are the most difficult years for growing children and their parents. Problems that may have simmered for years suddenly erupt. Overnight, it seems, boys discover girls and vice versa. They are sensitive, funny, argumentative, sweet, and vulnerable. Parents can help by realizing that the feelings experienced by their disabled child are not so different from those of other teenagers. They should do as they would for other children their age—allow them access to sex education, increasing freedom to move about their community as they show they can handle it, and access to activities involving other teenagers.

THE NEED FOR SEX EDUCATION

Sexuality embodies a world of loveliness and crudity, of the joy of beautiful manners, of growing self-awareness and the embarrassment of snickers. It is enthralling and exciting, a world of friendship and profound sharing. At the same time, it is a world of fear, fumbling, wanting, and frustration. And AIDS. I am sick at heart, as a parent and a teacher, to realize we must tell our children about this dreadful syndrome and how it is transmitted. You be the judge. If you believe there is the slightest possibility your child will need this information someday, see that she receives it.

How our disabled children handle their sexual awakening depends so much on the attitudes of parents and other adults who share in their rearing and education. The impetus for facing this reality early is that only by doing so can we prepare children for adapting realistically to a life outside the total protection of their homes.

Some parents treat the subject of sexuality and disabled persons by ignoring it. (If we ignored their social behavior, they would be animals by the time they reached adulthood!) Parents who ignore sexual training and education as children grow may be inviting sexual misbehavior. We need to think out and acknowledge future possibilities for our children, and then train them so that they will have confident, realistic attitudes and develop habits to ensure their safety. (Don't go down dark streets alone; don't accept invitations to go places with people you don't know; don't open the door to strangers.)

Profoundly retarded individuals usually have multiple handicapping conditions. Awareness of sexuality is minimal or nonexistent. Mildly retarded and mild-to-moderately retarded children may show nearly as much interest in sexuality and affectionate relationships as nondisabled children.

Understandably, the greatest fear of parents of adolescents with handicapping conditions is that they will be sexually exploited. By projecting fear on their children, parents may actually hinder their growth toward becoming careful, confident adults. Far better for their mental health to allow them expanding freedom accompanied by realistic training.

Aside from the mechanics of learning to get about in the community, which will be discussed in a later chapter, parents need to talk with their children about the whys behind these don'ts: Don't let strangers touch you. Don't touch them. If someone asks you to touch him, tell the adult you are with. If you are alone, tell someone else—the movie usher, the salesperson, the grocery clerk, a police officer if available.

Explain, and try to elicit responses from your child, that people *own* their own bodies. People have a right to say no when someone wants to touch their bodies.

An excellent book for parents and teenagers, developed through close cooperation by parents of many religious faiths, teachers, sex therapists, and medical personnel, is Mary H. Moore's *Parent Partnership Training Program, Book 5: Developing Responsible Sexuality*. It contains step-by-step instruction for teaching your disabled child to become an aware, sexually responsible adult.

Prominent among parental fears for boys is that if they are unable to attract girlfriends, they will become homosexual. Homosexuality does not exist among persons who are mentally retarded to any greater degree than among other persons. Many people while growing up have had minor or passing homosexual encounters. If we impart to our sons and daughters positive, healthy attitudes about the opposite sex and expose them to social activities involving both sexes, their attention will, a vast majority of the time, be directed to members of the other sex.

Parents of both boys and girls worry about the effects of masturbation. It is a natural act of self-exploration in the very young. In adolescence it becomes a pleasurable, conscious activity practiced to greater or lesser degree by both boys and girls.

Dr. Grace H. Ketterman, in *The Complete Book of Baby and Child Care for Christian Parents,* advises dealing with adolescents "wisely and gently about masturbation. Explain to them [in words they can understand] about their developing bodies and sexual feelings. Teach them that these are natural functions for a loving marriage."

Because not too many young adults with handicapping conditions will marry, telling them to refrain from self-stimulation until marriage is unrealistic. However, physicians and psychologists agree that unless practiced to excess, masturbation is not harmful at any age and need not cause parents undue concern.

Denying our children any exposure to outside influences will certainly cut down on risks but does little to help them become independent. We will do our children the greatest good by training them to recognize potential dangers in the community and to avoid them.

"When you are waiting to take the bus home, if anyone offers you a ride in a car, say no," a parent might say. "Stand out of reach, and don't get into a conversation. When you get on the bus, sit near the driver if you can. Sit by someone who looks like Grandma. If anyone bothers you, tell the driver. He will know what to do." Riding the bus a few times with the child helps to reinforce this training.

Complete risk avoidance, however, might mean sheltering the child from any social contacts that could conceivably develop into a deeper relationship. It unfortunately denies the child the chance to experience a social relationship with a young person of the opposite sex—and to cope through successful interaction. It may also have the effect of casting a mystique about girls or about boys that develops into an unnatural fear and fascination at the same time.

Girls should be told about menstruation before they are likely to start their periods. "This is what grown-up women do and you will, too," their mothers may tell them. Questions about where babies come from should be treated in a matter-of-fact, low-key manner.

The idea of sexual intercourse between unmarried people is counter to many parents' most deeply held beliefs. We do all we can to protect our children, even after they reach adulthood, from situations in which they could be exploited. The unfortunate truth is that parents will not always be around to supervise.

Adults who are mentally retarded are usually actively aware of their limitations. They can profit from counseling on problem behaviors, sexuality, interpersonal relationships, marriage, and their feelings about their disability. The role of counselor requires patience, flexibility, and communication skills that elicit frankness and comprehension.

When people who have mentally handicapping conditions do wed, they usually decide, when properly counseled, not to have children. A sperm count done on the young man may prove him sterile. If he is not sterile, the importance of using condoms should be impressed upon him. Parents and their doctors together may decide what form of contraceptive is best for a daughter.

Discussing topics like masturbation or other interesting topics related to the body was always easier with Mike than with his older brother. Partly, it was because my husband and I had gone through it once, but it was also because Mike has a beautiful and simple acceptance of all parts of his body. His penis is no more an object of embarrassment or pride to him than his arm, his pubic hair no less interesting than the hair on his head. (I was having coffee with a friend the day he first noticed the growth of pubic hair. He came running into the kitchen—fully clothed—and cried, "Mom, I have curly hair like Jim!")

THE IMPORTANCE OF ACCEPTABLE BEHAVIOR

As with other areas of social behavior, adolescents who are mentally retarded gain most of their knowledge about sexual-related behavior from watching others—but with one important difference. Frequently, they do not understand the social cues in context. They use what they have gleaned incorrectly.

Watching reruns of "Happy Days" on TV, for instance, young girls may get the idea that it's all right to swoon all over a table in a restaurant to impress a boy who is sitting there. A boy may believe it is "ba-a-ad" to stand in the middle of a restaurant and jerk both thumbs up, or to go up to a girl he doesn't know and throw his arms around her or even try to kiss her. Such behavior, more than just annoying its recipient, is likely to frighten her as well.

We parents can minimize this source of pain and embarrassment for our children by trying to foresee consequences and helping them learn correct behavior before something unfortunate happens.

Before his marriage, one young man who is mentally retarded spent at least half the time at the monthly dances getting girls to sit on his lap and kissing them. Since his marriage, he continues the same practice! His wife, no more socially adept and somewhat shyer, merely stands beside him and laughs at his behavior. He is not deliberately trying to be promiscuous. He is merely continuing patterns that were successful for him and that, to him, mean good social behavior at dances. And, of course, they are not.

Another example of incorrect application of social-sexual cues concerns our own son. Mike is a naturally affectionate young man. For a while last year, he was having an awful struggle trying to sort out family affection from sexual expression. It happened during a time of increased body awareness for him. We are a kissin' and huggin' family. So Mike went through a period of trying to kiss me on the lips in an embrace straight out of a TV soap opera. His hugs were accompanied by annoying pelvic moves. I almost bopped him a couple of times!

Each time he repeated the behavior, I told him in flat-out terms that that was not the way you hugged and kissed members of your family. Then we actually practiced affection-type embraces such as putting your arm around someone's waist or over a shoulder and giving a peck on the cheek. I threw in a few reminders along the way that, of course, we keep our hands to ourselves around other people. People have a right not to be touched.

When your child behaves in a manner that tells you she is picking up inappropriate sexual-social cues, for heaven's sake don't let her think it's cute, no matter what her age! And don't assume she'll grow out of it. She may not. It could get her in trouble! (But don't leave her with the impression it's horrible of her, either.)

Most parents try conscientiously to understand their children's behavior. They may be more tolerant of erratic behavior from their disabled child than they would from his siblings. If your child demonstrates sexual behavior that leaves you confused or puzzled about what your attitude or response should be, ask someone who works with adolescents, preferably in the field of disabilities—his teacher, therapist, doctor, or social worker. These people have the advantage of working with many other children and should be able to answer your questions, give you guidance, and set your mind at rest. If you are uncomfortable teaching your child about sex, find a professional or a trusted relative or friend who can help you out.

Whether or not to teach sex education in schools, and how much information to impart, is often a bitterly contested issue involving religious and moral beliefs with the sad result that there seem to be no uniformly accepted rules governing conduct or prevention of pregnancy or of disease. Some sheltered workshops sponsored by parent groups schedule "rap" sessions in sex education under the guidance of a counselor. Clients may sign up for these classes.

It is not a subject parents can safely ignore.

"FRIENDSHIP! FRIENDSHIP! WHAT A BEAUTIFUL FRIENDSHIP!"

The friends our children select from among people they know might leave us cold. We would be more comfortable if they preferred others we found more favored.

Yet we owe it to our children to respect their judgment. Why? Picture your child when his school years are past. What will he be doing and with whom?

It may be easy now to shut out that vision because, after all, his sisters and brothers and their friends are around constantly. And he's part of the action, even if on the fringe. He's enjoying himself. The burden of initiating the sociability is not yet his. But it will be. You cannot regard siblings always as entertainers, cheerer-uppers, and social directors for the disabled child—much less as surrogate parents. You must encourage him to seek friends among those who will share his enjoyment in simple pleasures, including cartoons on television.

I have always loved the words to the song "Nature Boy" about loving and being loved in return. I never dreamed then how we would apply the song as a measuring stick to what we held as possibilities for Mike's future.

When he was young, he played house like other children and was "Daddy" surrounded by his sister's dolls. He often said, "When I grow up and have children..." But as he grew older, I realized he was saying it as a question, as though awaiting—or dreading—affirmation or denial. I would usually hug him and say, "You probably won't be a daddy, but you'll be a super uncle." And sometimes we'd talk about when Jim or Laurie got married and had children and Daddy and I would become grandparents and everyone would come to our house for family dinners and all the kids would want to play with Uncle Mike. It was a happy, realistic picture that delighted us both.

I have skirted the possibility of marriage for Mike. We are not opposed to marriage for him any more than we are for our other children. But people are more accepting today of choices other than marriage. Individuals need not feel left out if they do not marry and have children. A young person may grow up, live alone or with a roommate, in an apartment, or marry and not have children, or live with several other people his own age in a communal living arrangement, all without causing a flicker of an eye. This freedom of choice makes living in the community easier for our children with handicapping conditions.

Whatever happens, we parents owe it to our children—disabled or not—and to ourselves to help each of them prepare realistically and positively for their futures. Healthy sexual and social adjustments can make the difference between young persons who are bewildered by a world in which nothing is happening the way they'd always been told and young persons aware of their limitations, who can trust their perception of the world.

CHAPTER 16

Gearing Up
for Letting Go

I was watching our Labrador retriever one day. Four weeks earlier she had given birth to eight pups, her first litter. Sassy little things now that their eyes were open, they were practicing barking and lurching about on all fours. Not long ago they could only squirm around like giant blind larvae. They were voraciously hungry and greedy about it, too. But Mama, despite eating almost continuously when she wasn't nursing, was becoming skin and bones. Finally, she began refusing to nurse. A little mouth would attach itself to her nipple, and she would walk unconcernedly away, dragging the hapless pup until he dropped in a graceless bundle. We began supplementing their feed with huge pans of warm milk three times a day. Mama lounged near with a disinterested expression while they lapped milk. She knew they were big enough to be weaned, and so she had begun it. Her calm attitude as much as said, "This is the way to grow up, children. You're big enough to eat alone now."

Though it takes years longer, human parents can help their children through their own natural weaning process in several ways, to help defuse the children's (and the parents') fears about eventual separation. I remember once when Mike came home after ten days at camp. He looked thinner when he climbed off the bus. I felt a surge of pity as I pushed forward to meet him. Poor kid! He was probably sick and lonesome, and I hadn't been there when he needed me. Right? Wrong. On the way home I heard about the hikes and swimming and super-duper desserts until finally I said, "I suppose you wish you were still there."

"You bet!" Mike said. Well, that shot me down!

But listening to the happiness and confidence in his voice, I thought, *That's a compliment to his dad and me that Mike can go away and manage without his family. It means to me that he knows he's loved. He doesn't fear that going away from home a few days means we don't want him around anymore.*

Occasionally, when you think about your child leaving home eventually, look for opportunities to do a bit of "weaning":

- Assure her that you love her and that she will always be your child, just as your own parents still love you and consider you their child. (The child may see the humor of her mother being a grown-up child.)
- Let her know you have faith in her ability to accomplish tasks by letting her do things without interference, within limits of safety and common sense.
- Grant her occasional times away from home: visiting relatives, sleeping over at a friend's, overnight camping, or times at home with a sitter while you are gone overnight or longer.

Over the years, you have been training her in simple skills involving self-care, clothing care, and house and yard work. Now in adolescence is the time to refine those skills and remind your child that she must learn to do these things because "we don't want to continue doing for you what you are old enough and capable enough to do for yourself."

Sometimes it takes an outsider to convince us how capable our children actually are. A ten-year-old went to stay at a family care home for three weeks while his parents took a trip. It was his first time away from home. When the parents returned, they discovered that the care-parent had managed to toilet train him, a feat they had given up on. "How did you ever do it?" the mother exclaimed with gratitude.

"Well, why not? He's a big boy, and I have five other children in my care! I don't have time to do things for them they can do for themselves," the care-parent replied. Yet she had taken the time and been patient to toilet train him because, comparing him with the dozens of others she had in her care, she felt he was capable.

INDEPENDENT LIVING STEPS

As your child becomes increasingly more capable, you can work together on several steps toward independent living. Not all young people will be able to master each with equal success. But kids surprise you.

Cooking Give her more and more responsibilities in the kitchen. As you use your appliances, take time to teach her how to use them correctly: what "warm" means, what "broil" means, when you turn on the oven; the difference between "simmer" and "boil" on the range top. Show her how boiling water looks opposed to water that is simmering.

I consider the microwave oven one of the safest and most versatile appliances for Mike to use. Dishes stay cool while the food warms, bacon and sausage covered with a paper towel do not spatter when "fried," and frozen dinners can be prepared with a minimum of fuss or extra dishes. In addition, microwave ovens are simple to operate.

When Mike began fixing his own breakfasts and lunches on weekends, I used them as teachable moments. He likes scrambled eggs. Therefore, he had to learn first how to handle eggs when taking them from the refrigerator, how to crack them into a bowl without getting them all over the counter, how to beat them, add milk and salt without spilling, and how to regulate the temperature of the skillet. Then he needed to become dexterous with a spatula, to learn that certain foods stick when the pan isn't oiled, and to manipulate a heavy skillet with potholders. He also learned to scrub out the skillet after letting it soak.

We went step by step through each food that Mike learned to prepare. To make a roast beef sandwich, he had to learn to use a large carving knife safely, and to wash and dry it without cutting himself or the tea towel. He learned to replace cold foods in the refrigerator after use, to replace lids before returning catsup or mustard to the cupboard, and to remind me when something is used up. Instead of having him tell me, eventually I encouraged him to write it down for our shopping list.

The natural time to help her build a file of simple favorite recipes is when your child is enthusiastic about learning to cook. Include plans for entire well-balanced meals and nutritional reminders. If her reading skills are limited, use pictures of processes and products, and color code the measurements. Fingernail enamel is available in all colors. Invest in a few colors to mark a set of measuring cups—red for the one-cup measure, blue for the one-half cup, and so on—and then paint the cup measures in recipes to correspond. Do the same for measuring spoon sizes. (Use one red cup of Bisquick and one blue cup of water.)

Shopping Grocery shopping makes the most sense when it's tied directly to the child's needs. If he has printing or writing skills, ask him to "please add milk to the shopping list." If he lacks these skills, begin using cut-out pictures of products and foods. You can sometimes find tiny pictures of appropriate products that you can paste on cards as part of the recipe. Use an old deck of playing cards for your shopping list. Glue pictures of products you commonly buy onto the cards for a permanent file. Then to shop, merely pull out the cards you need, and return them to the file after the shopping trip. Labels from cans are good for gluing on cards. Then he can look for brand and size as well as generic product.

In the beginning, take him shopping with you. Give him part of the list. Make a game of it. Meet back at the checkout. Eventually, let him shop alone. Later refinements of shopping coincide with budgeting: estimating how much each item will cost, counting his money to be sure he has enough, and using a calculator. Teach him not to buy items not on his list.

Learning housekeeping skills More than just making her bed or washing the dishes, you can add vacuuming (including how to change the bag), washing floors and windows, and cleaning bathrooms so that they are sanitary. Make sure she realizes that many cleaning products are poisonous, how to use them economically, and how to recognize the poison warning.

Maintaining personal hygiene Sloppy hygiene is not confined to disabled children, though they may be less aware than others when their body odor is offensive, their clothing is soiled, or their hair is dirty. From toilet-training days on, we showed Mike how to wash his hands with soap after using the bathroom or before working in the kitchen.

Graduating from the days of being bathed by Dad or Mom after dinner, Mike was very happy to shower himself—until we discovered that his shower was just that, equivalent to running under the lawn sprinklers! Then it was back to showing him how to lather a washcloth with soap and really scrub himself, especially the groin area, under the arms, the neck and ears, and to wash his hair with similar energy.

For years, Mike "forgot" to brush his teeth until reminded. Then an unexpected bonus of cavities one year helped him make the connection between clean teeth and sound teeth.

For girls, good personal hygiene must also include understanding how to use sanitary pads and tampons, when to change them, and how to dispose of them. Girls should also be taught how to wash out stained underwear.

Grooming The words *look nice* and *smell nice* always appealed to Mike's sensitivities. Also, becoming a young man has increased his desire to be attractive to young women. So it was with very little encouragement that Mike began using underarm deodorant, learning to use an electric razor and check his face for missed whiskers before he considered the job finished, and wanting to wash his hair often and carry a comb in his pocket.

Caring for clothing and shoes Becoming clothes-conscious is more than just buying good-looking clothes. A few years ago I demanded more help around the house. Among other things, it was agreed that each child would learn how to use the washing machine and dryer and either do a load of family wash a week or do personal laundry. It's the best thing I ever did! When Jim moved out at the age of twenty, he probably had fewer loads of ruined laundry at the Laundromat than any other young man newly out on his own.

Mike and Laurie learned how to sort laundry, how to wash dark cloths in cool water and whites in warm water, how to measure detergent, and how to clean out the filter traps. They also gradually began to hang up their clothes at night so that they wouldn't have to be washed after only one wearing if they were not dirty or perspiration-stained or wrinkled.

When it's time to buy new clothes, Mike is gradually taking more responsibility. A card he carries with him lists his clothing and shoe sizes. Before we shop, he tells me what he wants and we find it in a catalog. That gives him an idea what it will cost. We also discuss colors and where he plans to wear the item. It isn't always easy to be dressed appropriately for the occasion. He is still not yet comfortable locating a salesperson and asking permission to try on clothing; nor is he sure when he does try it on that it fits correctly (especially if it is the wrong size but he really wants it). We're working on it.

Taking medication Many developmentally disabled children are on daily medication. Mike is not. But when he has a headache, instead of playing ministering angel (he gets lots of loving without my having to award myself nurse points), I now ask him what he needs for it.

"Aspirin?" he suggests.

"Good idea. Bad headache or little headache?"

"Little headache. One aspirin. Right?"

"Right."

Children can learn to self-administer even complicated routines of medication. If your child will be on medication all his life, now may be the time to begin training, under your close scrutiny. Using the little pill boxes that come with seven separate compartments for the days of the week may help.

Developing problem-solving skills Informal sessions in which various problem situations are brought up can help the youngster learn to break down problems into simple steps. It may be human nature to put off facing problems until they occur, but a wiser move is to anticipate problems and discuss solutions with your child.

When we installed smoke alarms at home, we talked about what we would do if there were a fire. Mike had no idea. Laurie had learned at school about closing doors, feeling a door for heat before you open it, breaking a window, and laying a blanket or other protective item over the sill before attempting to climb out. We also talked about escape routes and walked through several alternate routes, depending on where the fire was. We also made sure current police, fire, and paramedic numbers were pasted to each telephone. Living in southern California, we also practiced earthquake safety "drop and cover" drills.

Since Mike was by then riding the city bus line, we talked about what he should do if he missed his stop or boarded the wrong bus. To my surprise, he said he wouldn't be lost; he'd be on the bus. His concept was that "the bus is the vehicle that takes you from school to workshop." It didn't embrace the idea that a network of buses went to all sorts of places. Finally, he decided that he would get off. "Then what?" I asked. First, he thought he would walk. Then, he decided he might get lost, so he should telephone home instead. That led to the idea that he should ride the bus until there were some stores where he could find a telephone; and that, in turn, led to the realization that he should have two "emergency quarters" with him all the time in case he did have to call.

Saint John's Child Study Center, a division of St. John's Hospital and HealthCare, in Santa Monica, California, has developed a series of situational problems useful in discussion sessions with developmentally disabled adults.

What should you do if:

- there's a fire at home?
- you realize you are on the wrong bus?
- you lose your bus money?
- you are home alone and a stranger comes to the door?
- you find a wallet or a purse?
- you feel sick and can't go to work?
- your good friend is very ill in the hospital?
- someone teases you?
- a stranger offers you a ride?

In discussing these situations with your child, don't try to tackle them all at the same time. When you ask her the question, accept the first answer seriously. Then break down the solution into steps that will follow logically for her: "You've lost your bus money. What would you do?" She may say something that isn't sensible as far as you're concerned, such as, "Ask somebody to give me more money." You say, "I see. What else could you do? Where do you take the bus?" If she takes the bus home from work, you might want to suggest she go back to work and attempt to borrow the money from someone she knows or use the telephone to call someone who could pick her up.

Learning to tackle problems a small step at a time may help your child to think clearly without panic when a problem does arise and she is on her own.

Using transportation   In midsummer of 1980 the Los Angeles Rapid Transit District announced that all of its new buses would be fitted to accept wheelchairs. Other cities have made or are making similar modifications. This trend speaks well for public awareness and regard for civil rights of citizens with handicapping conditions.

Several years before the time a child moves out on his own, his parent or foster parent can begin teaching him his way around the city. Start with short neighborhood walks, then go by car or bus into town. It can be a grand adventure. If he is able to read, teach him to "navigate" for you by reading all the street and road information signs you pass. Traveling by bus, he can look up routes and boarding times in bus schedules. He can familiarize himself with landmarks that help him locate his stop, learn to transfer, and make correct change. Make simple maps with the child, and he can color in his house and all the town's landmarks—the schools, churches, and shopping malls. The feeling of confidence imparted to the young person gives you a corresponding helping of pride and joy as you see independence coming a step closer for your child and for yourself.

Here are suggested steps for learning to ride the bus:

- Memorize correct bus number or numbers.
- Locate the number on the bus.
- Ride together to a preset destination.
- Let the youngster ride alone when he feels ready.
- See him off, then meet him at the destination.
- Split a hot fudge sundae to celebrate his victory.

Ordering food in a restaurant   If possible, collect menus from restaurants ahead of time. (You may want to visit McDonald's and similar places and copy down their prices and fare also.) Compare prices of similar items on several menus. Make up your own restaurant game. First, decide how much each person can spend. Then, "place" your order. A pocket calculator is handy to add it up to compare with your budgeted figure. Next is the trade-off. If the child's choices put her over budget, encourage her to substitute—a cola for a milk shake. If she simply must have the steak sandwich when everyone else is having a hamburger, she might use up her beverage money altogether.

When you go to a restaurant, go dutch. Take the calculator along to help your child resist waiters' suggestions to add expensive side dishes or drinks to the meal. Don't forget to compute tax and tip.

Knowing home safety   This knowledge is especially important for the child who will eventually live in an apartment alone or with another developmentally disabled person. Make up a poster list, using simple stick figures, of each set of routines your child will need to know. For instance, one poster might be "What to Do Before You Go to Bed or Leave Home" and show, with a combination of words and pictures, a stick figure locking each door, locking windows, turning off room heaters, turning down thermostats, checking that the range or oven is turned off, and that no water is running in the house.

Another poster might detail "What to Do in Case of Kitchen Fire." A stick figure observes a grease fire. He turns off the heat source and sprinkles bicarbonate of soda on the flames. (Keeping a box of soda handy to the range is always a good idea.)

Similar posters can be created giving step-by-step instructions for what to do if you smell gas, if you wake up and smell smoke, or if there is a fire.

Using the telephone   Help your child begin her own list of important telephone numbers, either on a poster or in a book. A small picture beside a number can help her easily recognize the appropriate numbers for police, fire, or paramedics. Add personal emergency numbers for family members, reliable neighbors, or social workers to this list. Fill a pocket-size address book with these numbers or even a list small enough to fit in the wallet so she can carry it with her.

Budgeting money   No matter how little money your child will be handling, he needs to learn that no one can spend more money than he actually has (even though the reverse often appears to be true). Mike is poor on math skills, but he uses a collection of envelopes marked "bowling," "snacks," "cassette tapes," "bus pass," and so on that make up his items of expenditure. On each envelope is marked the amount he needs to put inside each payday. The training will carry over to the time when the envelopes read "rent," "utilities," and "clothing."

After school Mike worked at a sheltered workshop, so called because workers are sheltered from the usual demands of a job. When he began receiving small checks for his work, we went to the market near home where I usually shopped, and he filled out a check-cashing card. Sometimes he stopped there after work by himself to cash his check and buy himself a soda or TV fan magazine. He also had a minuscule bank account and learned how to endorse his check for deposit and to fill out a deposit slip.

It is also desirable to get an identification card. In California this card is obtained from the Department of Motor Vehicles and resembles a license, with picture and physical description, and is valid identification for establishing identity when cashing checks.

Making full use of community resources   If the young person is to live in the same community as her parents or foster parents, they can help the transition in another way: explore with the young adult community resources that are free or relatively inexpensive and accessible by public transportation.

Near where we lived at that time was an enclosed shopping mall with two major department stores, several specialty stores, and fast-food stops. Mike loved to shop there. He walked there alone to buy a music tape or just to treat himself to a soda and popcorn. This advance in independence came naturally because the bus that brought Mike home from his workshop dropped him off at the mall. Walking home from the mall daily made solo shopping trips to the mall a logical extension.

A nearby community college offered extension classes for persons with disabilities, among them an afternoon swimming class. I talked it over with Mike, and he decided he'd like to join the class. We consulted the bus schedules. After workshop we found that instead of riding home on the bus, Mike could transfer to a second bus that went by the college. So he joined the class, taking his bathing suit and towel with him when he left in the morning.

Both activities, independent shopping and the swimming class, are outgrowths of activities closer to home. For some years, Mike had been walking the dog to a park a few blocks away, running down to the neighborhood grocery store to buy milk or eggs, or even getting himself to the bowling lanes in an emergency.

Especially good are community programs that are continuing, where a child of any age can feel a sense of familiarity and welcome, such as at church, the theater matinee on Saturday afternoon, or the local library's weekly story time or films.

For several years, the Parks and Recreation Department of West Covina has sponsored a monthly Friday night dance for young people who have mentally handicapping conditions and are age sixteen and over. Fifty to one hundred and fifty people eager for social interaction joyously attend the event. On their first visit they fill out an application, which adds their name to the mailing list for future dances. Each month they pay one dollar. Each month a theme is chosen. Games, decorations, and refreshments all reflect the theme. Young men and women arrive about seven, some from private homes, some from small family care homes, foster families, or fairly large facilities. Nearly all are well groomed. Good social behavior is stressed. Staff persons are assisted by chaperones who are young, friendly, and always ready to participate to draw in the lonely or shy or newcomer.

Parents can infect their about-to-fly young person with a sense of fun and adventure as they set about to see exactly how much in their communities the young adult can take advantage of later in safety and with confidence.

Reliving memories Most parents stow away mementos of their child's growing years. It's time to get out those shoe boxes and put those mementos to work. A scrapbook—it doesn't have to be elaborate, just durable—makes a wonderful family project. Some parents have always kept scrapbooks for each child. In these days of low-cost extra prints and accessible photocopying machines, it's no problem to duplicate grade cards, special awards, and programs as well as add photo reprints.

The child can see himself growing through the pages of his album even as the number of experiences grows. When he is living semi- or independently, his album will give him an unmeasurable sense of family and might ease lonely hours by bringing back happy memories and keeping fresh family occurrences he has forgotten. It might help him to realize that he is still part of the family, although he, like his brothers and sisters, now lives apart.

All the effort you now devote to enhancing a child's enjoyment of hobbies and sports will give you anxiety-free hours later when instead of picturing the child sitting alone and bored in an apartment somewhere, you can realistically visualize him bowling or swimming or taking pictures or bus rides and enjoying the company of others.

CHECK OUT FEDERAL PROGRAMS

When your child reaches eighteen (earlier if there is financial need), he is probably eligible for federal aid in the form of Supplemental Security Income (SSI). This program makes monthly cash payments to disabled people who don't own much in the way of property (home ownership does not count) or other assets and who don't have much income. A severely mentally retarded person may be eligible for these payments.

A parent, guardian, or other responsible person may apply on behalf of the mentally retarded person and get a formal decision on eligibility. The child's birth certificate and medical proof of his disability should be taken along when the application is made. Once eligibility is established, the amount received each month will vary with each person. Some people receive less because they have other income. Others receive more because they live in a state that adds money to the federal payment.

People living in a public institution generally are not eligible for SSI payments. However, people who live in publicly operated community residences serving no more than sixteen people may be eligible. People living in their own or their parents' home may also be eligible.

"HOW CAN I TELL IF MY CHILD QUALIFIES?"

A mentally retarded child under eighteen (or under twenty-one and attending school) is considered disabled if it is shown that his IQ is 59 or less, or 60 through 69 with marked dependence, in relation to age, upon others for meeting basic personal needs and a physical or other mental impairment that restricts function and development. He may also be eligible if it is seen that his level of achievement is less than half that of other children his age.

A mentally retarded adult is considered disabled if it is shown that his IQ is 49 or less, or 50 through 69 with an inability to perform routine, repetitive tasks and a physical or other mental impairment resulting in restriction of function. Severe mental or social incapacity with marked dependence on others may also be grounds for eligibility.

Children may be eligible and yet not qualify for funds because their parents' income is too high. When the children reach the age of eighteen, however, the parents' income is no longer a factor when deciding eligibility.

WHAT THE SCHOOLS CAN DO

Ten years ago, few schools considered it part of their job to teach disabled children essentials of getting along in the community. Now, working closely with neighborhood sheltered workshops, high schools with a student body that integrates slow learners and other children with special needs stress habit training in school and workshop programs that will help children get along better independently.

Being on time, being dependable, dressing appropriately, conversing in a manner that enables clear exchange of information, and getting along with others are only some of these habits. The workshop is designed to use the skills of the workers, no matter what their level. They contract for simple jobs in the community, such as assembling components of prepackaged kits, and the workers are paid a percentage of minimum wage based on their individual productivity. Many sheltered workshops, also called training workshops, are founded by parent groups.

Parents frequently complain that their youngsters learn nothing in sheltered workshops. They are under the impression that children are being trained in some particular skill that will lead them to an adequately paying job in the marketplace.

Workshop leaders believe it is better to train workers to achieve good work habits rather than learn specific skills. They contend that potential employers have made it clear that if they are given young men and women to work with who have good work habits, plus trustworthiness, honesty, and loyalty (those old-fashioned virtues again!) they, the employers, are happy to train them in the specific skills needed for specific jobs.

Mike came home from work one day, and as we were getting lunch together, he spilled some iced tea. "I can't do anything right," he blurted. Unusual for him.

"Who says?" I asked.

"The custodian."

At eighteen, Mike was experiencing his first summer job as part of a school workshop program sponsored by the federal Comprehensive Employment Training Act (CETA). His job was custodial work under a young man who was hired as a summer custodian for one of the schools.

We sat down for lunch, and I tried to get him to talk about it. Mike doesn't like to talk about unpleasant things that involve his feelings. He denied the custodian had said anything. Press though I might, he refused to say more.

I wasn't really surprised when, the next day, the director in charge of coordinating summer jobs called.

"Mike isn't doing well at his job," he said.

First reaction: If I was there, I know he could do it right. Second reaction: The supervisor probably isn't used to dealing with developmentally disabled kids and isn't getting through to him. Third reaction and the one I say: "What is the problem?"

"Do you have trouble with Mike being stubborn?"

"Yes," I said reluctantly. Once Mike gets it into his head he wants to do his work a certain way, it takes a herd of elephants to make him do it differently.

"The custodian says he gives Mike jobs like sweeping and raking. Mike tells him when he's finished. But he's not finishing the job the way the custodian wants it done."

Fourth reaction: Is he really saying the custodian wants him out? I say, "What shall we do?"

"We're willing to work with him, but it would help if you would talk to Mike on your end."

Relief. "We certainly will! When he's working for others, he must do things the way they want them done. He has to learn what it means to work for someone who is paying him good money."

"Well, I was hoping you'd feel that way. Talk to you next week."

I cradled the phone, thinking. It would be so easy to believe that that particular custodian got out of bed on the wrong side and was just picking on Mike. After all, Mike got along fine with the supervisor on his last job. Maybe he's not a person who should be supervising job training for people with handicapping conditions. Still, he's probably more interested in getting the job done than about hurting someone's feelings. He has to be.

Painful truth time: No matter what kind of a person the custodian is, he was temporarily Mike's supervisor. Though Mike will work for many different people, his jobs will have one thing in common: His work must please the employer, or he won't have a job very long.

And then I realized that was what the workshop leader meant when she said, "We don't teach skills. We teach work habits and attitudes." As if to underscore the point, Mike's supervisor sent home the following job rules, which embody this commonsense approach to job training for developmentally disabled persons.

Rules on the Job:

1. Always pay attention to us when we show you how to do a chore. Look at us; do not look elsewhere.
2. When we show you a way to do a chore, that is the way you are to do that chore.
3. Work at a steady pace. Do not stop every four minutes to wander around or tell us something that has nothing to do with the job.
4. The only time you are not to be working is when you are on your fifteen-minute break. You are not to be sitting down on the job.
5. Check your work. Does it look good? When you finish your work, come to us to see what to do next. Do not wait for us to come to you.
6. If you are not sure how to do a job, ask questions. Don't just say, "Right" or "I understand," when you don't understand.

Summer job experiences are important for young people while they are still living at home and possibly still attached, though only a couple of hours a day, to high school. In this way, though they may be made to feel they aren't performing well in one area, they have strong support in other areas of their lives, which helps them face and work on shortcomings—in job training in this case—with greater confidence.

GETTING A JOB

Parents sometimes hesitate to take advantage of job training programs in the community. They may be unable to conceive that their child will ever be capable of traveling by herself to a job training facility. Or they may fear that the job will make the child ineligible for federal and state aid to disabled persons. The Social Security Administration and state social services do not consider the performance of simple tasks under constant supervision—such as in a sheltered workshop—at nominal pay for such work as evidence that a person is capable of self-support. If a mildly retarded person does become self-supporting, she will be developing her own program of covered employment under Social Security.

Here are possibilities that may be available in your area.

Work-study programs These programs, also called work-experience programs, are actually part of the public school education at the high-school level. In regular high schools, students can receive grade credit for working in a local business or industry, such as food service, child care, or hospital training, or gaining skills as a paraprofessional, such as physical therapy aide or dental assistant.

Parents of a child with special needs can check with their child's teacher. Sometimes students are not given the opportunity to work in the community directly from school but instead have the option of attending a sheltered workshop part of their school day. There they are expected to learn work habits to prepare them for real jobs later.

Sheltered workshops Described earlier, sheltered workshops offer the largest opportunity for a child to gain experience working outside the home. Parents interested in locating a workshop can probably do so through several sources: a parent group (many community workshops were begun by parent groups and continue to be sponsored by Retarded Citizens Association affiliates); the district office of the local public high school; or the city or county social services office.

Many workshops call themselves training workshops, which

may be a misnomer, since it is the exception for workshops to actively train personnel to work elsewhere in the community. A dedicated, aggressive leadership that believes in the value of mainstreaming could survey community needs that workshop employees would be capable of filling and train them accordingly.

Workshops also may provide employee counseling and training in personal living skills. A few of them provide comprehensive projects outside the workshop, giving on-the-job training in farming, housework, gardening, and maintenance work.

Activity centers   Activity centers are designed to take a severely mentally retarded person out of isolation and help him become less dependent. Nonresidential, these centers are usually located in the heart of a city, accessible by private vans with lifts or community transportation. Social development, personal adjustment, grooming, and independent traveling are stressed. Saint John's Child Study Center is a good example of a well-run program.

Federal-state vocational rehabilitation programs   Voc-rehab programs are organized throughout the country on state, county, and local levels. There is a much greater emphasis on skill training toward specific employment than there is in sheltered workshops. Counselors may place clients in competitive jobs, sheltered workshops, or homebound work, according to skills.

To qualify for services, people must have a physical or mental handicapping condition that makes them substantially disabled for employment. There must also be a reasonable expectation that they will be employable after training.

Disability assessment, work evaluation, counseling, and job placement are free at any voc-rehab office. Voc-rehab agencies differ widely in ability to provide help. If persons are not receiving services the parents believe they are entitled to, they may appeal to the state director of vocational education for a grievance hearing.

Local vocational training programs   Parents willing to become actively involved can work to improve their children's community job opportunities. One effective means is to contact your child's high-school teacher and/or principal. If they are enthusiastic about mainstreaming, you should get cooperation. The next step is to gather a committee of like-minded citizens—parents like you and other interested parties—and look over your community. What jobs are out there that can be filled capably by your children? Pay a call on these businesses. Whether it's product oriented like a local bottling plant or service oriented like a custodial maintenance firm, there are jobs the children can fill.

Some groups have worked out arrangements whereby businesses agree to hire developmentally disabled persons at half salary for six months. At the end of that time, each employee is evaluated and either retained at full salary or let go.

"If a child is only mildly retarded," believes one high-school special education teacher, "his best chance of getting a job is through someone he knows: either at the plant where his father or his mother works, or through someone they know, who knows the kid as a person instead of a label."

Parents and strong parent groups can campaign in their communities for more jobs for their children by getting the word out that they are dependable and trustworthy. Newspaper campaigns, visits to the city council and to area businesses and clubs—all can make a positive difference in a community's awareness of and reception to its citizens who are mentally retarded.

HOW COMMUNITIES CAN HELP

Communities can help not only by allowing citizens with special needs access to jobs within their abilities. They can also lend support to decent housing. Legally, mentally retarded adults have as much right to live in safe neighborhoods as other citizens, to use public transportation and public recreation areas. Dr. Richard Koch has for years pleaded for a mix of low- and middle-income housing in all areas of the city so that all people may live close to their jobs, not only persons with handicapping conditions.

Americans like to think of themselves as fair people who live and let live. Yet, time after time, when community residents apply for licenses to care for a specified number of developmentally disabled adults, they are met by obstinate opposition from businesspeople, private citizens, politicians, and Realtors. They have no more idea about the lives of people who live in such homes than they do about operating nuclear power plants.

A common example is that of a home on a residential street in a Los Angeles suburb. A survey of the neighborhood in the spring of 1980 revealed no complaints by neighbors. The home that had been in operation for five years housed forty developmentally disabled adults, many of whom had jobs and came and went freely about the community. Suddenly, a city councilman instituted proceedings to rezone the area and deny the home a new license, citing complaints by neighbors that people from the home were "wandering around the neighborhood."

The city council voted 3–2 to rescind the house's license. But during a subsequent appeal, it was learned that the councilman who filed the original complaint had bought, just two months prior to the case, a house two doors from the home as a rental income property! Just one man, greedy to maximize profits on an investment, cared so little for his fellow humans that he willfully jeopardized the home of forty adults who had never harmed him in any way. The case had a happy ending: Los Angeles Superior Court handed down a decision in favor of the home that said that a city has no right to deny developmentally disabled citizens the right to live in a residential area.

Whether parents like it or not, they often find themselves crusading for the rights of all disabled people to secure those rights for their own child. Thus, even though your child may be living comfortably and loved and protected within the circle of his own family, you will look around the community—and look ahead—at job opportunities, housing potential, and transportation to determine where effort is needed now to make it the child's community tomorrow.

CHAPTER 17

*Independence
at Last*

Comes a point when children's confidence is at a peak. If you keep
them back, you gradually erode their confidence that they can
move ahead.

> —Evis M. Coda, M.D.
> Consultant and former medical director
> St. John's Child Study Center
> Santa Monica, California

T wo things happened that helped shape my thinking on independence for developmentally disabled adults. One was
seeing ten men sitting docilely on a bench in the sunshine.
They were all youngish and apparently able-bodied. They "lived" in
a moderate-size residential facility. They did nothing all day. Was
their somnolent state due to routine drugging each morning (a
practice now outlawed)?

"Well, what do you expect?" said the director, a rather scruffy,
take-it-or-leave-it person. "They've been in a state hospital all their
lives. We just got 'em mainstreamed."

If that was mainstreaming, I'm a Lilliputian mongoose! Had they
ever received training in independent living skills?

The other significant occurrence was reading a book written by
the father of a boy with Down's syndrome. The boy was high
functioning. The father was evidently well-off. After his wife's
death, he gave up his business because he thought he owed it to his
son. He spent the rest of his life traveling about the world with his

son. The father died when his son was in his thirties. The child died of a minor infection within a few months. *What a needless sacrifice of a father's life,* I thought. *Years of his life, thousands upon thousands of dollars, spent for the continuous entertainment of one person. Had the son been nondisabled,* I wondered, *would the father have felt the same sacrificial need?* Between these two extremes lies a wide range of possibilities for independent and semi-independent living.

The following is abridged from an editorial by Margaret Lewis that appeared in *Down's Syndrome News,* published by Down's Syndrome Congress, in October 1983:

On Being Tender

There is a dilemma between proving that children with Down's syndrome and other handicaps have potential, and running the risk of kicking, quite cruelly, some parent whose cherished child will never go to classes for the educable retarded or perhaps never speak at all.

The one thing we share as parents of handicapped children is the vulnerability we each inherited when our particular child was born. That automatic humbling creates a kinship of pain unlike any other.

If you were dealt a "high functioning" child, take a few minutes and role play the part of the parent whose child doesn't walk or even feed himself. How would you insulate yourself from the "what did I do wrong?" feelings, the insidious comparisons with some mother's child who does so many things so well? There is enormous need to contradict the public image of retarded children as helpless and hopeless. But in so doing let us remember to lift up our fellow parents whose children only too well fit the public's preconceived notion of what it is to be handicapped.

WHAT IS INDEPENDENT LIVING?

Independent living is usually considered living on one's own, managing one's own life, making one's own decisions. More and more young people with special needs are at present living independently. More young people are also living semi-independently and independently of their parents in numerous other ways. Some are mainstreamed, living in apartment buildings with a heterogeneous mixture of citizens but still receiving services from case managers, counselors, parents, or other advisors who help them out with such things as paperwork, problems of family living, transportation, and jobs.

Others live in apartments maintained expressly for persons with handicapping conditions. A director lives in the same building and oversees his clients' lives to a greater or lesser degree. Frequently, these apartments have general regulations, such as clients must be in their own apartments by ten, may not have visitors after that hour, and perhaps have their financial affairs supervised by the caretaker.

A shift is under way in living arrangements for developmentally disabled adults across the nation. Fewer placements are being sought in board-and-care homes (one to six clients), and demand is increasing for placement in apartments and other units that encourage greater personal responsibility and independence.

The growth of self-advocacy organizations is a sign of the new awareness among people about physical and mental disabilities and a willingness to recognize and deal with them.

"LABEL JARS, NOT PEOPLE"

The above advice comes to you from Richard, a young man who was born out of wedlock. Born with mental and physical disabilities, Richard was given up at birth and sent to a state hospital. There he remained until California began the move to take people out of institutions and place them in communities. Richard went to a family care home. He caused so much trouble he was moved out and sent to another home.

It was there that Richard says he learned how to love. At the age of twenty, he was accepted into a community independent living training program. Living on his SSI payments at first, Richard completed the training and is now self-supporting as a custodian in a large office building.

Richard is also a member of the Speaker's Bureau of People First of California. People First is a self-advocacy group begun in California, now with groups in Oregon and Colorado. Group members emphasize learning how to solve problems. Using this skill, they teach other disabled people how to start their own group, how to elect officials, and how to talk to politicians to get what they want and need in the community.

Individuals interested in starting their own branch of People First may write for a free copy of their newsletter. (See the address in the Appendix.)

"WHY CAN'T SHE JUST LIVE AT HOME AND BE INDEPENDENT?"

This question often comes from parents whose child has grown into a well-behaving, pleasant-to-be-around healthy young person. She is a delight to be with and often elicits comments from the parents' friends on what a good job they've done rearing her.

"She can be just as independent at home." When parents tell this to one social worker, he often responds by asking them, "Would you believe it if she were not developmentally disabled?"

"That's not the same thing," the parents protest.

But isn't it? We have struggled to rear our children just like nondisabled kids. Now are we to take away their feelings that they can also be semi-independent when they reach adulthood? The fact that "they are no trouble" is really not the issue. At issue is the fact that our disabled adult children still have a lot more growing they can do, and it will not happen unless they are given the opportunity. Parents cannot help being protective and involved with children, even adult children, under their own roof.

Once another parent asked me to accompany her to find a home for her daughter, who was twenty-six. We visited several places, some not bad and one about which the daughter was very enthusiastic. It was a former private school on generous grounds that housed an active coed population of sixty young mentally retarded adults.

But finally, after she had "forgotten" to keep several appointments with social workers and home directors, the mother admitted tearfully that she did not want Dottie to go: "She's all I have. What would I do without her? I need her check. And I would be alone." She would indeed be alone. Her teenage son had left the previous year without finishing high school. Her husband had vanished several years earlier.

Well-trained developmentally disabled adult children such as Dottie probably give parents the least trouble of all their children. Additionally, that Supplemental Security Income check, for which they may be eligible at age eighteen, goes to the parent or care provider until such time as the child is managing his own affairs. Sometimes it is more for the parents' convenience than they would care to admit that the child remains in the home past maturity.

Such parents have a beautifully behaved adult child who looks up to them and respects their decisions at a time when the other children are perhaps testing their authority. They have a steady trained worker who does many of the rote jobs around home. And they have that additional income.

But for parents to equate their desires with those of their adult child, or to put these considerations ahead of the adult child's continued growth toward independence, is selfish indeed. We do not rear our other children with an eye toward being repaid when they reach maturity. Why on earth would we think we "deserve" now to have a developmentally disabled child stay home, work for us for free, and bring in extra income?

There are no easy solutions. Dr. Richard Koch, in *Understanding the Mentally Retarded Child: A New Approach*, writes, "Years ago I didn't recommend routinely that the retarded adult move out of the home. But, I've learned by bitter experience that if you wait until there's a crisis, the adjustment is much worse for all concerned."[1]

Society generally disapproves of a clinging parent who keeps one child at home long after she should be out and about in the world. But the time is not quite here when society says to the parent of a developmentally disabled adult child, "Your child also has a right to her own life."

Richard, the young People First advocate, urged these words on parents: "You won't be on this earth forever. Don't treat your son or daughter like a child. Try to let go the apron strings. Let them be adult."

Why is it so hard to let go? Even though you may have believed in a general way that your child should leave home upon maturity, the closer it comes, the less welcome it may be. Your other children, emerging into adulthood, probably chafe for independence. (Many times the parents' feelings are mutual.) But your disabled child is still so dependent! You know his weaknesses and have fears about his ability to get along without you. You may even picture him being lonely, getting lost, eating poorly, or being hurt intentionally or unwittingly by insensitive strangers. Or even worry, as one overly conscientious mother did, about what the neighbors would think if she let go.

But there is another side, too. Most parents take vicarious pride in being seen with a son who excelled in sports or scholarship at school. In the same way, we parents of disabled children take pride when others, seeing us with our children, recognize the worthiness of our achievement. We have accomplished something few others have been privileged or called upon to do: We have successfully parented a well-adjusted disabled person, who is as ready as he'll ever be to step into the world—his world—without us.

"One of the easiest placements, with no bad emotional effects on either the parent or the child," recalls a California caseworker, "was of a young man who was eighteen. When he was just a baby, the parents had been advised to rear him in as normal a manner as possible, treating him like the other children, and to expect that he would leave their home when he was an adult, just like the other children. Now they wanted help in locating a nearby family home setting for him so that they could visit him on weekends. It worked out beautifully, with no complications. He's happy, he's emotionally independent, and he's still part of the family. And a large part of the credit is due to his family."

I remember one mother of a thirty-year-old insisting she'd never "put her child away." Heavens! To put a child away conjures visions of musty, moldy 1930s movies with saucer-eyed waifs in rags peering pathetically up at you! Realize that what you are doing is the same as you would be likely to do in similar circumstances with any of your other children, sharing the enjoyable task of helping them find their first outside home.

But when your child does move out, do not expect that everything will run smoothly. She will have times of homesickness and uncertainty. So will you! In addition, you may be plagued by a sense of "did I (or did we) do the right thing?"

One good antidote to such misgivings is to remind yourself with pride that she is able to move away now because of the emotional support and years of good training you parents provided.

If the first or the second or the fourth living arrangement doesn't work out, it seems to me that the wise parent would resist the impulse to suggest that the child move back home. (Erma Bombeck recommends, "When the child leaves the nest—move the nest.") However, if after a year or so the adult child, you, and his social worker or caseworker all feel it is in his best interests to return to your home, it's possible, isn't it?

What happens more frequently during this year, though, is that the parents discover the joy of personal freedom and of new freedom to be with each other. They lend increasing encouragement to their child to make the most of his new independence. He is still family. He will always be family. But they have made it possible, through love and sacrifice and self-discipline, for him to continue to grow as a unique person.

WHERE WILL HE MOVE?

Just as a single type of housing and community is not equally satisfactory to all citizens, so no single residential arrangement meets the needs of all adults with developmental disabilities. All states have social service agencies that list available residential facilities within the state. Many states have agencies like California's Regional Centers that maintain staffs to aid families in finding appropriate housing and provide a lifelong support system to undergird the child's independence. If you have trouble locating a helpful agency in your area, write to the National Association for Retarded Citizens (address listed in the Appendix).

As you consider possible types of housing, you will probably learn about family care homes, board-and-care, group homes, and residential facilities. A family care home is a private home licensed to care for up to six children or adults. A good family care home can provide a loving, secure environment. The term *board-and-care* refers to group homes. In California a small group home cares for six to fifteen individuals of any age. A large group home is licensed for sixteen to fifty or even seventy-five tenants, usually adults. *Residential facility* is a blanket term meaning any out-of-one's-own-home placement.

The small group home is becoming increasingly popular in the United States. In this setting, much emphasis is placed on being part of a family, on becoming responsible for oneself, and on sharing the duties of maintaining the home.

Although the close family atmosphere of a family care home may be lacking in the larger board-and-care homes, the good ones provide varying degrees of opportunities for independent growth. Parents need to be wary of unsupported claims by any residential facility operator that "we give them as much independence as they can handle." Some, but not all, large group homes have fine training programs and are well staffed and well qualified.

The type of residence your family member moves into may be limited by availability, cost, or distance. Does your family place great emphasis on living close enough for frequent gatherings of the clan? Does your adult child favor a coed setting? The smallest units, though licensed to serve both sexes, frequently limit themselves to accommodating only one sex as a way of avoiding problems. All vary greatly in the amount of responsibility given and independence allowed to each resident. In some places, tenants do most of their own cooking, cleaning, and shopping and—if on convenient bus runs—also get to and from jobs and appointments independently.

If your adult child is very capable, he may decide eventually to go out on his own.

LOOKING FOR AN APARTMENT

Before apartment hunting, the adult child and the parent may want to draw up a list of guidelines:

1. Cost. Will he be able to afford the apartment, alone or with a roommate?
2. Location. Is the apartment located on a bus route or within walking distance of his job and community facilities?
3. Safety. Is it located in a safe part of town? Are the apartment grounds well lighted?
4. Condition. Is the building well managed? Is the unit in good repair? Does the management agree to arrange for needed repairs when necessary?

An emerging problem of mainstreaming developmentally disabled adults into a regular apartment complex is their difficulty in forming abiding social relationships with others in the apartments. One young couple, Henry and Cleo, faced that challenge and are meeting it effectively.

Henry and Cleo married two years after they met at school in a small town in Illinois. Henry is the more aggressive, but Cleo has an infectious smile for all.

Cleo had lived with five other developmentally disabled girls in a board-and-care home run by an elderly couple. Henry had lived at home with his parents and two sisters. At the end of the school year in June, Henry asked his mother if Cleo couldn't come and live with them during the summer. Reluctantly, Henry's mother agreed.

"She was a cute girl in her early twenties, and Henry was attracted to her. When she came to stay with us, she would get up, eat, go to work (at the sheltered workshop), come home and sleep until supper was ready, eat, then go back to bed. That was all she did with her life," said Henry's mother.

"She was never taught to do anything when she lived at the home. She never changed her clothes, did not seem to understand about personal hygiene, never washed her hair. During the summer, we got her to be aware of herself. We got her hair cut and taught her to take care of it. We even had her teeth fixed. When summer was over, she didn't want to go back.

"Then Henry decided he wanted to marry Cleo. We talked about it, his dad, Cleo, Henry, and I. Our family doctor is now Cleo's doctor, and Henry and Cleo had several sessions with him before they married. Cleo understands that she would not be able to take care of a little baby properly, and she is on birth control pills.

"After they married, we found them an apartment only a block from a supermarket, and there are a few small shops there, too."

Cleo does not read or write, although Henry does. Henry and his parents are trying to teach Cleo to read simple phrases so that she can learn to follow a recipe when she cooks, for example. Henry can cook simple meals independently. His mother visits every afternoon before he comes home to check if everything is all right (Cleo is afraid to answer the telephone) and to help Cleo start the evening meal.

Once a month her mother-in-law takes Cleo shopping. She said, "Cleo is beginning to learn things now. She's motivated. She wants to be a good wife. We bought her some perfume. She bathes often now, and when she takes clothes off, she'll say they need to be washed and put them in the hamper."

The young couple's apartment is on a direct bus line to Henry's parents' home and his job. Cleo is not yet confident enough to travel alone by bus, but Henry buses to work. He is now employed in an advanced training workshop and hopes soon to move into an entry-level job on the "outside."

Henry's mother still receives both their SSI checks at her home because Henry's concept of money management is not developed. She observed, "But he's learning. We put their checks in small denominations and have envelopes marked "rent," "food," "bus tickets," and so forth. He won't touch the money in those envelopes. Right now we're working on them not just going down to the shopping mall and buying food and things until their money runs out. We budget all month; and then if there is something left, they can take that and spend it frivolously."

Henry and Cleo's favorite pastime is traveling by bus to a large shopping mall five miles away. They wander from one end to the other feasting on hot dogs, giant cookies, candy, and Orange Juliuses, and teasing each other continually.

Henry and Cleo experienced bouts of loneliness in their new apartment. As the only retarded couple in the complex, they were not too successful developing more than surface acquaintanceships with other tenants. They solved the problem recently by signing up for night classes for persons with handicapping conditions at a nearby school. Here, three nights a week, they are improving their reading and writing skills and making new friends with whom they can expect to develop lasting relationships.

It would be interesting to drop in on Henry and Cleo a year from now. I'm betting that Cleo is reading not only recipes but letters and circulars that come in the mail as well. And that Henry will have the job he aspires to. They are proud of each other, their home and their possessions, and each new skill delights them.

Just like any other young couple in love, starting out.

CHAPTER 18

Spiritual Growth

"Well, how is Mike doing in his new digs?" our minister asked us after church one day. And then he said, "You've no idea how many people you have helped through Mike."

I simply stared at him. Because of Mike there was so much we were unable to do! So much time, so many fights on his behalf, so many years when he was young during which I felt too exhausted to put forth that added effort for the church or the community or my husband. And especially, so many years of being blind to the needs of Laurie and Jim.

Mental exhaustion still crops up once in a while because the same problems don't go away but repeat endlessly: people—strangers—fearing to be around mentally retarded people; a few professionals still blithely telling parents "put them 'away'"; granite-hearted Realtors in the forefront of neighborhoods fighting to keep out any facilities for mentally retarded persons; chickenhearted potential employers; and—yes—tight-fisted educators and legislators.

"Helped how?" I asked.

"They see Mike and they see hope. God uses Mike."

When I think about all the ways that belief in God brings hope and comfort to us, I remember not the hope but the despair of those early years. Well-meaning people mouthed robot formulas: "God must have thought you were a pretty special family to give you such a special child." God deliberately created a child with imperfections because He had a special family to grace? No way! Hearing someone say it's God's will that you have a baby with a handicapping condition brings absolute misery to a parent.

Without knowing anything about disabilities, Christian friends who really want to help a family with a child with special needs can be invaluable. Let them lay aside themselves. Forget any question of why it happened. Help by expressing God's love as Jesus did: unconditionally. Nonjudgmental listening, to mother, to father, to siblings. A loving attitude toward the disabled child. Offers to care for the baby so the parents can take a breather, even for a few hours. Letting your children play together. In the beginning, words don't help! Being there does.

When you are a believer in Christ, He is there for you in time of trouble. If you are not a believer, all the words coming from your Christian friends will not comfort you or give you courage, strength, and faith in yourself to face the decades-long task of rearing a disabled child well.

This is what non-Christian parents find so unbearable when Christians say, "Give your cares to God." The unshakable faith of believers in God. Yes, their strength is apparent, and parents may long to have it for themselves, but in the attendant turmoil of bringing a baby with a handicapping condition into the world, their hearts are usually unable to receive the gift. They see mouths moving. Words. *Words.*

"Feed My lambs," said Jesus. First He fed, then He taught. "Love them," said Paul in 1 Corinthians 13. If Christians' direction was made any clearer, there would be no need for words at all.

Once when Mike was about ten, our family attended the wedding of one of our baby-sitters. After the wedding, while we were all enjoying cake on the church patio, a group of the bride's college friends came over to us and asked Guy if they could pray over Mike. They were sure they could heal him. Their faces were so earnest, so open. Guy looked at me, and we exchanged a smile. "Sure, go ahead," he said. To our knowledge, there had never been an instance of a person's medically documented Down's syndrome reversing itself after prayer for healing. We knew that with God nothing is impossible, of course, but we knew also that Mike would likely not be an exception.

Mike was delighted to be the center of all that attention. A little pool of sadness seeped into my heart because the young people firmly believed that they could bring about a miracle cure for Mike. I almost wished they wouldn't pray for healing. But then I thought that everyone has to learn that petitioning is a two-edged sword. Are we as prepared to accept *no* as *yes?*

Afterward, one of the group confidently predicted that Mike would shortly be healed—or maybe gradually. I cannot think of a greater miracle than to be the recipient of a spontaneous healing; yet the prayers of the millions who do not receive this healing are just as fervent. How easy to believe when you are healed! How wonderful to believe when you are not!

That must have been what our pastor meant when he asked, "Do you realize how many you've helped?" If Mike and the Ross family, with God's help, can survive whole and strong, with no special gifts, look what others can do, too!

There was—is—a miracle. Mike's nature is such that he takes each person at face value. Anyone who has ever worked with people who are mentally retarded knows that frequently this rare gift shines through them. Good people become better for knowing citizens like Mike. Where they might have teased or made double entendres, which they knew would not be understood, they have been chastened by a spirit of goodness that is totally unalterable. Mike is so trusting, it sometimes frightens us.

Even when he was just a toddler we sensed how completely he was God's child. Once he wandered away (as was his frequent delight). We lived in a rural area, and I found his go-cart about three streets away, abandoned in front of a house we had passed on walks, a sort of mini-farm with rabbit hutches, chicken yards, and all that good stuff. The owner lived in a house in front and was immediately alarmed when I knocked, looking for Mike. Behind his house was a cattle pen containing about two dozen cows and five or six horses. It was a dangerous place for any small creature and easily gotten into through the corral fencing.

We raced back to the pen. We stooped and looked between the legs of the animals. Mike was there, looking like a diminutive Daniel. I was terribly frightened. The owner was flabbergasted. "I don't see how he got in there without being trampled," he said. Before we could go after him, he tramped blithely toward us, under and around the animals' legs.

He has been in a number of dangerous situations and come through with that maddening unflappability of the person who believes he is in no danger at all. More than once he was lost in strange neighborhoods when he was learning the intricacies of bus transferring. Once he was dangerously ill with massive internal bleeding, and yet when I stood at the foot of his bed lined with the white and green gowns of hospital staff, the sense of God's presence was so palpable it nearly tore the roof off. Mike's eyes held mine, and we both knew he was in no danger.

When the first edition of *Our Special Child* came out, Mike accompanied me to Portland, Oregon, to the national convention of the Down's Syndrome Congress. He sat beside me at the book table. Together we autographed copies of his book.

For three days a parade of younger and older parents with babies and children with handicapping conditions streamed by, in and out of the workshops. Mike, so proudly signing his name under mine, would come around the table to greet little ones. He wanted to share with parents his understanding that their children looked just like he did when he was a baby. He told them about his job, about taking the bus, about his girlfriend and his music posters.

As Margaret Lewis has noted, not all children with disabilities have equal potential. No matter how diligently parents work with their children or how much money they spend pursuing the latest treatment, a small minority of the children will not show measurable improvement. But at the convention there were far too many parents whose doctors had told them that their babies could never be helped or expected to achieve anything. So many that I had to take a second look. What did the doctors see that I didn't? These were not youngsters with severe disabilities! I could see a young Mike in many of them: I saw good muscle tone, intelligent expressions, eagerness, and curiosity. The parents were reacting with disbelieving joy to the happy, well-adjusted young man perfectly at ease in a strange hotel in a strange town. Surely some of the doctors had misled the parents. Anyone could see there was indeed potential here!

Our spiritual growth as a family came about so gradually I do not believe any of us noticed. Slowly, we learned to lean on God. Mike as God's instrument has helped an older brother and a younger sister to become more aware and compassionate than other kids toward disabled or aged people. He has helped his father to become more broad-minded; me to learn humility and tenderness; all of us to appreciate simplicity, to admire those who struggle in adversity, to embrace those who are hurting.

If God had given in to us, or to those young people so many years ago, and created a physical miracle by healing Mike's disability, how many lives would have gone untouched? Mike is God's child. The miracle his life is becoming doesn't surprise me any longer.

I know God heard our prayer for Mike's healing, and I know He heard the prayers of the young people at the wedding. I heard His answer, too:

"No, My beloved, no."

CHAPTER 19

Affirmation

O
ne of the saddest tasks facing parents is affirming a child's fears. Beginning about the age of sixteen, Mike would once in a while come home from school and mention the word *crazy* or *retard*. I knew that there were occasional bad times in school. Being in the only classroom of developmentally disabled adolescents on a high-school campus of one thousand students, Mike could not possibly have avoided all unpleasant experiences.

Each time I tried gently to probe his hurt, he would withdraw. My heart ached. He knew that there were a lot of things that most kids do that he was not able to do well and that he was being teased because of what he was.

From his teacher, I learned of incidents of baiting and name-calling. What could I do? How could I armor him against such terrible hurts? I wanted to cry with him, to hold him close and never let him go. Few things hurt parents as badly as knowing that a child is being cruelly abused and that there really are some adults who don't care enough to intervene.

One day, when he had again made some reference to a *retard*, I took a few minutes to pray, then invited Mike to accompany me on a walk. It was just after dinner. Cool breezes were making music in the eucalyptus trees, setting their long golden shadows to dancing on cooling streets. I jammed my hands in my jeans pockets as we strolled along.

"Mike..."

"What?"

"About names people call other people. . . . Kids at school have been calling you names, haven't they, honey? . . . Is someone calling you retarded?"

"Yes, but I'm not!"

We walked along in silence. "Honey, being retarded isn't so bad. You are a nice boy, you're good-looking, and we all love you. . . . Do you know what *retarded* means?"

"No."

"It means that it's harder for you to learn things than it is for most people."

"I'm not retarded!"

"Mike, yes, you are, honey. But not very much. You are a healthy young man. And you are going to have a long, happy life. So what if things are harder? You're strong."

"I'm stronger than they are!" A lost, fleeting look of bewilderment crossed his face.

"You know that Daddy and I are very proud of you, don't you?"

"Uh, huh."

"And we don't care if you are retarded . . . or if you have twelve toes growing out your ears."

"Mo-om!" Mike gave my shoulder a playful shove.

That was it for about six months. During that time if the word *retarded* fit into conversations in Mike's presence, I used it anyway. I wanted him to get used to hearing the word in a nonthreatening setting, comfortably said, so that its use would not throw him into despair.

Then one day when we were driving home from the store, he asked me what made him retarded.

"What disease, you mean? It's something called Down's syndrome. It's just something that happens to some babies."

"Did other babies get it?"

"Yes. Your friend Larry has it."

"Larry has Down's syndrome?"

"Yes."

A week later a young woman called who had a six-week-old son with Down's. She apologized for calling and said she had heard through a friend of a friend about our son. She wanted to know if she might visit us. We were delighted, naturally. (It gave us a chance to show off our son.) We immediately invited her to visit. Mike was genuinely excited about actually seeing a little baby who looked like he did when he was a baby.

Mike was fascinated by Sammy, an adorable baby with a full head of dark hair and good muscle tone.

"The doctor told us just to take him home and love him, that there was really nothing they could do for him," the mother said wistfully.

Oh, no! I thought. *Not after twenty years! Not that same tired line!*

Mike to the rescue. "Sammy's like me," he said. And for the next several minutes he told Sammy's mother everything she wanted to know (and probably more) about his job, his school, his swim class, girls, and his favorite rock group.

After she ran out of questions for him, Mike went off to his own pursuits. Sammy's mother looked shell-shocked. Mike certainly did not epitomize the bleak picture the doctor had painted.

She left our home a far more joyous, more hopeful person than she had come.

It was only a few days after Sammy's visit when Mike, his dad, and I were relaxing on the patio. Mike was having some job problems, and we were telling him not to be discouraged.

"I wish I didn't get born with Down's syndrome," he blurted.

Tears blurred my eyes. "I wish you didn't, either, honey."

His dad added, "You're having a tough time at work just now but look how well you're doing in swimming." (He had swum thirty-eight laps that afternoon.)

Mike straightened in his chair. He seemed to struggle with his thoughts. Finally, he said with dignity and firmness, "My strength is stronger than my Down's syndrome."

CHAPTER 20

Ole Dad

H i, Ole Dad!" Mike always calls his father Ole Dad the first time he sees him when he comes home for a weekend.

"Hi, Miker!" This affectionate nickname started in high school when Mike's teacher made the three Mikes in the class add their last initial to their papers. Mike began signing his name with a small *r* attached to the end and refused to change it.

The father-son relationship was not always so unforced on Guy's part. Recently, Guy shared with me how, in spite of appearing in my eyes as a loving and caring father, it took years before he really felt as comfortable as he seemed to be. These next pages are his words.

When our first child, Jim, was born, it was an *event*. My feet did not touch ground for days. Everything fit. All the pieces were in place, and life was beautiful. But when I first saw Mike, I thought they had brought out the wrong baby. But the name tag read BOY ROSS so that seemed to settle it. I remember thinking he wasn't very pretty, but he sure was feisty, and that is a good asset in a new baby. The next day was the worst of my life. We were told about Down's syndrome, mental retardation, and institutions. Our beautiful world had cracked.

In an early chapter Bette describes how the doctor advised us to place our son in an institution and forget him—forget him for the good of our marriage and our family. In some cases that may be the best thing to do. For us, it was not right. He was my son—my responsibility! Like my marriage, for better or for worse, until God do us part. At the time, my position seemed very clear to me. It was my duty to be the provider, the husband, the father. I am very good in that role. I understand responsibility, obligations, dedication to the work principle. Besides, when you are busy, you don't have time to feel sorry for yourself. Plunging into these obligations and tasks meant I could forget about Mike sometimes.

It was not until years later that I allowed myself to cry over my loss. The loss of a son as perfect as the first one, the loss of the feeling that made Jim's birth such a glorious day.

I suppose every parent fantasizes about his children before they are born. They are going to be everything you ever imagined or wanted to be yourself—the best baseball player, the smartest lawyer. When Mike was born, I didn't understand the enormity of these psychological hurts. I am from an era when big boys didn't cry.

Today, it's allowable, but I'm not sure it's any easier for a man to own up to his grief, to confront it and deal with it in a healthy way. When Mike was born, I buried it and let it fester; I refused to look at my feelings of rage, revulsion, fear, and helplessness. It took me nearly twenty years to discover that having felt that way did not make me a monster.

When Mike was eighteen, I happened to sit in on a two-hour session with a psychologist and other fathers, most of them younger than I was. (I didn't want to go, but I was supposed to be setting an example.) One father was painfully uncomfortable. Everyone listened to the leader, but only two or three spoke up. I saw heads nod in agreement when the leader spoke about the feelings of powerlessness that overwhelm the father of a disabled child. I could identify with everything he said. You want to do so much to help, but nothing you can do alters the fact that one of your children is mentally retarded.

Today, trained parent-support groups and professional counselors are available to help parents through this time as soon as the little ones are born. My advice: Get into a support group right away. It helps.

My greatest help came from parent group sessions, listening and talking with other dads and moms, sharing common problems in trying to help our children. I can never begin to thank those other parents whose courage and strength taught me so much.

I am still amazed today when people congratulate me on what a fine job I have done being a father to Mike. That he is successfully coping with his disability is obvious to those who know him and are familiar with the world of special needs. But Jim and Laurie are also coping, successful human beings, and no one has asked me to share my secrets in rearing them. True, they were not born with a handicapping condition, nor do they deal with that condition in day-to-day life, but they have had to face up to their weaknesses and struggle in their daily living, too.

If I have been instrumental in my children's development into useful and independent citizens, it is because I loved and cared enough for them to be the best father I knew how. I am there for them. If that sounds noble, don't be misled. There are millions of other dads and moms doing the same thing, day in and day out, and some doing a better job.

Having someone to be a caring, loving father figure is an essential in child development. Sociologists think that the lack of a father figure in the family may be a causative factor in the growing rash of guiltless antisocial behavior among young people. Raising a family is a full-time job for two parents. For a single parent, it is really tough, and if one of the children happens to have a disability, the task can be overwhelming. There is a much higher divorce rate among parents with disabled children, and deeper levels of poverty and family problems.

Too many fathers cop out before they give themselves a chance. Fathers, you need to be aware of this and *hang on;* work through your problems. *You can do it!* After all, God does not give us more in our lives than we can cope with. With faith, with strong family support and community support, fathers and mothers can ride out the rough period after their child is born and look forward to the future with confidence. Successfully rearing a child with a handicapping condition—or any other child—enriches a man's life forever. To misquote a popular commercial, when you care enough to give the very best, give yourself.

I remember a time Bette and I were asked to share our experiences with a parent-support group whose children lived in a large board-and-care facility. We arrived in the middle of the business part of their meeting, and as we listened to the problems they were discussing, I realized that the degree of impairment and mental retardation was much more involved with their children than with mine. I doubted if their children had experienced a tenth of the freedom and variety of life our son enjoyed. What could we possibly say that would encourage them? The words almost stuck in my mouth as I shared our plans for Mike to complete high school in special education and our future thinking about his independent living.

After the meeting, one of the women told me how glad she was to hear of other active parent groups working for their children, and that it was possible for some kids to mainstream in life. She told me her daughter's long-term goal was to be more self-sufficient in a wheelchair and to learn to feed herself. And the smiling woman was thanking me. I should have thanked her and the other members for the lesson in true courage and committed love.

Probably our most important fundamental decision in Mike's early years was to let him share and experience everything he could to the limit of his capabilities. Some of it wasn't easy, all of it was challenging, and quite a bit of it was fun.

I recall sprawling out in a meadow in the High Sierras one summer, gasping for breath, while Mike was busily collecting rocks to throw in the stream, a favorite pastime of his. I had just backpacked him three miles up the trail because at six he lacked the coordination and stamina to get up there by himself. Eleven years later Mike was at summer camp carrying his own backpack on a three-day excursion with his peers.

Knowing how to promote independence is not information you are automatically given as a parent. If you are lucky, you recognize the need for it and learn how to cultivate it. It's natural to want to protect and shield your young from harm, but in doing so with disabled children, we must be careful to allow them their right to explore and to sometimes experience failure.

Mike has always loved sports, second only to his love for music. In terms of coordination and strength, he could not compete with his age peers in Pop Warner football or Little League baseball. Mike, Jim, Laurie, and I spent many a happy hour shooting baskets at the hoop over the garage. We played a game called HORSE. You choose a spot and shoot a basket, and if you make it, you get an *H* and the others have to imitate your throw. When you miss, the next player gets to set up the shot. The winner is the one who shoots five baskets (*H-O-R-S-E*) from different spots on the court first. It was an ideal game for Mike and didn't require running and skillful twisting.

In the beginning, competition was not the purpose. But as Mike grew and his skill increased, it was soon evident that he was out to clean my socks. He wasn't above rubbing it in a little if he won an after-dinner shootout.

Bowling opened up a time for out-of-school socialization. Tournaments and award dinners gave him an opportunity to hang up trophies next to Jim's baseball awards and Laurie's Western Riding ribbons. Mike's greatest sports achievement and pleasure came in swimming. The joy he experiences in swimming, I think, is comparable to mine standing hip-deep in a trout stream with a fly rod in my hands. He won gold medals in the Special Olympics for swimming, but as much fun and excitement as this grand event generated, I believe he gets as much joy from just doing laps in the pool by his apartment.

Providing your son with the opportunity to participate in sports is just one small way of turning loose. It extends through childhood, the teen years, and right into adulthood. You have to keep tuning yourself in to where your child is in his life. What is he capable of? What does he want? Not what *you* think he is capable of and what *you* want for him. We need to help our children think about what they want and how and to what degree it may be achieved by them. The day is arriving when neither Mom nor Dad is there. Can your child survive in life with dignity and zest without you?

No thoughts on my relationship with my son would be complete without acknowledging what he has given me in my life. Admittedly, I did not start out loving my infant son with the red countenance. Pity and a sense of obligation and unrealized resentment were closer to the truth. But watching Mike struggle to learn to do things that most of us take for granted changed my attitude. Admiration for his doggedness and determination changed my respect into love.

Anything I have ever given him has returned a thousandfold. Mike helped me learn about God. When he was born, I was a sometimes Christian. Sometimes I went to church. Sometimes I thought about God. I thought more and more about God and myself and why things happen after Mike was born. If God was a merciful, loving God, why did He let him be born this way? Truly, if prayer changed things, our prayers would have changed Mike's condition. How naive my thinking was. God does not purposely create imperfections. He creates life and He creates the total opportunity to live that life with or without His influence. As Mike turns to his father with trust and love and receives help, I turn to my Father and seek love, encouragement, and strength.

This faith has been a sustaining element of our lives. Through our experiences, our family has grown stronger and, individually, I believe, more compassionate and willing to help others. In this area we are still growing and have a lot to learn. Mike has his own relationship with God and becomes swept up in stories about Jesus.

It is gratifying to me to know that Mike prays in time of need to One of whom he can ask anything and not fear rebuff, criticism, or pity, but is assured of acceptance, love, and comfort.

JUST LIKE JIM

One day when Mike was about twenty-five, I received the shock of my life. Mike and I had been talking with a psychologist, which is a good thing to do now and then. She complimented Mike on what a fine young man he was.

He said, "I'm not like Jim yet."

"In what way?" she inquired.

"You both have jobs, you both live on your own, you're both fine young men," I put in.

"Mom," Mike said patiently, "you know what I mean."

I glanced at the psychologist, then said, "I really don't, honey."

"I'm not like Jim. I still have my Down's syndrome. When am I going to grow out of my Down's syndrome?"

"But, Mike, you were born with it. It isn't something you grow out of."

"Yes, I am!" His voice began to rise.

"Mike—"

"You said! You said do this, do that, this is what Jim does, and I'd do that and I'd be like Jim!" Mike grew more agitated.

"Oh, Mike—" I shook my head.

Mike refused to look at me. He looked panic-stricken. "You promised!"

"No...I meant..."

"You said I would be just like Jim. Jim doesn't have Down's syndrome. And 'member that time at church when the pretty girls prayed over me? They said my Down's syndrome would go away, and I still have it! You promised, Mom!"

"I never said you'd outgrow your Down's syndrome!"

"You said I'd be just like Jim. Jim doesn't have Down's syndrome!"

"I said—" Ah, God! It was all I could do not to shriek with rage at the Down's syndrome that had robbed Mike of so much. This fine young man! This sensitive, caring, humorous human being! What awful irony. What had I done? I tried to be so careful not to plant false illusions, tried to keep Mike focused on what was possible in his life. Just like Jim...Jim without Down's syndrome.

All the way home in the car, Mike kept talking, talking, reminding me of all the things he'd learned to do just like Jim. I could only utter the well-worn phrases of all he had done, all he had overcome, how much he was loved, but there, there it was—the ever-present Down's syndrome.

CHAPTER 21

Life Goes On

M ike lives now in Canoga Park, an urban-suburban area northwest of Los Angeles in the San Fernando Valley, seventy miles away from our home. His only income is a monthly SSI check for $662, which pays for his half of the rent, utilities, quarters for the Laundromat, and groceries. What is left he uses for entertainment (and occasionally, grudgingly, for new clothing—"laundry," he calls it). He swims almost daily in the apartment complex pool, which is just below his second-floor apartment. He likes to rent wrestling videos and films like *Batman* or *E.T.* at Sam Goody's rentals. He also likes to eat out at Carl's Jr., sometimes with his roommate or other friends. He has his hair cut at a cut-rate barber "where the girls are real pretty, Mom," and he sees a local dentist and doctor who accept MediCal patients. He still loves to take pictures, and extra rolls of Polaroid film are always welcome gifts.

A caseworker from the Work Training Program drops by once a week to see how things are going: apartment sanitary, the food in the kitchen fresh, enough money in Mike's account to pay the bills. She says she always enjoys visiting Mike. On Halloween she brings her grandchild to visit because Mike's always in costume for the trick or treaters.

Mike feels badly that he has been unable to get a "real job for money." For two years, he has worked fifteen hours a week at a senior citizens complex a mile from the apartment. In wet weather he gets to work by bus, but he likes to walk most of the time. He is well thought of by his supervisor and loved by the residents. He takes nonambulatory residents to and from their apartments in their wheelchairs to the dining room. He helps serve lunch, bus tables, and clean up the dining room. His lunch is provided.

I asked Mike once what was the worst thing about living on his own.

"Being lonely."

"What do you do when you feel that way?"

"I get happy, Mom." Mike said it so matter-of-factly. Just like, of course, you do something about it. Nobody has to stay lonely. "I go get a drink."

"At Carl's Jr.?"

"Yeah. And go to Sam Goody's."

"Ever call up a friend?"

That apparently was not one of Mike's options. He is very congenial in company but has great difficulty initiating the action. Mike and his roommate have fights sometimes, but his roommate is better at thinking up things to do when they are bored. His roommate loves to go to Universal Studios, and his parents gave him a pass. Now he and Mike go there several times a year by bus.

Mike needed all his courage and skill to master bus travel in Los Angeles. He visits us once a month, more often if there is something to celebrate. He must travel on the RTD bus through Los Angeles and change buses at Sixth and Main where it's not always safe from thieves. Twice he has had his pocket picked, been robbed of his Handicapped Bus Pass and his California identification card and all his money. Now he carries all but change in a shoe, in a fanny pack, or in his luggage.

One afternoon Guy drove to the Disneyland Hotel bus stop where he was to meet Mike's bus from Los Angeles. It was Thanksgiving eve, and Mike's bus was due around five. Guy called an hour later. The freeways were jammed. Mike hadn't come in yet. The other family members were assembled—Jim, Laurie, and her husband, Misha, waiting. Another hour passed with no word. The turkey went back in the refrigerator, unstuffed. All we could think about was, *Where is Mike?* It started to rain.

As the evening wore on, all the RTD bus drivers passed the word along their intercoms. We didn't know if he'd even gotten on his first bus. Finally, at eleven o'clock, the bus dispatcher called us. They had not located Mike on any of their buses. They thought we should know that no more buses would be traveling that night.

Wherever Mike was, he was alone. I didn't dare unleash my

imagination. Guy drove back home. It was horrible for him to come home alone. At least, waiting at the bus stop, he'd felt somehow tied to Mike. By that time, the Los Angeles Police Department was also looking for him.

Misha knows Los Angeles well, having spent an adventurous but carless adolescence getting around by bus. He said he knew all the bus stops, and he was going to look for Mike.

At 1:30 Thanksgiving morning Misha called us. He had found Mike, huddled in a doorway near Sixth and Main in his trench coat, waiting for a bus that would not come. Misha and Mike arrived home an hour and a half later. Mike muddy to his knees. He was exhausted and shaken. At 3:00 A.M. we were sitting around the kitchen listening as bits and pieces of Mike's story came out.

Somehow he had gotten off the first bus short of his transfer point. For the next four hours he had wandered around Los Angeles looking for familiar landmarks. There was a lot of construction going on, and nothing looked the same. He crossed barren lots and freeway overpasses. Once he approached a policeman for help, but the officer was "talking tough to some guys" and Mike was afraid. Then he tried to use a telephone, but the two he found were broken. About eight o'clock he spent the last of his money on a burrito. Finally, he found Sixth Street and followed it to Main. He recognized his bus stop and so he waited there.

That day we had more to celebrate than Thanksgiving. We celebrated Mike for his courage and bravery and Misha for refusing to give up. We celebrated being together and whole again.

For the next two months, Mike and his dad and I were afraid for him to ride the buses. We drove to his apartment to pick him up and drove him back. We knew Mike was dreading making the journey by bus. Finally, we talked it over, and Mike felt ready to try again. Now, it's almost as if he's put that night out of his thoughts, and he comes home by bus regularly again.

We still spend birthdays, holidays, and many vacations together as a family. I asked Jim and Laurie one time if they ever resented Mike for all the extra attention he received. They insist not. "It would have been different," Jim said, "if you guys had given Mike special treatment, you know, so that he was a spoiled brat or something."

"I never felt he was 'special.' He was my brother, just like Jim. We used to fight with him as much as with each other," Laurie added. "You always made him do Saturday chores right along with the rest of us. But not all kids with disabilities are as capable as Mike is. We were lucky because Mike could do so much."

Mike has continued to mature in many ways. He has learned to work through tough problems. Last summer we took Laurie and Mike to Mexico for a week. Mike had always wanted to see King Tut's tomb. I told him Mexico had pyramids and ancient tombs, too, and he agreed to visit the ones in Mexico instead. He had saved for two years for part of the money to pay his way.

We stayed at a hotel in Oaxaca that had been a monastery in the fifteenth century. We visited archaeological sites and craft markets and street vendors and the zócalo. We had a terrific time. On the last day of our trip, Mike grew increasingly pensive.

Coming home on the plane, he wanted to talk. He said that his roommate yelled at him a lot. Through his eyes, I could see the roommate following him through their cramped apartment obsessionally talking.

Mike said his roommate said that Mike didn't do things right. "And he wouldn't stop. He wouldn't let me talk! And I'm the one who can read and write. I have good ideas, too. And he wouldn't let me say them!"

Mike said he couldn't stand it anymore. He didn't want him as a roommate anymore. Then he said that everything was falling apart. A lot of the staff at Work Training were leaving, too.

"The workers?" I asked.

"No, not the workers. The big guys, the guys at the head."

"Like Walter, who was your crew chief when you were on the janitorial maintenance crew?"

"Yes, he left to get married. Why are they leaving? They don't get paid enough, Mom. And so they get jobs that pay better."

Mike looked very worried. After a few minutes he said, "Jim got to come home."

What he meant was that he wanted to come home, like his brother Jim. Over the course of seven years, Mike has endured poor placements, a never-ending series of social workers and staff workers, and the disappointment of seeing jobs he liked disappear under him. Before going to work at the Senior Center, it seemed that every time he got into a job where he felt comfortable and able to do the work, with congenial coworkers, and that was close to his apartment, the job dissolved.

His staff person, Lisa, had just left on maternity leave. Her sub, Teresa, also his roommate's staff person, turned Mike over to another worker. The roommate told Mike that Teresa did it because she didn't want to be his worker anymore. It sounded like something he would make up. He is more verbal than Mike, thinks faster, and I think is less honest. But since Mike is honest, he believes that everything everyone tells him is also true. He felt very low when he talked about this, very hurt.

The staff at Work Training Program, with whom Mike continues to be associated since he graduated to independent living, are wonderful. Most of them are terrifically caring people. Many have master's degrees in social work. Yet they are paid near to minimum wage. It is no wonder they are chronically understaffed. One of the fallouts is the lack of personnel for the ongoing pursuit of suitable jobs for the clients as they successfully complete the years of independent living and job training.

Mike has seen us move to a new city. He has seen Laurie move back home and stay a few months. Then she married and moved away, and Guy and I had a few short months of couplehood, the first in nearly thirty years. Then Jim's marriage and his business broke up, and he moved back home for some healing and mending. Jim was here over a year. We were glad to have him, to be able to help him. When he was healthy again, he moved out again.

Riding home from Mexico in the darkened plane with Guy, Laurie, and Mike, I could see Mike's face in profile, looking glum, deep in thought. "What is it, Mike?" I said.

"I'm worried about my future."

I found his hand, rough, thick skin, stubby fingers, and bitten fingernails. I squeezed it. I loved him so much. "Mike, I can't ask you to come back home. That would be a step backward. Jim was home, yes. When his marriage broke up, Jim felt very bad. He lost his business and his wife at the same time. We wanted him to come home so we could help him get over it and start to feel good again. Laurie was home, too, for a while. But now she's married and on her own, and that's the way it should be.

"When we get back, I'll help you find a new roommate. Do you want your roommate to move out? Are you willing to look for another apartment if he won't?"

"Yes."

"Okay. But your job, Mike, I thought you were happy with it."

"I don't get paid money. My roommate makes fun of me."

"His jobs don't last. You've worked at your job a long time and you are good at it and everyone likes you there."

"I could look."

"Do you want to get together with staff and see if we can help you get a new job? Shall we do that? Will you call Work Training and see if you can get us an appointment?"

"Yes."

Our plane got in late Saturday night. The following Wednesday was Fourth of July, and Mike was to stay with us until after the holiday. Monday morning, I reminded Mike to call his staff person at Work Training and make our appointment.

"Mom, I've been thinking." Now that he had been able to get his problems off his chest and I had turned aside his bid to come back home, Mike appeared to have reconsidered his options. "We are on the list for a two-bedroom apartment in the same apartment building. If we had our own bedrooms, it wouldn't be so bad."

"I see."

"His parents want me to be his roommate. His other roommates couldn't stand him."

"You don't have to, honey."

"Well . . ."

"You still like him?"

"He needs me, Mom."

"That doesn't mean you have to stay with him."

"I know that."

"You think you want to?"

"Yeah, I think so."

"Shall we still talk to Work Training and see if we can get the job ball moving again?"

Mike hesitated.

"Do you want to think about that more, too?"

"I guess so."

Throughout this, what I wanted Mike to realize was that life always presents options. And that, as always, we were there as a backup. To me, being a backup means being there to help solve problems, not to take them over. More specifically, to help point the way for Mike to solve his own problems so that he won't panic when problems of daily living come and we are no longer there for him to lean on. A kind of "this is how you do it." Mike had done superbly. He had been able to talk about his concerns, unleash the emotions, and then come around in a cooler mood and look at things again. He had made reasonable decisions.

Mike's ability to live so close to the limit of his capacity awes me. Where does he get the strength? "I have courage," he says once in a while. He certainly does. He also has a strong individual personality.

I still had to ask myself, How could I let Jim come home and not Mike? Because for a time Jim was broken in spirit. The problems

225

Mike faced were those all people face from time to time, not getting along with roommates, not being able to find the right job.

Mike still has in place a working support system that oversees daily living concerns for the hundreds of mentally retarded adults linked to the Regional Center and Work Training Program. He has a neighborhood that he trusts himself in and friends he sees every day. He walks or occasionally rides a bus to work, markets, doctor and dentist, the barber, the video store.

Yes, Mike has problems now and then. Don't we all? But he's blessed with good health, and as each year passes, he becomes more mature in understanding his world and more capable of coping with it.

Recommended Reading

Bracey, Gerald W. "Why Can't They Be Like We Were?" *Phi Delta Kappan,* October 1991, pp. 104–17.

Bricker, Diane D. *An Activity-Based Approach to Early Intervention.* Baltimore: P. H. Brookes, 1992.

Bricker, Diane, and Casuso, Valerie. "Family Involvement: A Critical Component of Early Intervention." *The Council for Exceptional Children,* October 1979.

Buschman, Larry. "Katie's Computer." *Instructor* magazine, February 1992, p. 33.

C.B.I., Community-Based Instructional Handbook for the Huntington Beach Union High School District, Edison High School, 21400 Magnolia, Huntington Beach, California 92646.

Cohen, Felice. "Learning Disabled Students Boost Scores, Self-Esteem." *T.H.E. Journal* (Technological Horizons in Education), March 1992, p. 36.

Des Jardins, Charlotte. *How to Organize an Effective Parents Advocacy Group and Move Bureaucracies.* 1980. Coordinating Council for Handicapped Children, 407 South Dearborn, Room 680, Chicago, Illinois 60605.

———. *How to Get Services by Being Assertive.* Chicago: Coordinating Council for Handicapped Children, 1980. These two volumes by Des Jardins should be in every parent's library.

The Education of Students with Disabilities: Where Do We Stand?: A report to the President and the Congress of the United States. National Council on Disability. Washington, D.C.: The Council, 1989.

Evans, Jerome, R., Ph.D. "A Report of Mental Health Problems Among California Regional Centers." 1979. Communications with the author should be directed to Mental Health Services, 300 Hillmont Avenue, Ventura, California 93003.

Garwood, S. Gray. *Designing a Comprehensive Early Intervention System: The Challenge of PL 99-457.* Austin, Tex.: PRO-ED, 1989.

Gordon, Sol. *Living Fully: A Guide for Young People with a Handicap, Their Parents, Their Teachers, and Professionals.* New York: The John Day Co., 1975. An excellent, easy-to-understand, well-written book addressed directly to young people.

———. *Raising a Child Conservatively in a Sexually Promiscuous World.* New York: Simon & Schuster, 1989.

Gordon, Sol, and Snyder, Craig. *Personal Issues in Human Sexuality.* 2d ed. Boston: Allyn & Bacon, 1989.

Koch, Richard, M.D., and Koch, Kathryn Jean. *Understanding the Mentally Retarded Child: A New Approach.* New York: Random House, 1974.

Levy, Dr. Janine. *The Baby Exercise Book: For the First Fifteen Months.* Translated from the French by Eira Gleasure. New York: Pantheon Books, 1975.

Ludlow, Barbara L., et al., eds. *Transitions to Adult Life for People with Mental Retardation: Principles and Practices.* Baltimore: P. H. Brookes, 1988.

Mittler, P., ed. *Research to Practice in Mental Retardation.* Vols. 1, 2, 3. Baltimore: University Park Press, 1977. Vol. 1: *Care and Intervention: The Acceleration and Maintenance of Developmental Gains in Down's Syndrome School-Age Children.* This ongoing study of early intervention describes the results of the Model Preschool Center for Handicapped Children and the Child Development and Mental Retardation Center, University of Washington, Seattle.

Mittler, Peter, and McConachie, Helen, eds. *Parents, Professionals and Mentally Handicapped People: Approaches to Partnership.* Cambridge: Brookine Books, 1984. Co-published in UK by Croom Helm Ltd. 800-666-2665.

———. *A Parent's Guide to Accessing Parent Groups, Community Services, and to Keeping Records.* Washington, D.C.: U.S. Dept. of Education, Office of Educational Research and Improvement, Ed. Res. Informational Center, 1989.

Schultz, Jane B., Carpenter, C. Dale, and Turnbull, Ann P. *Mainstreaming Exceptional Students: A Guide for Classroom Teachers.* 3d ed. Boston: Allyn & Bacon, 1991.

Sparling, Joseph, and Lewis, Isabelle. *Learningames for the First Three Years.* New York: Berkley Publishers, 1986. This book is ideal for the parent or teacher of disabled children. Games, simply described and well-photographed, are arranged by developmental age rather than by chronological age.

———. *Learningames for Threes and Fours.* New York: A Guide to Adult-Child Play. New York: Walker & Co., 1984.

Spock, Benjamin, M.D. *Baby and Child Care.* New York: Pocket Books, 1989.

Springen, Karen, and Kantrowitz, Barbara. "The Long Goodby." *Newsweek,* October 22, 1990, pp. 77–80. When parents give up a disabled child for adoption, the pain often lingers.

S.S.I. for Retarded People. Washington, D.C.: U.S. Department of Health, Education and Welfare, Social Security Administration, HEW Publication.

The Task Force on Concerns of Physically Disabled Women. *Toward Intimacy: Family Planning and Sexuality Concerns of Physically Disabled Women.* 1977. Planned Parenthood of Snohomish County, Inc., 2730 Hoyt, Everett, Washington 98201.

Transition Services Language Survival Guide for California. California State Publication. California State Printing Office, Dept. of General Services, 344 N. 7th, Sacramento, CA 95814.

Travers, Joanne M. *We've Been There...Can We Help?* Ontario-Pomona Association for Retarded Citizens, 9160 Monte Vista Avenue, Montclair, California 91763. This manual is for training parents to become community outreach educators.

Turnbull, H. Rutherford III. *Free Appropriate Public Education: The Law and Children with Disabilities.* 3d ed. Denver: LOVE Publishing Company, 1990.

Van Wogner, Dr. Benjamin, Professor of Science Education. "Guidelines for Working with Students with Disabilities." *AIMS Newsletter,* May-June 1991.

Weiner, Roberta. "The REI Movement." *Electronic Learning,* March 1992, p. 12.

Parents and others seeking a variety of good books about children with special needs may want to contact Woodbine House, a company that publishes books for new parents, such as *Children with Down's Syndrome: A Parent's Guide* (1989) and *The Language of Toys* (1989). Similar titles include books on autism, cerebral palsy, epilepsy, and many others. The address is 5615 Fishers Lane, Rockville, Maryland 20852. The telephone number is 800-843-7323.

Educational Software

for Students with Special Needs

Broderbund Software, Inc.
500 Redwood Blvd.
Novato, CA 94948-6121
"The Playroom" for early learning, available for Macintosh, Apple, and
IBM-compatible computers

Edmark's Early Childhood Software Catalog
P.O. Box 3218
Redmond, WA 98073-3218
800-426-0856 for free catalog

Educational Resources
800-624-2926 (or in Illinois 708-888-8300) for free educational Macintosh
catalog

Learning Lab Software
20301 Ventura Blvd., Suite 214
Woodland Hills, CA 91364
800-899-3475
Specializes in special needs technology

MacWarehouse
Special Education Public Domain Software
Technology for Language and Learning, Inc.
P.O. Box 3013
1690 Oak St.
Lakewood, NJ 08701-3013
800-925-6227

MECC
3490 Lexington Ave. N.
St. Paul, MN 55126-8097
800-228-3504
An early and continuing leader in educational technology

Multisensory Curriculum Catalog
Creative Learning, Inc.
P.O. Box 829
North San Juan, CA 95960
800-842-5360

Sunburst
800-321-7511

Troll Associates
100 Corporate Drive
Mahwah, NJ 07498-0025

Appendix

National Organizations Serving Children with Special Needs

American Council on Rural Special Education (ACRES), Western Washington University, National Rural Development Inst., Miller Hall 359, Bellingham, Washington 98225. Telephone: 206-676-3576. For educators, parents, and university and state department personnel. Rural electronic bulletin board, telephone referrals for resource linkage. Publishes ACRES newsletter every six weeks.

Computer Access Center, 2425 Sixteenth Street, Room 23, Santa Monica, California 90405. Telephone: 213-450-8827. This organization specializes in classes for children with special needs, their parents, and other professionals.

Council for Exceptional Children (CEC), 1920 Association Drive, Reston, Virginia 22091. Telephone: 703-620-3660; 800-873-8255.

Divisions of CEC:
- Center for Special Education Technology (CSET), electronic bulletin board, SpecialNet TECH.LINE.
- Council for Children with Behavioral Disorders (CCBD)
- Division of Career Development of the Council for Exceptional Children (DCD)
- Division for Early Childhood (DEC)
- Foundation for Exceptional Children (FEC)

Directory for Exceptional Children. Boston: Porter Sargent Publishers, Inc., 1991. Lists over 2,600 public and private schools, clinics, and treatment centers for children and young adults with emotional, developmental, and organic disabilities. Lists resident and day schools. Lists associations, societies, foundations, and state and federal agencies and personnel.

Directory of Residential Centers for Adults with Developmental Disabilities. Phoenix: Oryx Press, 1989. The address is 2214 North Central at Encanto, Phoenix, Arizona 85004-1483.

Exceptional Children's Foundation, 2225 West Adams Boulevard, Los Angeles, California 90018. Telephone: 213-731-6366. One of the nation's oldest and largest nonsectarian organizations serving mentally retarded people of all ages.

National Association for Retarded Citizens, 2709 Avenue E East, P.O. Box 6109, Arlington, Texas 76011.

National Association of Private Schools for Exceptional Children, 1522 K Street, NW, Suite 1032, Washington, D.C. 20005. Telephone: 202-408-3338.

National Down's Syndrome Congress, 1800 Dempster Street, Park Ridge, Illinois 60068-1146. Publishes a newsletter, reviews books, ten times yearly for parents and professionals.

National Information Center for Children and Youth with Disabilities, Box 1492, Washington, D.C. 20013. Telephone: 703-893-6061; 800-999-5599. Publishes newsletters and informational bulletins.

National Network of Learning Disabled Adults (NNLDA), 808 North Eighty-Second Street, Suite F2, Scottsdale, Arizona 85257. Telephone: 602-941-5112. A self-advocacy group.

People First International, P.O. Box 12642, Salem, Oregon 97309. Telephone: 503-362-0336. Write for copy of newsletter. A self-advocacy group.

People-To-People Commission for the Handicapped, P.O. Box 18131, Washington, D.C. 20036. Telephone: 301-774-7446.

Regional Centers of California, Department of Developmental Services, 744 P Street, Sacramento, California 95814.

Special Olympics, 1350 New York Avenue, NW, Suite 500, Washington, D.C. 20005. Telephone: 202-628-3630. Board Chairman Sargent Shriver. Informational brochures, instructional manuals, and lists of state programs available upon request.

Notes

Chapter 1

1. Richard Koch, M.D., "Feelings and Their Medical Significance," *Ross Timesaver,* September–October 1974, pp. 1ff.
2. Koch, "Feelings and Significance," pp. 1ff.

Chapter 2

1. Benjamin Spock, M.D., *Baby and Child Care* (New York: Pocket Books, 1976), p. 4.
2. Spock, *Baby and Child Care,* p. 2.
3. Spock, *Baby and Child Care,* p. 2.

Chapter 3

1. Sol Gordon, *Living Fully: A Guide for Young People with a Handicap, Their Parents, Their Teachers, and Professionals* (New York: The John Day Co., 1975), p. 84.
2. Simon Olshansky, "Chronic Sorrow: A Response to Having a Mentally Defective Child," *Social Casework,* April 1962, pp. 190–93.
3. Richard Koch, M.D., "Feelings and Their Medical Significance," *Ross Timesaver,* September–October 1974, pp. 1ff.
4. Ann P. Turnbull and H. Rutherford Turnbull III, *Parents Speak Out: Views from the Other Side of the Two-Way Mirror* (Columbus, Ohio: Charles E. Merrill Publishing Co., 1978), p. 138.
5. Koch, "Feelings and Significance," pp. 1ff.

Chapter 4

1. Adapted from *How to Organize an Effective Parent Group and Move Bureaucracies* (Chicago: The Coordinating Council for Handicapped Children, 1971), p. 11.

Chapter 5

1. Joyce R. Ludlow and L. M. Allen, "The Effect of Early Intervention and Pre-School Stimulus on the Development of the Down's Syndrome Child" (Birchington, Kent, England: J. R. Ludlow, 1979), p. 31.
2. Timothy J. Teyler, quoted in Judith Brody Saks, "Latest Brain Research Offers Lesson in Learning," *The Executive Educator,* October 1979, p. 28.
3. "Overprotectiveness," *Patient Care,* November 15, 1978, p. 208.

Chapter 7

1. Senator S. I. Hayakawa, "Our Son Mark," *McCall's,* December 1969, p. 79.

Chapter 9

1. Kathryn A. Gorham, "A Lost Generation of Parents," *Exceptional Parent*, May 1975, p. 521.
2. Ann P. Turnbull and H. Rutherford Turnbull III, "Jay's Story," in *Parents Speak Out: Views from the Other Side of the Two-Way Mirror* (Columbus, Ohio: Charles E. Merrill Publishing Co., 1978), p. 119.

Chapter 10

1. Gay L. Parrish, M.A., Chief of Community Development, North Los Angeles Regional Center, 8353 Sepulveda Blvd., Sepulveda, California 91343.
2. Tami Yamaga, Edison High School teacher and co-coordinator of Community Based Instruction program (a mainstreaming project) for the Huntington Beach Union High School District, Huntington Beach, California.

Chapter 12

1. Bev Carhart, "High Country Classroom," Special Education Program, Park City, Utah, 1977–78.

Chapter 13

1. The Helsels, "The Helsels's Story of Robin," in *Parents Speak Out: Views from the Other Side of the Two-Way Mirror* (Columbus, Ohio: Charles E. Merrill Publishing Co., 1978), p. 110.

Chapter 15

1. Jerome R. Evans, Ph.D., "A Report of Mental Health Problems Among California Regional Center Clients," Mental Health Services, Ventura, California, 1979, p. 1.
2. Evans, "A Report," p. 6.
3. Evans, "A Report," p. 11.
4. Evans, "A Report," p. 12.

Chapter 17

1. Richard Koch, M.D., quoted in "Independent Living," *Patient Care*, November 1978, p. 235.

Index